BLACK SON RISING
Rising Up, Fighting Back, and Breaking Free!

BY MICHAEL CURTIS JONES
(MICHAEL SAMIR MOHAMED)

Chicago, Illinois

First Edition, First Printing

Front cover illustration by Harold Carr

Copyright © 2006 by Michael Curtis Jones (Michael Samir Mohamed)

All rights reserved.

Printed in the United States of America

ISBN #: 0-974900-07-9

BLACK SON RISING

I am a Black *Son* Rising!

I am rising up, fighting back, and breaking free.

I am rising up as a man, and taking responsibility for educating, uplifting, and empowering Black men.

I am fighting back against the systems of oppression that perpetuate the cycle of Black-on-Black crime and violence.

I am breaking free from the chains of mental, physical, and emotional bondage that were placed on my people through the institution of American slavery.

I am a Black *Son* Rising!

Together, we can become Black *Men* Rising!

Together, we can rise up, fight back, and break free!

Freedom is the Goal. Knowledge is the Key. Faith is the Way.

This book is dedicated to the following groups of people:

- The African men, women, and children – our ancestors – who lost their lives and their freedom as the result of the "Slave Trade Holocaust," which destroyed the lives of some 15 million+ Africans, for no other reasons than the capitalist greed and false doctrine of white supremacy.

- The Black men, women, and children who have become the unfortunate victims of black-on-black crime and violence, which has its historical roots in the chains of mental, physical, and emotional bondage that were placed on our people through the institution of European and American slavery.

- The Black fathers, sons, and brothers who, instead of being at home to support and protect their Black families and communities, are locked up and "locked down" in prisons around the country, because no one ever taught them the knowledge of how to set themselves free.

- The freedom fighters, Black and White, past and present, who have sacrificed their lives and died in the struggle to liberate their Brothers and Sisters from the systems of institutionalized racism.

For all of these people, I cry out with my whole heart!

This book is a tribute to the strength, courage, and intelligence of The Three Black Kings: *Marcus Garvey, Malcolm X, and Dr. Martin Luther King, Jr.*, all of whom are my Spiritual Fathers and my Brothers in the struggle for freedom, peace, and justice.

I love you and miss you all.

CONTENTS

ACKNOWLEDGMENTS

Where are the black writers who will dare to confront this racist nation? Who will illuminate the dream of the disenfranchised and sing the song of the voiceless?
- **Maya Angelou, Novelist and Poet**

As you know, the causes and effects of black-on-black crime and violence have been and will be studied, examined, and debated by count-less thousands of individuals and groups, before me and after me.

I don't assume to know or pretend to know everything about the history, sociology, or psychology of African and African American people. My knowledge is very limited and I am still woefully ignorant on many subjects pertaining to the history and heritage of the African in America. In fact, the things I *don't* know would fill several oceans, but I'm willing and ready to learn.

Yet, it's one thing to study and know and debate the causes and effects of black-on-black crime and violence, but it's another thing to do something positive and constructive to end it.

In the proud tradition of some of our greatest contemporary heroes including, *Dr. Jawanza Kunjufu, Na'im Akbar,* and the late *Professor Amos N. Wilson,* I have chosen to make it my life's mission to not only understand the causes and effects of black-on-black crime and violence, but to assume a proactive role in breaking its cycle.

However, none of us can do this extremely difficult work alone.

That's why I'd like to take this opportunity to thank the dozens of family members, friends, mentors, and teachers who provide me with the moral and emotional support that I need to continue doing the difficult work of educating, uplifting, and empowering Black men. We need another 10,000 foot soldiers on the frontline doing this work, so that we can break this cycle of black-on-black crime and violence once and for all.

I am honored to have been chosen to be one of the few, the proud, the free – a freedom fighter and a soldier in the struggle for peace and justice.

First and foremost, I give thanks to God, my Father, for this extraordinary gift of life, and the strength, courage, and intelligence to do His works. Next, I'd like to give thanks to my mother, the late *Rose Elaine Curtis,* my best friend and mentor, whose untimely passing is felt every day of my life.

I'd like to express my gratitude to my family and friends who continue to give their valuable time and support in practically everything I do: *Angela Caesar, Aliya Curtis, Gina Chambliss, Valerie Dent, Shannan Martin, Kim Speed, Imara Solwasi, Edwin Sloane,* and *Reggie Bradshaw.*

A special thanks goes out to all of my students, the administrative staff, and the Correctional Officers at the Metropolitan Transitional Center (MTC) in Baltimore, Maryland.

Finally, I'd like to give a special thanks to Dr. Jawanza Kunjufu, and the staff at African American Images, for believing in me and supporting my latest effort to bring the message of truth and hope to the Brothers who are still struggling to be free.

Thank you and God bless you all!

A SPECIAL ACKNOWLEDGMENT

Surround yourself only with people who are going to lift you higher.
- **Oprah Winfrey, Entertainer and Media Mogul**

I only have a handful of really good friends whom I can count on when the going gets rough. I am very grateful to have these people in my life, for I would truly be lost without them. I don't have to call out your names. You know who are. But if you're one of the so-called "friends" who is wondering whether or not I'm referring to you, chances are I'm not, because a true friend knows whether or not he or she is one.

However, there are good friends and there are "great" friends. Of great friends, I only have one.

This person is a great friend because no matter where I am or what I am doing, I can always count on that person to be there for me and to have my back. Friends like that usually come along once in a lifetime, and when you get them you hold onto them for dear life.

But how do you say thank you to such a friend? It seems that words alone are not adequate to convey your gratitude and deepest appreciation.

How do you say thank you to someone who believes in you more than you believe in yourself?

How do you say thank you to someone who just won't let you quit on yourself no matter how hard you try?

How do you say thank you to someone who just won't accept less than your best?

How do you say thank you to someone who takes the time to call you every single day, three or four times a day, just to make sure you are still on track with your goals?

How do you say thank you to someone who puts everything on the line to help you fulfill *your* dreams instead of theirs?

How do you say thank you to someone who constantly puts your needs before their own?

How do you say thank you to someone who does everything in their power to lift you higher and higher?

How do you say thank you to someone who does all of these things without asking for or expecting anything in return?

Honestly, I don't know how you say thank you to such a unique and wonderful friend, but I have to try.

Angela, you are my very best friend in the whole world. I thank God every day for sending you into my life. I hope you know that I am more grateful to you, and for you, than words alone can express. I can tell you, however, with the utmost sincerity, without your unfailing love, guidance, energy, and support, this book would never have been written.

Thank you so deeply!

Forever your friend,
Mike

INTRODUCTION

We have survived the Middle Passage and we have survived slavery. We have survived the deadly arbitrariness of Jim Crow and the hatefulness of Northern discrimination. But now we face a danger more covert, more insidious, more threatening and potentially more final even than these: the apparently sly conspiracy to do away with Black men as a troublesome presence in America.
- **William Strickland, Activist**

It "ain't" easy being a Black man in America, because it seems as though our very existence is a threat to everyone around us.

It seems that we are either a threat to ourselves on the streets where we die from our own hands; or a threat to our Black women whom we mentally and physically abuse and disrespect; or a threat to our Black children whom we sire and then abandon; or a threat to the white power structure in this racially hostile nation we call "America."

Apparently, the only place where we are not a threat to anyone is on the basketball courts, the football fields, the boxing rings, and the music studios, where our anger, hostility, and aggression can be used to earn ourselves and our new "mastas" millions of dollars.

It seems that it's okay for Black men to be angry, hostile, and aggressive as long as we are channeling that energy and aggression into profitable white business ventures, like sports franchises and record labels.

It seems that it's okay for Black men to be violent, crude, and abusive as long as we're selling stadium tickets, filling theatre seats, and drawing patrons to music stores and concerts.

But what happens to the Black men who don't get lucrative basketball or football contracts?

What happens to the Black men who never make it to the boxing rings or the music studios?

Question:

Where is all that violence, anger, and aggression supposed to go – that same violence, anger, and aggression that makes us such great athletes and entertainers?
Without an outlet for it, where does it go?

Answer: It goes nowhere!

It stays right inside of our Black men who have been socially and economically barred from mainstream society and denied the opportunity, through the systems of institutionalized racism, to provide a reasonable standard of living for ourselves and our families.

It stays right inside of our streets, where it physically destroys anyone hungry enough to compete against these Black men for the few breadcrumbs the "hood" has to offer.

It stays right inside of our homes, where it emotionally damages the women who love and support these Black men, and the children who call these men "father."

It stays right inside of our communities, where it psychologically terrorizes the honest, hard-working men and women, and the innocent children and teens, who become the unwitting victims of these angry Black men.

It stays right inside of our minds, where the seeds of our self-destruction were first planted in Black men, and Black people, through the institution of American slavery.

It stays right inside of our hearts, where a Black man's fear, greed, and self-hatred reside. This is the place where it does the most damage, because this is the place that is hardest to reach and where the real cycle of black-on-black crime and violence begins, and ends.

These are all the places this anger, hostility, and aggression will stay if we don't start teaching Black men how to break these chains of mental, physical, and emotional bondage that alienate them from mainstream society and marginalize them into narrowly defined, self-perpetuating negative stereotypes as thugs, gangstas, playas, pimps, hustlers, and "niggas."

Black-on-Black

According to the latest Department of Justice, Bureau of Justice Statistics homicide and incarceration rates for Black males:

- There are 2 million people in prison or jail in America. Of the 2 million, 60% (1.2 million) are Black males.

- 1 out of every 3 Black males, between the ages 20-29, are either in prison, on parole, or on probation.

- The rate of incarceration for Black males is 7 times higher than the rate for White males.

- AIDS is the #1 cause of death among young Black men aged 15 to 24.

- 1 out of every 21 Black males in America will be murdered and most of them will die at the hands of another Black male.

- Black males, between 15 and 24 years of age, are 7 times more likely to be killed by violence than White males.

- Black males are 7 times more likely to commit homicides than Whites... nearly 94% of all the Black homicide victims are killed by other Blacks.

- 65% of the homicides committed by Black males against other Black males are committed using a handgun...more than 1/2 of the Black youth homicides in the nation are gang-related.

Cause & Effect

After reading the above statistics on black-on-black crime and violence, you have to shake your head in disgust and amazement at how many Black men are locked up or murdered in this country.

However, we already know that a lot of Black men are violent, hostile, and aggressive; we don't need statistics to tell us that. All you have to do is read a newspaper or listen to the news every day, to know that a lot of us are dying or getting locked up over drugs and gang wars.

But the question is: Why?

Why are we killing each other like dogs in the street?

Why are we robbing each other, and peddling that chemical slavery to our own people?

Why are Black men so ruthless and dangerous toward other blacks?

Think about it for a minute:

After everything we have suffered at the hands of White men through racism and American slavery, including whippings, lynchings, and burnings, what kind of self-respecting Black man kills another Black man, or sells deadly drugs to his own people?

Why are we so quick to inflict harm on our own people, yet we won't raise a hand against the very people who created the deplorable conditions in which we live and suffer?

Why do we hate and hurt each other so much?

I have been asking myself these same questions for the past ten years. So then what's the answer?

I believe with my whole heart that the violence, hostility, and aggression that fester inside Black men, like an open seeping wound, are the symptoms of seven destructive characteristics that are typically found in people who have been subjected to various forms of oppression over a significant period of time: *fear, false pride, material greed, mental laziness, social ignorance, self-hatred, and misplaced anger.*

I further believe that these seven destructive characteristics, which give rise to black-on-black crime and violence, have their historical roots in seven separate but related conditions:

1. The slave mentality that was programmed into the Black race through the institution of American slavery, and the "Willie Lynch" process.

2. The psychological effects of racism and racial oppression, and the personality traits that oppressed people develop in response to them.

3. The post-traumatic stress of White-on-Black crime and violence to which the Black race has been subjected for more than 400 years.

4. The absence of strong, positive Black father figures, and other positive role models in the lives of Black males.

5. The role reversal of Black mothers who have been forced to assume the duties of the father and the head of the household, due to the absence of strong Black fathers from the Black family dynamic.

6.   The constant bombardment of negative images in the mass media (i.e., news, TV, and movies) depicting Black people as lazy, ignorant, dangerous, and dishonest criminals and thugs.

7.   The absence of a strong spiritual foundation that is rooted in Black cultural identity, and that instills in a person a sense of morality based on a healthy respect for God, life, truth, peace, freedom, justice, wisdom, and love.

There is no conclusive, scientific evidence to support my theory that all seven of these conditions together contribute to black-on-black crime and violence. However, there is a significant body of research on each individual condition, and its relation-ship to crime and violence in general, that gives weight and credibility to my theory.

I also have my own personal life experiences, some common sense, and conversations with hundreds of Black prison inmates, juvenile offenders, social workers, and psychologists, and my own extensive, independent research that has helped me to reach these conclusions.

The "Black Experiment"

It occurred to me one day while conducting my research that the crime and violence in the Black community bears a striking resemblance to a lab experiment I once heard about.

Apparently, there was a study done once in a laboratory that put several rats in a closed box, with only one chunk of cheese that was only big enough for one rat. After only a few hours in the box, the rats tore themselves to bloody pieces fighting over that one little chunk of cheese.

Now, I know people are supposed to be better than rats, but if you constantly strip them of their dignity, subject them to mental and physical abuses, divest them of any positive examples of appropriate behavior and bombard them with only negative images of themselves, and then insulate them against any moral or ethical training that appeals to their cultural identity – what are you left with? A load of angry, hostile, violent, aggressive, and psychologically traumatized lab animals, instead of human beings. Every behavioral scientist on the planet knows that if you constantly treat people like animals, sooner or later, they are going to start acting like them.

And that is exactly what's happening with the Black race in general, and Black men in particular.

We have become the human lab rats in some sick, twisted white racist capitalist idea of an interesting sociological and psychological experiment. I can just imagine a group of rich, fat White men in a smoke-filled room discussing the strategy for carrying out the "Black Experiment." I suspect that the conversation probably goes something like this:

We'll put these niggers in boxes called "ghettos"; deliberately exclude them from mainstream society; bombard them with images that depict them as ignorant savages; inundate them with false ideas about black manhood through music and videos; have them bow down to false images of a White God who looks like us; throw a few breadcrumbs in the box; and then sit back and watch Darwin's dog-eat-dog theory of natural selection (i.e., survival of the fittest) become the law of the land.

We'll force them to accept menial low-paying jobs that are nothing more than cheap slave labor, or bar them from employment altogether, and then watch them tear themselves to pieces for a few of the breadcrumbs we throw their way from time to time.

We'll watch in utter amazement, and amusement, as their homes and communities become places where murder, crime, rape, and other forms of violence are the rule -and kindness, self-respect, human decency, and compassion are the exception.

We'll call this experiment 'capitalism' and then sit back and reap the profits that expand our white business enterprises, that build our white financial empires, and that send our white children to college so that they can learn how to keep the 'Black Experiment' alive, from one successive generation to the next.

And if anybody should start asking questions like, "Why are Black men so violent, hostile, and aggressive?" we'll blame these niggers for their condition, and have our social scientists show the world, with "scientific" proof mind you, that that's the black man's natural state, and as a result he's not much good for anything else other than providing manual labor for our businesses and profits for our sports franchises.

And we'll tell the whole world that we are actually doing these niggers a favor by providing homes (ghettos) and jobs (slave labor) for them that they couldn't, or wouldn't, otherwise provide for themselves.

Let me just say this on behalf of all of us Black nigga lab rats, "Thank you, massa, we sure does appreciate you helping us poor ignorant colored folk out, cauz' we dunno what we would do without you."

Wake up, Black man!

You are a living, breathing lab experiment and it's time to get out of the lab, for too many of us lab rats are dying, and it ain't interesting or amusing anymore, at least not to us.

And the fear, false pride, material greed, social ignorance, self-hatred, and misplaced anger that has been socialized into us via this lab experiment is creating and perpetuating this deadly cycle of black-on-black crime and violence in our own families and communities.

The key to getting out of this lab box (the mental and physical ghetto) and breaking this cycle of black-on-black crime and violence, is to liberate yourself from the slave mentality that you have been "taught" from birth.

That means that you are going to have to start taking responsibility for educating yourself on how and why and when you became a "slave," and what steps you need to take and what knowledge you need to learn in order to become "free."

That's the short-term solution.

The long-term solution is to start learning, and teaching others, the basic life skills and the marketable employment and business skills that are necessary for us to successfully compete in this racially hostile nation.

We also have to start pulling all of our mental, physical, and financial resources together so that we can start building the kinds of institutions and infrastructures that can protect future generations of Black men, women, and children from falling victim to the "Black Experiment."

How to Read *Black Son Rising*

Black Son Rising is organized into five (5) parts and forty chapters. Each chapter is a separate essay that can be read independently, or they can be read together as a collective work:

- **Part I – The Cause** – contains 11 essays which describe the psychological and sociological conditions that give rise to black-on-black crime and violence.
- **Part II – The Effect** – contains 7 essays which highlight the devastating effects of black-on-black crime and violence in Black communities.
- **Part III – The Solution** – contains 16 essays that propose the changes that Black men can make as individuals, and as organizations, to break the cycle of black-on-black crime and violence, and restore peace and harmony in the Black community.
- **Part IV – The Three Black Kings** – contains the biographies and written works of Marcus Garvey, Malcolm X, and Dr. Martin Luther King, Jr. It is a tribute to the legacy of the strength, courage, and intelligence these men used to lift the Black community to new heights of peace and prosperity.
- **Part V – The Final Call!** – contains 2 essays which summarize the whole message and purpose of the book, and really drives home the point of our need to come together as men, and as a community, to break this cycle of black-on-black crime and violence.

Black Son Rising can be read from start to finish, or it can be read chapter by chapter, from the beginning, the middle, or the end. However, for continuity's sake and for a complete understanding of the causes and effects of and solutions to black-on-black crime and violence, I recommend that you read it from the beginning straight through to the end.

PREFACE

Anytime there is a self-loving, self-respecting, and self-determining Black man or woman, he or she is one of the most dangerous folks in America. Because it means you are free enough to speak your mind, you're free enough to speak the truth.
- **Cornel West, Philosopher and Activist**

From this point forward, a lot of people, both Black and White, are going to be offended by what they are about to read. The good news is that if you *are* offended, that means you are at least *thinking* about what I have said. I can't offend you unless you're thinking, and *thinking is* the first step toward freedom.

Make no mistake, I am going to offend someone when I use terms like "house niggas" and "field niggas."

I'm probably going to offend someone when I refer to them as drug-dealing, gun-toting, gang-banging, back-stabbing murderers of their own people.

I'm probably going to offend someone by telling them that their ignorance and slave mentality is at the root of all of their criminal, violent, and irresponsible behavior.

I'm probably going to offend someone by telling them that their fear and ignorance keep them enslaved.

I am definitely going to offend someone when I demonstrate to them, with cold hard facts, that their whole life has been one big lie after another, and that they have swallowed the lie hook, line, and sinker, and as a result have they been led down the path to their own self-destruction.

Whatever it is that offends you, you're going to have to get over it, because:

I will not apologize for speaking the truth!

And the truth must be told, because black-on-black crime and violence is destroying the Black race.

The truth must be told!

The truth is, Black man:

Black-on-black crime and violence is not an accident. It is the direct result of the efforts of the white racist power structure in this country to exterminate the Black man and the Black race.
The truth is, Black man:

From one generation to the next, and from the day you were born, you have been psychologically conditioned to hate, fear, disrespect, and destroy the Black race and to perpetuate a system of mental and physical slavery.
You are being *used* as a pawn of the white racist power structure to commit Black racial genocide, because:

- Every time you commit a crime, you give the white racist power structure in this country the excuse to put you where they want you: *in graves* or *in prisons*. The laws and policies of this country – written by White men, for White men – were designed to rob Black men of their freedom, their respect, and their manhood.

- Every time a Black man goes to prison, that's one less Black man to raise and support his Black children, thereby creating a new generation of fatherless Black children who are now more likely to become the victims, and the perpetrators, of black-on-black crime and violence.

- Every time you abandon your child, and your child's mother, you are reinforcing negative stereotypes of Black men as immature, irresponsible, trifling, and disloyal fathers and mates, thereby giving our Black women the excuse to date White men, or to date any other man outside our race.

- Every time you commit a crime of violence, you are reinforcing negative stereotypes of Black men as ruthless, dangerous, and out-of-control hoodlums, thereby giving other races the excuse to disrespect us, because we don't even respect ourselves.

- Every time you sell crack, cocaine, heroin, or some other dangerous drug to another Black man or woman, you are helping to destroy at least two generations of Black families: the drug addicts themselves and their children who now have to grow up in households with strung-out, unemployed, and unfit dope-fiend parents.

- Every time you put a liquor bottle to your lips, or a crack pipe in your mouth, or a heroin needle in your veins, you weaken your mind, body, and spirit, and destroy any chance of uplifting yourself, your children, the Black family, or the Black community.

- Every time you kill another Black man, you are killing another potential Black father, and making it more difficult for the Black race to reproduce itself, thereby facilitating the process of Black racial genocide.

- Every time you kill another Black man, you are killing the next Malcolm X, Marcus Garvey, Dr. Martin Luther King, Jr., or some other potential great Black leader who could lead us into social and economic prosperity, and lead us out of mental and physical bondage.

- Every time you kill another Black man, you are helping the white racist power structure is this country and hate groups like the KKK become more powerful, because there's strength in numbers, and as their numbers continue to grow, our numbers keep getting smaller and smaller, because we are dying before our time.

This is why I must speak out, because our ignorance of the truth is perpetuating this cycle of black-on-black crime and violence and facilitating the white supremacist's goal of Black racial genocide.

Be forewarned, I'm going hard, and I'm not going to sugarcoat the truth just to keep from offending the "sensitive" little pride and ego of any man, Black or White.

If you don't want it hard and raw and real, then go read a damn comic book, because I came here today to call a spade a spade, and a rose a rose;

and I will no longer bite my tongue, for I have grown sick of the taste of blood in my mouth.

If I say something to offend you, you are welcome to stop listening or stop reading. I'll understand, because the truth hurts.

However, I advise you to keep listening and keep reading, because you just might learn something that could save your life, or the life of someone you love.

A lot of what I say might not even apply to you, but if the shoe fits, damn it, then wear it; but if you're Black, everything I say here applies to you, one way or another.

Some of you "house niggas" and "field niggas" are going to be very, very angry with me for bringing the truth because I'm challenging the *status quo* and messing with your little "thang" you got going, but as you're reading *Black Son Rising* and hating on me and judging me for my actions, ask yourself the following questions:

1. **How much courage does it take to stand up and openly confront racism and the white power structure in this country, knowing full well that it could cost you your life or your freedom?**

2. **Is there *any* truth to what I am telling you, and what can you do to confirm the truth for yourself?**

3. **What are my motives for teaching you this "truth"? Am I trying to help you or am I trying to hurt you?**

4. **Aside from the drug game and the rap game, or whatever other hustle you're into, what struggle are you ready to die for?**

5. **What steps and actions have you personally taken to break this cycle of black-on-black crime and violence?**

Until you can answer these questions with complete honesty and without feeling ashamed of yourself for taking part in this "racist shell game," don't sit there and judge me, or hate on me, for having the courage to speak the truth that you could and should speak, but won't because you're too afraid of the consequences of voicing your opinion in front of your White "mastas."

When you are done asking and answering these questions, and done reading *Black Son Rising*, take a good hard look at yourself in the mirror, and then ask yourself one last question:

Am I a slave or am I free?
You can say what you want to say, or think what you want to think about me, but I'm taking a stand, and I'm ready to fight for my freedom and yours, and I'm ready to die for my beliefs.

Are you?
I'm only offering you the truth, but you're the one who has to decide if you want to know what the truth is, and how you will use it after you hear it.

I'm not trying to save your life. I'm only trying to help you save your own life, because you're the only one who can do that.

I can only show you the door, but you're the one who has to walk through it.

You can take the red pill and wake up from this living nightmare, or you can take the blue pill and stay asleep as a slave in *The Matrix*, but the choice is yours.

PART I

THE CAUSE

When you control a man's thinking you do not have to worry about his actions. You do not have to tell him not to stand here or go yonder. He will find his "proper place" and will stay in it. You do not need to send him to the back door. He will go without being told. In fact, if there is no back door, he will cut one for his special benefit. His education makes it necessary.

History shows that it does not matter who is in power . . . Those who have not learned to do for themselves and have to depend solely on others never obtain any more rights or privileges in the end than they did in the beginning.

- Dr. Carter G. Woodson, Historian

1

BLACK SON RISING

Rising Up, Fighting Back, and Breaking Free!

Once a people are truly educated, they will not ask for power, they will take it.
- **John Henrik Clarke, Historian**

My name is Michael Samir Mohamed and I am a *Black Son Rising*. I was born into bondage in a country that calls itself "the land of the *free*," yet for nearly 40 years of my life, I have been living, working, and thinking like a slave.

I am an African, born and raised in America. My parents are African. Their parents are African. And their parents' parents are African too. Unfortunately, none of them knows they are African, because in their minds they are simply "American," with no love or desire to embrace their African history and heritage.

Like a lot of so-called "African Americans," my parents, and grandparents, and great grandparents were raised as "free slaves" (*i.e., a slave who thinks he or she is free*), and they passed their "free slave" mentality down from one generation to the next. As a result, I too was raised to think and act like a "free slave," and I did so until I received my first *awakening* six years ago and started the long, difficult, and perilous journey to personal freedom.

Contrary to what you might think because of the name I am using, I am not a Muslim. The name Samir Mohamed was bestowed upon me by a very powerful, brilliant, and honorable Nubian Egyptian elder named Samir Shakur, whom I met and studied under during my visit to Aswan, Egypt, in February 2004.

I was honored with that Nubian and Arabic name because Samir, my spiritual father, recognized in me my burning desire to be free from my ignorance, self-hatred, and fear. And in Samir's Nubian Egyptian philosophy, changing one's name to reflect his African cultural identity is one of the first steps toward freedom.

I agree with that philosophy wholeheartedly.

Thanks to strong, courageous, and intelligent Black men like Samir, and other mentors, past and present, I am no longer a "free slave," but a *Black Son Rising* – a freedom fighter and a man of God; a seeker of Truth and Wisdom; and a soldier in the struggle for Peace and Justice.

I am just one of the many thousands of *Rising Sons,* here and abroad, who are breaking free from the chains of mental, physical, and emotional bondage that were placed on our people through the institution of American slavery.

BLACK SON RISING

Now, as a Rising Son, I am using the strength, the courage, and the intelligence given to me by God, to speak truth to power, and to awaken the rest of my Brothers from their long, deep slumber.

That is the solemn duty and obligation of every Rising Son.

The Rising Son Speaks

I came here to tell you that it's time for you to wake up, Black man!
I came here to tell you that it's time for you to get up off your back, for you have been sleeping far too long!
I came here to tell you that it's time for you to rise up and open your eyes to the truth, which has been hidden from you by your oppressors!
Why?
Because your people, the Black race, the first race, the "hue-man" race, is in deep, heart-wrenching trouble.
We are spiraling downward into a perpetual state of mental, physical, and economic slavery, instead of striving upward toward a permanent state of peace, prosperity, and social freedom.
This downward spiral is the direct result of the deliberate efforts of your oppressor, the White racist power structure (*"whips"*) in this country to mentally weaken, emotionally cripple, and physically kill the Black male.
For thousands of years, history has demonstrated that when you kill the male of the race, the race itself will eventually die. And the death of the Black race is the terrifying "final solution" to the problem of the "White man's burden" in this country, and in fact, the world.
The Black race in America stands as a constant reminder to all of the monumental hypocrisy of the American pledge "with liberty and justice for all." We are the living, breathing proof of that *great white lie*.
Therefore, to remove the proof and conceal the truth, the Black race in America must necessarily die. And for the "whips," the sooner we go the better.
The overt and covert efforts to kill the Black male, and consequently the Black race, have been successful thus far, because Black people in this country have been sleep-walking for a very long time, and we are overwhelmingly ignorant about the extent to which the *"whips"* labor to fulfill their dark and clandestine policy of Black racial *genocide*.
The Black race is in deep, heart-wrenching trouble, not because the *"whips"* are trying to exterminate us, but because too many of us have turned a blind eye to the truth and are still pretending that everything is "all right." And it's not!
Every time we see a handful of successful Black athletes and entertainers parading around on white-owned fields, courts, and stages, we are further lulled into a false sense of peace and prosperity – *knowing* full well that right outside our doors lie our Black men, women, and children who are dying from the drugs, the crime, and the violence that are tearing our Black communities to pieces.
Crime, poverty, unemployment, illiteracy, prison, violence, and *death* are the truest measures of the state of the Black race in America, not the illusionary images of the fame and the fortune of the few.
As long as our athletes (the field niggas) and entertainers are shucking and jiving and prostituting themselves for their white masters, and as long

as the uppity, bourgeoisie Blacks (the house niggas) are strutting around like peacocks in their little token 9 to 5 jobs that the "masta" was gracious enough to "give" them, then we really don't give a damn about what's happening to the rest of our Black Brothers and Sisters, do we?

After all, "I got mine, you need to get yours." Right?

Wrong! Our token, mediocre success means nothing, and is only temporary at best.

As long as the "whips" continue to subject our Black men to the worst kinds of injustices, without us house and field niggas so much as raising an eyebrow, or parting our lips in protest, there can be no permanent peace, prosperity, or freedom for the Black race in America.

Because if they can destroy our men, who are the strong and natural protectors of the race, then how much more will they do with our women and children when all the strong Black men are locked down or dead?

Do you honestly believe that it is by accident or coincidence that our Black women are growing mentally and financially stronger every day and succeeding where so many Black men are failing?

I tell you truthfully:

The psychological blueprint for the strengthening of the Black female and the corresponding weakening of the Black male was planned, foretold, and carried out more than 300 years ago in this country (see _Let's Make a Slave_).

Do you so-called "educated" house niggas honestly think that just because you have good jobs, and fancy degrees, and big houses, and expensive cars right now that the Black family in America has finally achieved the mythical "American Dream"?

I tell you truthfully:

Without Black men, there is no Black family! And not one Black man or woman in America will be able to keep what he or she now owns and covets, once every strong Black male in this country has been stripped of his freedom and/or his life.

They will take everything you have, just as quick as they gave it! That's right, I said "gave it," because many of you so-called "educated" house niggas are foolish enough to believe that you have actually earned these token possessions and positions you hold so dear.

Make no mistake, you only have what they have allowed you to have.

"But what about our civil rights and the Constitution?" you ask.

"They can't just take our possessions! The law will protect us!" you say.

Do you honestly think that the laws and policies of this country were designed to protect the rights of _all_ of it's so-called "citizens"?

I tell you truthfully:

The laws and policies of this country - written by White men, for White men – were designed to rob Black men of their freedom, their

respect, and their manhood – facilitating the subjugation of the entire Black race, and keeping the mantle of power in White hands.

Do you honestly believe that it is by accident or coincidence that hundreds of Black men are killed and incarcerated on a daily basis?

I tell you truthfully:

The psychological blueprint for the death, incarceration, castration, and annihilation of every strong Black male in this country was planned, foretold, and carried out more than 300 years ago in this country (*see Let's Make a Slave*).

The man is the natural head of the family, and the family is the collective body of the race.

Therefore, if you kill the head, you kill the body!
Consequently, if you kill the Black male, you kill the Black race!

That's why in order to save the Black race, it is imperative that we first save the Black male – the natural head of the body of the Black race.
But how do we save the Black male?
To save the Black male, we must first remove from his consciousness the ignorance about the extent to which the *"whips"* have willfully and deliberately robbed him of his strength, his pride, and his dignity and made it nearly impossible for him to realize any significant measure of success for himself or his family.
And contrary to the ignorant and popular belief, which says, "it's easier to teach a child than to repair an adult" (*which in my opinion is just a pathetic justification for giving up on our incarcerated Black men and women)*, to save the Black race, we must first save those Black males who have already fallen victim to the "masta's" plan.
That means that the common street thug, the hustler, the gang-banger, the brothers on lock-down, the ex-offenders, and the other so-called "wretched of the earth" must be saved first, for they are our greatest hope of salvation as a race.

It is the so-called "wretched of the earth" that shall be our ultimate salvation.

If we are to have any chance of saving the Black race from its continuous psychological enslavement and physical genocide, we must first save our fallen Black brethren by imparting the brutal and honest truth about the process and method by which they have become the fallen.
Once you tell a man how he has been manipulated and deceived into a condition of lack and suffering, and who it was that did the manipulating and deceiving, a man will of his own accord strive to pull himself up out of those conditions, and then make it his life mission to teach his fellow man to do the same (*Brother Malcolm X being the perfect and finest example of this maxim*).

4

In other words, once you unplug someone from *The Matrix*, they become your most zealous soldiers in the struggle to liberate others from *The Matrix*.

Accordingly – for the few mentally liberated Black men and Black women that have finally awakened to the truth – our sole (*soul*) purpose in life is to go about, domestically and abroad, liberating the minds of our mentally enslaved Brothers and Sisters, and uplifting the Black race to its natural state of peace, prosperity, and freedom.

This is our original state!

This is how we used to live in the dynasties of Egypt and Ethiopia, and the kingdoms of Ghana, Mali, and Songhay, before the European hordes swarmed into Africa and took by force all of its wealth, natural resources, and intellectual creations like math and science.

God bestowed upon us, the Black race, the first race, the "hue-man" race, and the gifts of strength, courage, compassion, dignity, insight, intelligence, wisdom, and respect for all of His creations.

This is our natural state!

We as a race only learned to be ruthless, and selfish, and ignorant after our exposure to and subjugation by the European races.

We became dangerous to ourselves only after we "learned" through European systems of mis-education that we are inferior, sub-human savages that need the moral and intellectual guidance of the "superior" White man.

The time has come. No! The time is long overdue for us to rise up, fight back, and break free from these false teachings that keep us in a perpetual state of terror, confusion, and ignorance, while simultaneously deceiving us into a false sense of peace, prosperity, and social freedom.

Despite what we see happening around us every single day with drugs, violence, and prison rates at epidemic proportions in Black communities, there are still those ignorant Blacks among us who are quick to claim that the Black race in America has made significant progress, and has experienced tremendous success in this country.

Usually this backward, uninformed way of thinking comes out of the mouths of those who are blind to the obvious truth around them, or too scared to speak the truth for what it is.

I tell you truthfully:

For every so-called "successful" Black person in this country, there are 1000 more who are failing miserably, and who are subjected to the worst kinds of poverty, crime, violence, racism, and other forms of oppression on a daily basis.

Should we be content with the mediocre success of the few, when so many others are failing?

No! The freedom and success of one means nothing without the freedom and success of all!

That's the mistake *we*, meaning Black people, keep making. It ain't about *you*. It's about *us*.

The Black race in America, and in fact around the world, needs to develop, cultivate, and embrace a philosophy of "collective destiny consciousness."

BLACK SON RISING

As an example of this philosophy of "collective destiny consciousness," look at the overwhelming success of the White race in America. Despite their individual differences and personal conflicts with each other, at the end of the day, in every way, they shamelessly empower, promote, support, uplift, and advance their own.

This is why they are 75% of the U.S. population.

This is why they own 85% of all the businesses in this country.

This is why they control 90% of the wealth of this country.

This is why 75% of their children attend and graduate from college.

This is why the unemployment rate among Whites is less than 5%.

Therefore, until we can claim this kind of collective success for the Black race as a whole, we cannot be appeased or pacified by the limited token success of a very small percentage of Blacks.

As long as the unemployment and homelessness rates for Blacks is 5 times what it is for Whites, we are not yet prosperous.

As long as the murder rate for Black men is 7 times higher than the murder rate for White males, we are not yet at peace.

As long as the prison rate for Black males is 7 times higher than the prison rate for White males, we are not yet free.

As long as Black people in America are dying on the streets, or living in abject poverty, or rotting away in state-funded prison warehouses – while the United States government spends hundreds of billions of dollars of the taxpayers' money to wage war on countries that haven't waged war on us – the so-called "American Dream" will remain for most Black people, the perpetual "American Nightmare."

Prayerfully, it is my greatest desire, hope, and vision that one day every Black man and woman in America will awake to the truth, get up off their knees and their backs, stand tall and erect with dignity, shake from their shoulders the dust of oppression, and resume their rightful places in the world as strong, courageous, and responsible protectors of the Black family, the Black community, and the Black race in America.

To that end we must work diligently, night and day, to manifest this, our collective destiny. And we must do whatever is necessary, but lawful within the confines of the Constitution of this nation, to accomplish these ends.

I believe there is a *Black Son Rising* in our midst. The time is ripe. The moment is at hand....

Let the revolution begin!

Creed of the Rising Son

I am a Black Son Rising!

I am rising up, fighting back, and breaking free!

I am rising up as a man, and taking responsibility for educating, uplifting, and empowering Black men.

I am fighting back against the systems of oppression that perpetuate the cycle of black-on-black crime and violence.

2

MANCHILD IN THE PROMISED LAND

The Journey from Slavery to Freedom

For where does one run to when he's already in the promised land?
- **Claude Brown, *Manchild in the Promised Land***

There is an old saying, "To know the free man, you must first know the slave." With that thought in mind, I will briefly share with you my own slave history, so that you can see for yourself that every man carries within himself the seeds of his own personal freedom.

Despite my rough beginnings as a youth, I have been very fortunate in life. I have had several successful careers as an adult, and made an awful lot of money. I was a corporate prostitute for several Fortune 100 companies, a military puppet in the armed services of the United Snakes of America, a law enforcement officer (*i.e., overseer*) for a federal law enforcement agency, and a slave-minded "step-n-fetchit" house nigga for most of my adult life.

I admit I had it good as an adult and a "free slave," but like way too many young Black males in America, I grew up on welfare, without a father or a male role model in my life, in a city infested with poverty, drugs, crime, and violence. For a brief time I too was seduced by the streets and I did the same stupid things that most young men do who don't have positive influences in their lives:

I stole cars and went joyriding, shoplifted from the corner store, sold and smoked weed, got high on malt liquor while hanging out on street corners, and jumped on Brothers who didn't belong in my neighborhood.

At the time I was running around like a young hoodlum, I knew what I was doing was wrong but I was doing what just about every young Black male in my neighborhood was doing:

I was modeling my environment and doing what I saw done around me every single day.

It never occurred to me until many years later that the overwhelming poverty, drugs, crime, and violence in Black neighborhoods, and the sense of hopelessness and despair they breed, was not an accident or coincidence, but the deliberate efforts of the white power structure in this country to rob Black men of their freedom, their respect, and their manhood.

I later learned during my *awakening* that these things were done in order to keep the Black race divided and subservient, while keeping the mantle of power in white hands.

7

BLACK SON RISING

Prior to that, I never gave any consideration to the plight of Black people or Black men or Black families, until I became a law enforcement officer and saw firsthand the inherent racial discrimination that is rampant in the criminal (in)justice system.

It's one thing to stand outside the criminal justice system and speculate that its adherents are racist, it's quite another thing to see the proof of it firsthand.

That was the beginning of my *awakening*, because it was then that I started asking questions like, "Why are there so many Black people being locked up? Don't white people commit any crimes in this city?"

For ten years, I was helping the "system" by locking up dozens of young Black men every single day in Washington, DC, before I woke up to the realization that prison is modern day slavery, and that we, meaning Black men, are perpetuating this system of slavery through the fear, false pride, material greed, social ignorance, and self-hatred that was bred into us through the institutions of racial oppression.

After I received my *awakening*, I began searching for ways to reach out to young Black men in hopes of turning them away from drugs, crime, and violence, and this whole "thug" and "gangsta" lifestyle that's destroying their lives, as well as the Black family and Black community.

With that mission in mind, I wrote a book titled, *The 1ST Challenge: Stop Acting Like Thugs, Gangstas, & Hustlers, And Start Acting Like Men!* which proposed a positive and powerful new definition of "manhood" for Black men in America.

I resigned from law enforcement 2 years ago to pursue a career as a speaker, author, and educator with a mission to educate, uplift, and empower Black men, and to break this cycle of black-on-black crime and violence that sends Black men to one of two places: *prisons or graveyards.*

Currently, I serve as a life skills instructor at a men's prison in Baltimore, MD. Not surprisingly, the prison population there is 95% Black. I am trying desperately to awaken these Brothers to the truth about the causes and effects of black-on-black crime and violence.

Ever since I started speaking out against black-on-black crime and violence, and how white racism and institutionalized racial oppression are at the root of it, I have been called everything in the book: *militant, trouble maker, radical,* and *racist.*

Racist?

I gladly concede to the other labels, but *racist?*

Is it racist to tell the truth?

Is a school teacher a racist when she teaches her students about the Jewish Holocaust, and how the Germans tried to exterminate the Jewish people?

Does she hate Germans simply because she recounts their atrocities?

Is it okay for White teachers to teach Black students about Black history?

Are our school teachers racists for telling Black students that their forefathers were once slaves?

Then what is the difference between what those teachers do and what I am doing?

Contrary to popular belief, I don't hate White people. I am a Child of God. I don't waste my God-given spiritual and emotional energy hating any man. That runs contrary to God's nature.

However, I do hate injustice, I hate the evil that men do, and I hate to see any man or woman, Black or White, treated as "less than human."

Therefore, I am not a racist. I am merely teaching "White history" and recounting the numerous atrocities that White people have heaped upon the Black race, and continue to heap upon them to this day.

I wonder if people would feel better if I were a White man teaching the history of white racism and racial oppression to Black students?

People ask me, "If you're not a racist, then why are you only trying to help Black people? White people suffer from drugs and crime and violence too."

They are absolutely correct in this fact. White people do suffer from drugs and crime and violence, but to answer that question for them, and for anyone else who might ask it in the future, here is where I stand on the issue:

1. I will help anyone who wants my help, regardless of their race, but they have to be open to the truth, and be willing to shed their long-held stereotypes and misperceptions about both races, Black and White.

2. White people in this country seem to be doing just fine without my help. They are 75% of the U.S. population. They own 85% of the businesses. They control 90% of the wealth. And yet they represent less than 20% of the prison population.

   On the other hand, Blacks are only 12% of the U.S. population. They own less than 5% of the businesses. They control less than 5% of the wealth. And yet they represent 60% of the total prison population.

3. When you go to the emergency room, who does the doctor treat first: *the person with the gunshot wound, or the person with a migraine headache*? Black people are suffering the greatest in this country. Ours is a gunshot wound compared to the migraine headache of Whites.

4. If more people stood up and spoke out against black-on-black crime and violence, and took action to get rid of it, instead of complaining about it, then we might be able to keep our Black men and women out of the prisons, off of the drugs, and away from the streets that are encouraging their criminal and violent behavior.

That's why I focus my efforts on Black people in general, and Black men in particular, because they are the ones who need my help the most.

Journey to Freedom

As a former law enforcement officer (*overseer*), I used to think that everybody I locked up deserved to be locked up. It took nearly ten years for me to realize that these so-called criminals and "thugs" are people just like you and me, with families and friends, and people who love them, need them, and want them in their lives, instead of in prisons and graveyards.

BLACK SON RISING

More importantly, I began to realize that their criminal actions were not born in a vacuum, but that there is a cause and effect relationship for their behavior.

After talking with and listening to the hundreds of Black drug dealers, thieves, and murderers I had locked up previously, and taught in prison more recently, I have discovered from their personal stories that these men have suffered the worst kinds of mental, physical, and emotional anguish you can imagine.

Is it any wonder that they are angry, hostile, and violent?

Make no mistake, I'm not condoning the criminal lifestyle of these men, and I'm not making excuses for their irresponsible and anti-social behavior. I still believe that "If you do the crime, you've got to do the time."

However, I do understand why these men do what they do, because I have been where they have been: *fatherless, penniless, hopeless,* and *full of rage and despair at the injustices we constantly endure.*

And more importantly, I now understand how, from birth, we have been socialized into these conditions.

My personal journey to freedom first began when I read the most powerful book ever written by a Black man, or any other man in my opinion, the *Autobiography of Malcolm X,* with Alex Haley.

That book changed my life forever.

I read the *Autobiography* for the first time in 1998, and it blew my mind and really opened my eyes to the truth about the condition of the Black race in America. It was Malcolm who inspired me to embrace all things Black and African, instead of glorifying all things white and European.

A year later I took my first trip to Kenya, Africa, where I saw beautiful Black African people who literally had nothing, yet they carried themselves with the bearing and dignity of kings and queens.

It was then that I started seeing Black people all over the world as my extended family, for they *are* my brothers, sisters, aunts, uncles, and cousins, and I have a responsibility to them, because they *are* family, and I love them as such.

I had to go all the way to Kenya to learn that lesson.

It was after reading the *Autobiography,* and visiting Kenya, that I began looking seriously at the negative attitudes and behavior of Black people in America.

I really wanted to know more about what happened to us, and why we are not more respectful and loving of each other like the Kenyans in Africa.

After reading Malcolm and going to Africa, I started asking questions like:

Why is it that no matter where you go in America, Black people have higher rates of poverty, unemployment, crime, violence, and imprisonment than any other ethnic group in the country?
Why is crime and violence so rampant in our own communities?

Is it by accident or coincidence that Black people on the West Coast suffer the same impoverished conditions as those on the East Coast, or in the South, thousands of miles away from each other?

What is the common denominator in our criminal, violent, and impoverished mindset?

Those questions, and the subsequent answers, opened a lot of doors to the kind of knowledge that eventually set me on the path to freedom from my own slave mentality.

For most of my adult life, I harbored the most horrible thoughts about Black people:

"Black people are just lazy, stupid, greedy fools, who don't know anything, don't want to know anything, don't have anything, and don't want any better than what they currently have."

What on earth could cause me to think and feel that way about my own people?

What I have learned in the last five years of my search for the answers to my questions about the "Black condition" has turned my world upside down, and has set me on fire to teach these truths to anyone brave enough to listen and act on them.

A wise man once said, "Ignorance is no longer an excuse for the man who has learned the truth. When you know better, you must do better."

I now know better. Therefore, I must do better than what I have done in the past, for those with the knowledge to the path of freedom have a responsibility to lead others to that path, less they become a slave of a new kind: the kind we call *coward.*

And now that I am no longer afraid to speak the truth, and no longer fear the consequences of my actions, I must tell you what I know:

Black man, you are suffering from a dis-ease called mental slavery. Your dis-ease has made you weak and cruel and irresponsible, and it is your dis-ease that perpetuates black-on-black crime and violence.

The symptoms of this dis-ease are fear, false pride, material greed, mental laziness, social ignorance, self-hatred, and misplaced anger.

The effects of this dis-ease are drug addiction, alcoholism, gangs and gang violence, murder, prison, unemployment, illiteracy, poverty, welfare, homelessness, fatherless kids, teenage pregnancies, child abuse and neglect, and domestic violence.

The true cause of this dis-ease is the psychological conditioning that has been passed down from one Black generation to the next, for the last 400 years, which your forefathers received through the institution of American slavery and the "Willie Lynch Process."

As a result of your dis-ease, your slave mentality, you have become angry, hostile, and violent, and you have become your own worst enemy.

I am going to show you how you have been deceived, manipulated, and mis-educated into your slave mentality. But once I teach you how you came to be in this condition, it is your responsibility, from that point forward, to free your own mind and get yourself out of this condition.

Once you know the truth, you can no longer claim ignorance as an excuse.

Once you know better, you must do better.

Let the lessons begin!

3

RACE MATTERS

The Politics and Origins of Racism and Racial Oppression

To talk about race in America is to explore the wilderness inside ourselves and to come to terms with a history we'd rather conceal.
-   **Cornel West, Philosopher and Activist**

Black people in this country have been, and continue to be subjected to every form of racism, racial discrimination, and racial oppression in every social venue you can think of including housing, education, business, employment, financing, entertainment, and the law. The only possible exception to this rule is sports, but I'm not sure that's entirely true either.

Yet, despite the long sordid history of racism, discrimination, and racial oppression, very few Black people actually understand what racism or discrimination is or *how* and *why* and *when* and by *whom* they are being oppressed.

You hear Black people talking about racism, discrimination, and oppression all the time, and it's true that we are oppressed as a race and as individuals. However, I'm not entirely convinced that Black people really understand that there is a big difference between racism, discrimination, and oppression, or why it is important to know the difference.

Why is it so important to know the difference?

First of all, one of the central themes of this book is that racism, racial discrimination, and racial oppression are, historically, the biggest contributors to black-on-black crime and violence, so understanding what the differences are will help you understand the points I'm trying to make.

Second of all, I think it is vitally important to understand the difference between these concepts, because people have a tendency to use words and ideas incorrectly and as a result end up sounding foolish to people who do know the difference.

With that being said, I'm going to clarify as best I can what the differences are between racism, discrimination, and oppression.

Let's start with the word *racism* which gets used, and often overused, incorrectly, just about every day.

Racism is a negative attitude or belief about a group of people based solely on the color of their skin, or their ethnic origin. These attitudes can be expressed in many different ways including the way people talk to you, the way people look at you, and ultimately the way people treat you.

Most people are racist to some degree. It's an unfortunate fact of human psychology that you feel some degree of animosity or discomfort toward people who look different from you.

But here's the important part: racism is about what you *think*, not what you *do*.

If you think all Black people are lazy and ignorant, that's *racist thinking*. If you think all White people are racists, that too is *racist thinking*.

And it doesn't have to be between different races. White people can have racist attitudes about Whites, and Black people can have racist attitudes about Blacks, and they both often do.

However, *racism* is not *discrimination*.

Discrimination is the unfavorable treatment of a person because of some recognizable characteristics about that person. The key words are *unfavorable treatment*. That means you have to take some adverse or harmful action against a person as a result of your negative attitudes about them, or their particular group.

For example, a White person can hate or dislike Black people simply because they are Black, and with no other justification for their feelings. That's *racism*.

But if that same White person denies you a job simply because you are Black, that's *discrimination* in general, and *racial discrimination* in particular.

As another example, if the Asian convenience store owner follows the Black customers around the store, but doesn't follow the White customers, that's discrimination. It's his attitude toward Blacks that makes its racism, because he *thinks* all Black people steal. But it's his actions that make it *racial discrimination,* because he only follows (*harasses*) Blacks.

People are discriminated against for all types of absurd reasons: *race, nationality, ethnicity, gender, religion, height, weight,* and *political affiliation,* just to name a few.

Racist views can and often do result in discrimination, but not necessarily. The bottom line is: you can *think* whatever you want to think about a person, but you better not take any negative *actions* against them to show it. That's *discrimination*, and that's illegal. Yet, racism and discrimination, as ugly as they are by themselves, are different from oppression.

Oppression is much, much worse. It is the "evil big brother" of the three. Discrimination and oppression are similar in that they both require adverse or harmful actions, but the major difference between the two is that discrimination is aimed at individuals, whereas oppression is aimed at entire groups of people with some common characteristic (*i.e., skin color*).

Oppression is the relentless systematic mistreatment of one group of people (Black) by another group of people (White), in which there is an imbalance of power within the social institutions that control both groups. The *imbalance of power within the social institutions* is a critical component in the definition of oppression.

Institutions of power are legally established entities that control different aspects of our lives such as, the financial institutions like the banking system, or the legal institutions like the courts and criminal justice system, or the educational institutions like the public school systems and colleges.

These are institutions of power.

Oppression can only occur where institutional power exists and where there is an imbalance in the institutional power.

BLACK SON RISING

In other words, if there is no institutional power to begin with, or there is no imbalance of power within the institution, then you cannot claim oppression.

For example, if Blacks had equal 50-50 power in financial institutions like banks, then you could not say that financial institutions were oppressing Blacks simply because they were being denied loans from the banks, because there is a balance of power within the institution

However, if Blacks only held 10% of the power of the financial institutions and were being denied loans at a significant rate, you could then make the argument for oppression, because there is an imbalance of power, 90% versus 10%, within the institution, and there is an adverse or harmful action against Blacks as a specifically targeted group.

Systematic mistreatment refers to the deliberate and widespread way in which mental, physical, and/or verbal forms of abuse are directed at particular groups targeted for oppression.

This systematic mistreatment has to occur at an institutional level, not on an individual level, and it must be directed toward a targeted group. In our case, we, meaning Black people, are the targeted group.

For example, the man who owns the local convenience store can't oppress you, even if he is mistreating you and discriminating against you, because he is not part of a larger system of institutional power. He's one man, with one little store. By himself, he is not a social institution. He may be a racist, but he is not an oppressor, and you have not been oppressed by him, even if he takes negative actions against you solely because of your race.

As another example, let's say you applied to a college that has an Equal Opportunity policy, meaning that "students shall be admitted without regard to race, gender, or religion."

Yet, you were denied admission because of the racist beliefs of that one particular admissions officer who reviewed your application. You have definitely been discriminated against, but you have not been *oppressed*.

However, if that same college has a majority White admissions board (*an imbalance of power*), and consistently denies admission to Black people specifically (*a targeted group*), then you can argue that Black people are being oppressed by that particular institution, because the institution as a whole discriminates against Blacks.

See the difference?

The discrimination has to be widespread throughout the college and overtly or covertly approved by the institution's policy makers, in order for it to be considered *oppression*.

Furthermore, if the majority of the colleges in the country have a majority White admissions board, which consistently denies admissions to Black people overall, then you could argue that the educational system (*an institution of power*) oppresses Blacks by denying them the same educational opportunities as Whites.

This too is illegal and it happens all the time. However, this kind of discrimination and oppression is very difficult to prove, because the institutions have argued that the Blacks didn't meet the admission standards, which are usually based on tests designed to exclude Blacks.

Oppression is institutionalized, in that it is enforced and sanctioned through the nation's legal, economic, social, welfare, and education

14

institutions. It is this institutionalization of oppression that perpetuates the imbalance of power.

Big businesses determine what products should be produced, the means and quality of their production, who will produce them, and for whom they will be produced.

The educational institutions decide what knowledge will be taught, how it will be taught, and who will teach it.

The legal and political institutions decide what laws to implement, who these laws will impact, and how these laws will be enforced.

The way oppression works in institutions is by penalizing particular groups of people by denying them career opportunities and prohibiting access to education, political influence, productive employment, decent housing, and fair and equal treatment by the law; all of which happens to Black people every day in this country.

Institutions of power are the ones that decide which non-target groups will be rewarded and which target groups will be penalized. The target groups are usually identified by race, nationality, ethnicity, gender, age, religion, sexual orientation, and other physical characteristics.

Your physical characteristics are very important to the institutions of power, because they make it that much easier to identify you as belonging to the target group.

In White America, the non-target groups of people who receive the majority of the rewards from the institutions of power are overwhelmingly middle and upper-class, white Christian men. This unequal distribution of rewards creates the imbalance of power necessary for the oppression of Blacks and other target groups.

Institutionalized oppression occurs in a self-perpetuating cycle that is designed to support and justify the imbalance of power in economic, political, legal, educational, financial, and other social institutions. This cycle begins with the deliberate, willful, and systematic process of misinforming the masses in general, and the target groups in particular.

This self-perpetuating cycle creates a social condition in which both the target groups (Blacks) and the non-target groups (Whites) are socialized to accept as "gospel truth" the misinformation they have been fed through the institutions of power.

A perfect example of this is the educational institutions' willful and deliberate false depiction of Black history as the history of a race of backward, ignorant savages. This false Black history has been taught to Black and White students as "truth" and is used to justify White people's sense of superiority and the Black's sense of inferiority, which is necessary for racial oppression to exist and persist.

The next step in this socialization process is blaming the victim of oppression for being oppressed, which cements the self-perpetuating cycle.

In other words, it's your fault that you are oppressed, because you are oppressed. It's that kind of backward, racist circular logic that uses the effects of oppression to justify continued oppression.

For example, poverty, unemployment, crime, violence, low academic achievement, and under-employment in low income, menial occupations are all the effects of racist beliefs that spawn acts of discrimination that give rise to institutionalized oppression, but they are also used as justification for further acts of racism, discrimination, and oppression.

BLACK SON RISING

The self-perpetuating cycle of racial oppression works like this:

I'm Black and I come to you looking for a job. You're white and hold the racist belief that all Blacks are ignorant and too lazy to work. You deny me the job, because of your racist beliefs, so now I am actually unemployed thanks to you. You then use my unemployed status as proof of your racist beliefs that I'm too lazy to work.

Next, I go looking for the education and training you say I need to get a job. However, before I can get into the training program, I have to pass a test that you created, which tests for knowledge you know I'm not likely to possess, thereby confirming your racist beliefs that Black people are ignorant. Yet you're the one who set up the under-funded school systems in Black neighborhoods, with inadequate books and unqualified teachers, that fail to teach Black people the bare minimum knowledge they need to pass the test you created in order to bar me from the training I need to get a job that you never wanted me to have in the first place.

So now I am truly ignorant, and unemployed, and forced to work in the underground economies that give rise to crime and violence that you think all Black people engage in; all because your racist attitudes toward me have created the conditions and the institutions that perpetuate my ignorance and unemployment, and my criminal and violent conduct, and reconfirm your racist beliefs.
Then you tell me it's all my fault to begin with, because I'm too ignorant and too lazy to know any better or do any different.

That's the real danger of institutionalized racial oppression:

It cements in the minds of the oppressed the notion that they deserve the conditions from which they are suffering, even though the conditions have been deliberately created by the systems of institutionalized racial oppression to begin with.

The Origins of Racism and Racial Oppression

There has always been some form of racism in the world, ever since modern man recognized his own physical differences from people in other groups and tribes.

However, the colonial form of racism we know and see today emerged out of the European and American slave trade during the 17th and 18th centuries. It was at the height of the European and American slave trade that Black people could be bought and sold like chattel property – and subjected to rape and mutilation – because they were regarded as sub-humans, and as being no better than cattle or any other livestock.

The basis for this racist concept of Blacks as less than human already existed in European culture in general, and in the Catholic Church specifically, which held that those who were not believers in the "one true Christian church" were obviously inferior beings and therefore, "less than human."

As a result of the Church's "heathen" doctrine, a whole new system of racist beliefs was developed which attempted to prove that Blacks were less intelligent than Whites, with smaller brains and a capacity only for manual labor.

It was during this era of colonial and Church rule, that Blacks began being depicted as uncivilized savages, despite the Church's knowledge of the existence of the world's greatest Black civilizations in Ethiopia, Egypt, Ghana, Mali, and Songhai. The significant contributions of these civilizations to the advancement of the Western World, in the form of math, architecture, science, medicine, and astronomy, have been deliberately hidden by the Church, and from the rest of the world, to this present day.

Contrary to popular belief, racial oppression was historically rooted in capitalism first, and racism second. Capitalism is an economic system in which the laborers do all of the work of production and the capitalists collect all the profits from their efforts. Think of it this way: you do all the work at the factory or warehouse, but the guy who owns the factory gets all the profits that your labor produces. The factory worker who works at the Ford car manufacturing plant doesn't get rich, but the guy who owns Ford does.

In order for capitalism to work, you need huge quantities of physical labor to produce the goods you want to sell. That means you need workers, especially ones you don't have to pay much, so that you can keep most of the profits from whatever you produce and sell. Next, you need somebody who wants to buy whatever it is you're producing, so you need consumers. But the consumers need material wealth and resources to buy the things you're producing and selling.

That's how this whole slavery thing got kicked off in Europe to begin with:

Spain and Portugal wanted to buy the luxury items that were being produced by England, France, Holland, and Germany, so they sent their armies under the supervision of Christopher Columbus to the Americas (i.e., the New World) to steal the gold and silver from the native Americans, to buy those luxury items, and then pave the way for future European colonists to use the native Americans' lands for crop production to create future revenue to buy European goods.

In order to plunder the gold and silver of the native Americans, and later rob them of their tribal lands in order to establish plantations to grow sugar, tobacco, and rice for commercial export to Europe, the European colonists had to exterminate millions of native Americans, because the native Americans were not going to just sit back and watch the colonists take over their land and resources without a fight.

For awhile the colonists were using the native Americans to plant and grow the crops of sugar, tobacco, and rice that were shipped and sold to Europe. However, from the time they arrived in the "New World" to about 50 years later, the Spanish conquistadors had exterminated about 15 million native Americans. Consequently, densely populated areas like Haiti, Cuba, Nicaragua, and the coast of Venezuela were completely destroyed and the inhabitants raped, tortured, and murdered, or infected with deadly diseases.

17

As a result, the European colonists (plantation owners) were suddenly faced with a serious shortage of cheap labor.

The colonists had to figure out a way to get free bonded (forced) labor over to the new lands to replace the native Americans they had massacred. At first, the colonists relied upon the importation of indentured servants, or serfs, from different European countries. But that didn't last long because the indentured servants were either dying from sicknesses or constantly running away, and unless they were marked or branded, you couldn't tell an indentured servant from a colonial master, because they all looked alike (i.e., white).

The crops the colonists produced in the New World were shipped to Europe for sale to other countries around the world, including African countries. The more crops that were sold, the richer Europe became. The richer Europe became, the more crops they wanted. The more crops they wanted, the more workers were needed to grow the crops at a faster pace and in greater quantities. However, the colonists were running out of indentured servants, because the word had spread that life was too hard in the New World, and that people were dying left and right. As the number of indentured servants got smaller, it became increasingly urgent to find new, more abundant, and more easily identifiable sources of forced, free labor.

Enter the African slave trade.

Someone came up with the "brilliant" idea to use Africans as free slave labor, and the African slave trade worked out extremely well for the colonists, because African slaves could be purchased cheaply and brought in unlimited numbers from the west coast of Africa. And by keeping them scattered, ignorant, and terrorized, the colonial plantation owners could keep the Africans in perpetual subjugation.

Furthermore, the color of their skin made Black Africans easily identifiable, stopping them from escaping and merging with the rest of the colonial population. Consequently, the skin color of all Black people became the sign and symbol of our servitude, for generations to come.

This was in fact the true origin of colonial racism toward Africans and the beginning of economic-based racial oppression.

Slavery was not motivated by racism initially. White racism, the view that those with non-white skins were inferior to those with white skins, was gradually developed over time to justify the particular form of slave labor that was introduced in the New World through capitalism.

Slavery, and slave trade for economic purposes, existed long before the European conquest of the Americas. Slavery was a common practice in Spain and Portugal. The Spaniards have a long history of enslaving the people they conquered. The Spanish armies engaged in the slave trade for hundreds of years, and often carried African slaves in their crews. In fact, Christopher Columbus had African slaves in his crew on his first voyage across the Atlantic.

However, the form of slavery that was commonly practiced in Spain and Portugal was not chattel slavery, but serfdom. Serfs were agricultural laborers who were not allowed to leave the land until they satisfied some contractual obligation.

Initially, Spain and Portugal did not enslave people based on their skin color. Instead the differences between slaves and slave owners were, at first, defined by the person's religion, in other words, if they were Christians versus "heathens." Heathens could be enslaved but Christians could not.

The non-white people the Spanish and Portuguese enslaved were considered "infidels" (non-Christians), subject by "Divine Law" to serve Christian masters. As late as the middle of the 15th century, when the slave trade to Portugal first began, the rationalization for the enslavement of Africans was not that they were dark-skinned, but that they were not Christians.

Furthermore, the Portuguese and Spanish rulers' social control of colonized peoples depended on their conversion to Christianity (the dominant religion of the ruling class). Many Africans during the early slave trade in Portugal did convert to Christianity and were subsequently freed and intermarried with the Portuguese.

But slavery based on religious beliefs was too difficult to enforce from one generation to the next, because you could not look at a person and tell whether or not they were Christian or heathen, but you could look at them and tell whether they were Black or White very easily. It was that first realization of skin differences as an easily identifiable marker, that made race a factor for enslavement instead of religion.

Once skin color became a useful symbol of enslavement, it seemed only "natural" for Africans to be forced into a subordinate social status. The next logical step was to conclude that Blacks must have been "naturally" inferior to Whites to begin with, because "If Blacks were not inferior to Whites how else could they have been enslaved by them?"

This racist view was necessary for justifying the use of Black slave labor by the capitalist plantation owners in the southern states of the U.S.

Slavery in the U.S.

The southern plantation owners in the U.S. could not condone or allow "White slavery" because it was clearly in contradiction to the Declaration of Independence ("We hold these Truths to be self-evident, that all Men are created equal, that they are endowed by their Creator with certain unalienable Rights, that among these are Life, Liberty and the Pursuit of Happiness...").

But "Black slavery" could be justified through the racist idea that people of African ancestry were not *men* anyway, but a *childlike, inferior race of sub-human beings who are undeserving of equal rights with White men.*

However, even after the abolition of chattel slavery in the late 19th century, racism still continued to serve the interests of capitalists by justifying the creation of cheap wage laborers. In fact, racism became much more prevalent (*common*) after the abolition of chattel slavery in America.

With the emancipation of Black slaves in 1865, their transformation into wage-based workers required the introduction of a new system of legalized slavery (i.e., *segregation through Jim Crow laws*) that would effectively nullify their status as "free" laborers, and justify the denial of the equal rights that they were formally "entitled" to under the U.S. Constitution.

Therefore, racism became even more useful as a justification for discrimination and racial oppression.

And contrary to popular belief, slavery in America wasn't abolished because of Abraham Lincoln's sense of humanitarianism, or his belief in the inherent equality between Black people and Whites. Lincoln's decision to abolish slavery was based on purely economic reasons, because slavery was no longer profitable and stood in the way of the economic development of the North.

Slaves were too expensive to feed and maintain, and the newly developing capitalist economies needed a mobile workforce and consumers who could afford to buy the goods now being produced in capitalist factories. Slaves, who were not a mobile workforce and had no wages with which to buy capitalist products, were standing in the way of the North's "economic progress."

Economic issues of capitalist greed created the conditions that led to the American Civil War - not the issue of racial equality. It was the North's desire to industrialize itself and the need to challenge the power of the Southern plantation owners that led to war, not whether or not slaves should be set free. Very few gave a damn about the Black slaves. They were merely pawns in the White racists' struggle for economic power over fellow White racist brethren.

Slavery did finally end as a result of the Civil War and the ratification of the Thirteenth Amendment. But it was simply replaced with cheap wage labor - and the U.S. Constitution continued to regard Black people as only three-fifths of a human.

Colonialism and slavery may have ended officially, but it was no longer necessary to colonize or enslave people in order to exploit them. It is largely racism, the enduring sense of Black people, and other people of color, as somehow inferior and uncivilized, which allows the white power structure in this country to continue exploiting poor Blacks and other minorities.

Make no mistake, racism, discrimination, and oppression in the U.S. are just as rampant today as in the 17th, 18th, and 19th centuries, although not as blatant and in your face as before, and that's only because it's supposedly illegal to openly discriminate against individuals or groups of people. That's why it's done on the institutional level, because it's harder to prove discrimination there.

Nonetheless, even to this present day, Black people are still more likely to be unemployed than Whites, and for longer periods of time, still earning less money in menial, low-wage jobs, and living in the absolute worst housing conditions imaginable.

The Slavery Issue in Modern Times

Some people, both Black and White, are wondering, "Why is it that in 2006, we are still discussing issues of racism, discrimination, and oppression?"

Because unfortunately racism is forever, discrimination is here to stay, and as long as people have the institutional power to oppress others, they will. That's a fact of human nature.

That means that for Black people in America, as long as we're living in this racially hostile nation that's run primarily by "undercover" white supremacists – and as long as we remain ignorant of our true history and heritage – we will always be on the receiving end of race-based hostility, discrimination, and oppression.

To this day, White people look at Black people like we are crazy for even mentioning the word "slavery." To them, we are still using slavery and racism as an excuse to justify our poverty, unemployment, drug abuse, criminal behavior, and violence toward each other. They want us to go around pretending that slavery never happened, or that it happened "so long ago" that we should "just let it go and move on."

Wake up, White people! That's not going to happen. We are not going to forget about it and we are not going to let you forget about it either, because even though slavery officially ended 140 years ago, the effects are still evident to this day in the form of "Black suffering" and "White privilege."

To make the point as to why Black people can't and shouldn't "just let it go," I quote a useful and informative dialogue on the "slave issue" and "White privilege" that was proffered by Dr. Claud Anderson, president of the Harvest Institute, and author of *Black Labor, White Wealth.* The dialogue is between Dr. Anderson and an imaginary White person who questions Black people's reluctance to let go of their slave past:

QUESTION: Slavery happened so long ago. I am not responsible for it. Why can't we just forget it?

ANSWER: The nation's race problem, a structural economic inequality between the races, is directly traceable back to and across four centuries of slavery and Jim Crow apartheid (semi-slavery). Slavery and Jim Crow established and maintained imbalances between the races. Under these social and economic systems, nearly 100 percent of this nation's wealth and power resources, and controls of all levels of government, were maldistributed into the hands of dominant white society. The advantages, preferences and wealth assets, in the form of stocks, bonds, shares, businesses, land, insurance benefits and trust accounts, are passed from one generation to the next through inheritance laws. Though whites today continue to enjoy the advantages of centuries of government-supported preferences for Whites, most live in a state of denial about how their group's wealth and power were acquired.

QUESTION: Why should the U.S. government apologize to Blacks for slavery?

ANSWER: For centuries, this nation's "Government of, by and for the people" did not include the Black race. Without government support, neither slavery nor Jim Crow segregation could have long endured. The government has apologized to all other groups to whom it has committed offenses, except Blacks. Yet, Black Americans have borne the burden of every obligation this nation has had since 1619. Black Americans did not confiscate nearly two billion acres of land from Native Americans. However, for more than four centuries, Blacks paid taxes and their life blood so that Whites who did confiscate the land could develop and enjoy it. Money out of Black pockets supported a federal Indian bureau and state commissions that gave Indians benefits that Blacks never received. Blacks did not start WWII, but money from their pockets made up the $13 billion that rebuilt Germany under the Marshall Plan and Japan under the Point Four Plan. Blacks did not intern Japanese Americans in the 1940s but helped to pay $22,000 in reparations awarded to each descendant in 1992. Real racial equality for Blacks in America begins with an apology and acknowledgment from the government that millions of Blacks were wrongfully used and killed. Economic justice and reparations must naturally follow.

QUESTION: Were not the Civil War, the 13th 14th and 15th Amendments to the Constitution an apology?

ANSWER: History itself provides the answer to this question. The Civil War was fought for a number of reasons, but not to free black slaves. A primary reason was to relocate the slave-produced wealth and industries of the South to the North. Attitude surveys conducted on the eve of the Civil War reported that less than 2% of white Americans were willing to go to war with the South to free Black slaves. Ironically, the Civil War and the enactment of the 13th, 14th, and 15th Amendments, ended full slavery, but allowed Jim Crow semi-slavery to replace it within two years. Jim Crow semi-slavery continued until the late 1960s.

QUESTION: How is the Dred Scott decision related to today's controversies about racism and whether to issue an apology to Blacks for slavery?

ANSWER: The Dred Scott decision issued in 1854 said that "Blacks had no rights that a White person was bound to respect." That decision established a legal dictum that was a common thread through slavery, Jim Crow apartheid, and the period of benign neglect and continues to be reflected in policies to this day. The Dred Scott decision was never reversed by the courts. The dominant society's practice of equating and confusing Black experiences with those of gender, class, ethnicity and physical handicaps continues the legal legacy of the Dred Scott decision.

QUESTION: What is racism?

ANSWER: Racism is a power relationship between groups based upon color. It is a group concept and occurs when one group has so much power that it can force another group to do what it wants. Its purpose is the uneven and unfair distribution of power, privilege, land and wealth to Whites. Contrary to the arguments of conservatives, racism is not fundamentally about individual actions and beliefs. The concept of racism did not exist until the 16th century commercial enslavement of Blacks began. Because Blacks as a group do not have the power, the black race has no racists, only Blacks re-acting racism.

QUESTION: What is the best way to frame a national discussion on race?
ANSWER: Any constructive look at race must be based upon an analysis of history. It is an examination of history that tells why the race issue exists, how it came to be, the social laws and customs that form the legacy that we see today in disparities between Blacks and Whites. A serious discussion would also seek to quantify the harm that was done to Black people. The uninformed opinions and misinformation that usually characterize racial discussions, result from an unwilling-ness to examine history and to approach the topic intellectually rather than emotionally.
QUESTION: Instead of race, why can't we focus more on the indivi-dual and individual accomplishment?

ANSWER: Race by definition refers to a group. Blacks as a group were subjected to the cruelties of slavery and Jim Crow apartheid. It was because they were members of a group that Blacks were enslaved, lynched, castrated. It is because of race that Whites, as a group, have advantages and preferences. It is easier for Whites to be attracted to the concept of individualism because with their wealth, power and population monopolies, they have not been and cannot be the victims of racism.

The Little Mouse Who Couldn't

I saw something the other day that really put this whole idea of slavery, racism, discrimination, and racial oppression into perspective for me.

Have you ever put down those sticky paper traps around the house to catch a mouse?

About a week ago, I saw a mouse in my home, so I decided to lay down a few of the sticky traps around the kitchen, before the mouse could get too comfortable with his new surroundings.

I went to the kitchen the next morning and sure enough, there was this poor little mouse stuck to the trap. My first reaction was pride and satisfaction: "I caught that little sucker! He's getting the hell up out of here! That'll teach his little butt about invading my home!"

I stood there for awhile and watched, in amusement at first, while that little mouse tried his best to get off that sticky paper.

He struggled as hard as he could, but no matter how hard he tried, that sticky trap just held him down, and would not let him go.

As he struggled in vain, you could see his little heart pounding in his chest from absolute terror and frenzied physical exertion. Eventually he died, but he died a long, slow painful death. He bled from the mouth, and urinated all over that trap. I don't know if it was fear that finally made his heart give out, or the recognition that despite his best efforts, he was not getting off that trap.

Either way, the end result was the same: *his physical death, which was preceded by his mental death.*

It was truly a sickening thing to watch, and it broke my heart that I was the one who caused his death.

As I watched in horror at what I had done to this little mouse, it dawned on me that this mouse's struggle was not unlike the struggle of Black men.

The sticky trap in our case is racism and racial oppression, to which Black men have been stuck for the past 400 years; but no matter how hard we struggle to get off the trap, the trap just will not let go.

And eventually we die.

First in the spirit, then in the mind, and finally in the body, as our hearts burst in our chests, and as the pain, anguish, and hopelessness of our condition takes hold.

I felt really bad for that little mouse and how he died struggling in vain, for no other reason than the fact that he was a mouse. If he had been a cat or dog, he would have been welcome in my home. But no, he was a rodent, a foul disgusting little "Black" creature that lived off the garbage of others. Or so I was "taught" to believe.

Like the little mouse, Black men have been mislabeled and portrayed as foul, disgusting, and nasty little creatures who can't or won't do for themselves, but who live off the efforts of others. Thus, traps have been laid out for our demise, because who needs such creatures in existence anyway?

However, after watching the little mouse squirm around on that trap, it occurred to me that the one advantage Black men have that the little mouse didn't, is the brains to learn how to avoid the traps of racism, discrimination, and racial oppression altogether.

Freedom from the trap of racism and oppression is our ultimate goal, but knowledge and education is the key to avoiding the trap in the first place!

Who would have ever thought the death of that "little mouse who couldn't" would make the real tragedy of racism and racial oppression, and their solution, so crystal clear?

4

STOLEN LEGACY

The Rape, Murder, and Theft of
African Knowledge, History, and Culture

*America's greatest crime against the black man was not slavery or lynchings,
but that he was taught to wear a mask of self-hate and self-doubt.*
- **Malcolm X, Nationalist Leader**

Because of racism and white supremacy ideology, the greatest lie ever told
in the history of the human race is that the Black race is inferior to the White
race. The greatest crime ever committed in history is the intellectual theft of
Africa's knowledge of arts and sciences, and the material theft of Africa's
vast natural resources like gold and diamonds.

First, not only are Blacks not inferior to Whites, but Black Africans
taught the European Whites everything they know about the arts and sciences.
Everything, and I mean absolutely everything the White European race knows
about anything – including math, science, architecture, ch(k)emistry,
medicine, philosophy, psychology, religion, and astronomy - they learned, or
rather they stole, from the Black race in Egypt (read *Stolen Legacy* by George
G.M. James).

Second, contrary to what some ignorant, uneducated people might tell
you, the original race in Egypt was Black, unlike the Arabic Egyptians you
see today. The original Egyptians were Ethiopians and Nubians, who migrated
from Ethiopia to Sudan and from Sudan to Nubia, and finally from Nubia
they developed the land and culture of Egypt, the greatest civilization known
to man. This is a proven anthropological fact.

Another proven anthropological fact is that while the Black race in
Egypt, Ethiopia, and Nubia was building pyramids, temples, monuments,
universities, and libraries, the White European race (Caucasians) was still
living as backward savages in caves, in the Caucasus mountains of eastern
Europe.

They were the wild, uncivilized man, running around buck-naked, eating
raw meat while the Egyptian astronomers and mathematicians were charting
and plotting the stars, and developing the world's first comprehensive,
organized religion called the Mysteries (*the basis of Judaism, Christianity,
and Islam*).

For the last 2000 years, white supremacists have been willfully and
deliberately trying to convince Africans and African Americans that they
were ignorant, backward, and uncivilized savages who ran around in grass
skirts before the Europeans arrived on the scene to liberate them from their
lowly, "heathen" existence.

When in fact, the Caucasian races of man are the original savages
they've been trying to convince us we were. They have utterly and completely

reversed the truth. Advanced civilizations didn't start with the Caucasian or European races. They started with the Black race, the original "hue-man" race, in Africa.

The subjugation of Africans, and subsequently African Americans, began with the deliberate rewriting and reversal of the true history of both the African and European races.

As Black people, we've been conditioned, or rather colonized, through the numerous systems of institutionalized racism, to believe that prior to slavery, the African was as a nobody, a non-entity, and an insignificant footnote in the pages of a "glorious white world history."

The Black race has been willfully miseducated, through an intricate socialization process, into believing the most despicable lie ever told:

That as a race, African people were weak, lazy, and ignorant savages who didn't know anything of any importance, never produced anything of any significance, and had always depended on the charity and generosity of other nations for their survival.

And that today, Black people all over the world, the descendants of these African savages, are no better off, or any smarter than their ancestors.

This is the white racist message that Black people are still being bombarded by, to this very day!

The Europeans fabricated this false history of Africa as a backward, uncivilized continent of dark-skinned, sub-human beings to justify their looting of African resources, their murdering and plundering of entire African villages, and their enslavement of millions of native Africans in order to build their white racist empires and satisfy their capitalist greed.

This whole socialization and miseducation process was achieved by deliberately falsifying the history of the world's greatest African civilization of Kemet (which Europeans call Egypt). The ancient Egyptians actually called themselves Kemmui, which meant "Black," written in their language of Medu – Neter. For years, Western historians have tried to divorce Black Africans from their Kemetic roots, while at the same time attributing the accomplishments of the ancient Kemmui to the Greeks, their cousins.

Although the Kemmui were a grand and glorious civilization, they were, in fact, preceded by a much earlier civilization called Ta-Seti (Nubia), which meant "Land of the Bow" because the Nubians were world renowned for their skill with the bow and arrow.

The Ta-Seti peoples (Nubians) were the original cultural developers of Kemet, who migrated north from Ethiopia into Sudan, eventually settling in the "Land of the Bow."

Where is that kind of information found in the white racists' history books that are used to teach our Black children in the public miseducation system?

It's not there, because the White people who make up public education policy don't want you or our children to know these facts about their own race. They want you and our children to swallow the European racist view of white supremacy which grew out of the false notion that the Greeks, their cousins, invented the arts and the sciences.

Stolen Legacy

The sole basis of their racial arrogance is that the Greeks were the originators of religious and philosophical thought, and the developers of modern concepts of philosophy, math, science, architecture, and astronomy.

For centuries, so-called Greek philosophers like Socrates, Plato, and Aristotle have been falsely credited for mankind's greatest intellectual advancements.

Nothing could be further from the truth.

The funny part is that the Greeks themselves never attempted to take credit for these developments. In fact, they did just the opposite; they praised and glorified the ancient Kemmui:

And upon his return to Greece, they gathered around and asked, "Tell us about this great land of the Blacks called Ethiopia." And Herodotus said, "There are two great Ethiopian nations, one in Sind (India) and the other in Egypt."
   - **Recorded by Diodorus (Greek historian 100 B.C.)**

They tell you in their own historical accounts, written by their own historians and so-called philosophers, that they learned everything they know from the Egyptians:

Compared with the Egyptians, the Greeks are childish mathematicians.
   - **Plato**

So then why are we still giving credit to the Greeks for the development of the arts and sciences?

Why are Black college students, even those in so-called Historically Black Colleges and Universities, still pledging Greek fraternities and sororities, and flashing Greek letters with such false pride and arrogance?

Greeks didn't develop the arts and sciences that are taught in colleges and universities; Black Africans did.

Black college students attending HBCUs are supposed to be some of the brightest students in the country, and the biggest supporters of Afrocentric lifestyles. I don't see it. I have friends who graduated from HBCUs who know very little, if anything about true African history, and still run around calling out the Greek letters of their respective fraternities and sororities.

If they are so Afrocentric, then:

Where are the African fraternities, sororities, and letters?

How many of these Black frat bothers have actually read books about African history, written by African historians?

How many college professors actually teach true African history?

Why are we selling ourselves short of our rich African heritage and accomplishments?

Why are we so damned impressed with everything white and European?

Why do we continue to persist in our own humiliation?

I've been to Egypt. I've seen the pyramids, and the temples, and the monuments with my own eyes and the carvings of the images of the pharaohs, with prominent Negroid features, who built them. I've been to Abu Simbel where the hollowed out stone mountain temple of Ramses II, Egypt's greatest pharaoh and a Brother, rises up majestically to tower over the landscape of the kingdom of Nubia.

I've seen the libraries and universities of Luxor and Aswan, Egypt, that have stood there in antiquity for thousands of years before the arrival of the Caucasian and Mediterranean races.

You can't feed me any kind of bull about European this and European that. You can't trick me into thinking that everybody in Africa is running around in grass skirts and carrying spears, and that the Europeans "liberated the backward African savage from his ignorance."

I've been to eight different African nations, and despite what the white racist media would have you believe, not all Africans are poor, illiterate, or starving.

But you don't have to take *my* word for anything that I say about the rape of African knowledge and history. In fact, I encourage you to challenge everything I tell you about anything, and try to prove me wrong. I freely admit that I am not a historian. Nor have I learned everything I need to know about African and European history myself.

However, there are hundreds of Black historians, men like Dr. Maulana Karenga, George G.M. James, J.A. Rogers, Molefi Kete Asante, Dr. John Henrik Clarke, Dr. Chancellor Williams, and others too numerous to name, that have spent half their lives researching our history, and have all reached the same conclusions:

European white supremacists stole the knowledge, history, and culture of ancient Africa, and claimed it as their own. Worse yet, they used the knowledge to perpetuate a mythology of white racial superiority, and to create a system of world economic slavery.

Dr. John Henrik Clarke, one of the world's most beloved and respected Black historians, had this to say about European contact with African civilizations and the alteration of African history:

Africa and its people are the most written about and the least understood of all of the world's people. This condition started in the 15th and the 16th centuries with the beginning of the slave trade system. The Europeans not only colonialized most of the world, they began to colonialize information about the world and its people. In order to do this, they had to forget, or pretend to forget, all they had previously known about the Africans... Contrary to a misconception which still prevails, the Africans were familiar with literature and art for many years before their contact with the Western World. Before the breaking-up of the social structure of the West African states of Ghana, Mali and Songhay and the internal strife and chaos that made the slave trade possible, the forefathers of the Africans who eventually became slaves in the United States, lived in a society where university life was fairly common and scholars were held in reverence.

Of the soldiers in the struggle to completely eradicate the pervasive racial myths clinging to the origins of African history, few scholars have had the impact of Dr. Chancellor James Williams (1898-1992). Chancellor

Williams achieved wide acclaim as the author of the 1971 publication, *The Destruction of Black Civilization—Great Issues of a Race from 4500 B.C. to 2000 A.D.*

In *The Destruction of Black Civilization*, Chancellor Williams effectively described white supremacist efforts to alter African history and deny Africans any credit for contributing to world civilization. He called this systematic method of denying and altering Black African heritage, *The 7 Criteria of White Supremacy in Dealing with Black History*, which is described below:

The 7 Criteria of White Supremacy in Dealing with Black History:

1.   Ignore or refuse to publish any facts on African history that would not support their racist theories.

2.   Create a religious and scientific doctrine to ease the white conscience for oppression and enslavement of African people.

3.   Flood the world with hastily thrown together histories that contain European perspectives only.

4.   Start renaming people and places. Replace African names of persons, places and things with Arabic and European names; this will disguise their true black identity.

5.   Change the criteria for defining race. For example, one drop of Negro blood in America makes you Negro no matter how light your skin, but when reporting ancient history reverse the standard. Make one drop of white [non-Negro] blood render someone Caucasian no matter how dark his skin is.

6.   When Black civilization is so obvious your best schemes cannot hide it, find a way to attribute the success to outside white influence [or aliens from outer space].

7.   When all the ancient historians contradict your theory, seek to discredit them.

As Africans and African Americans, we have been humiliated and ridiculed because our history and heritage was stolen by Europeans, and our knowledge of the arts and sciences wrongly attributed to people who themselves deny the honor.

However, no one can humiliate you without your consent.

That means, if we continue to be ridiculed, it is because we allow ourselves to be ridiculed, by not taking the time to learn about our own history and heritage.

The only way we are ever going to be able to hold our heads high as a race, is to stop letting other people who don't have our best interest at heart teach us a false history about our own people and start taking personal responsibility for learning the truth about our significant African heritage for ourselves.

It is only then that we can begin to remove this sense of racial inferiority that has been bred into us through the systems of institutionalized racism that were created to perpetuate the myth of white racial superiority.

5

AMERIKKKAN HISTORY

The Psychological Effects of White-on-Black Violence

The most potent weapon in the hands of the oppressor, is the mind of the oppressed.
- Steven Biko, South Afrikan Revolutionary

Black-on-black crime and violence has reached epidemic proportions in hundreds of cities all over the country. Young Black men are dying every single day in America from violence we inflict on ourselves. This is a national crisis, with seemingly no end in sight!

At the root of black-on-black crime and violence are the fear, false pride, material greed, mental laziness, social ignorance, self-hatred, and misplaced anger of the perpetrators. However, if you really want to understand the true *causes* of black-on-black crime and violence, you must first learn and understand the history of White-on-Black crime and violence, and the devastating psychological *effect* it has had upon the mental, physical, and emotional condition of the Black race.

From the brutality of the American slave trade in the 1600s, through the vicious mob attacks during the civil rights era of the 1960s, and right on up to the police brutality of the 80s and 90s, and the 21st century, "AmeriKKKan History" is a history of racism, discrimination, and violence against Black Americans. For more than 400 years, Black Americans have been subjected to the worst kinds of racial hostility and physical brutality in history.

For centuries the White race has raped our Black women; lynched, castrated, and otherwise mutilated our Black men; and mentally and physically traumatized our people in the concentration-camp-like conditions of the slave plantations, the ghettos, and the prisons that they have created.

This mentally and physically oppressive environment has finally seeped into the social and psychological consciousness of the Black race. As a result of the constant and violent oppression by Whites, the Black race has become socially and psychologically conditioned to hate, fear, and destroy other Blacks. So that Blacks, once the victims, are now the victimizers.

It is through the psychological trauma of White-on-Black violence that we have become, in effect, our own worst enemies!

Although the systematic process of instilling self-hatred and fear and violence in the Black race began with the African slave trade, the scientific method of conditioning Blacks to hate and fear and brutalize each other, was eventually codified and honed to precision in the 1700s with the assistance of a British West Indies slave trader by the name of Willie Lynch.

Willie Lynch formulated a brilliant blueprint for not only the physical, but more importantly, the psychological enslavement of Blacks for generations to come.

He literally guaranteed the slave masters and plantation owners that if implemented, this slave-making doctrine would keep the Black race fearful of and dependent on the White race, and distrustful of and disloyal to itself, for at least 300 years, and possibly 1000 years or more.

His words have proven all too prophetic, because even unto this day, 300 years later, the Black race is still ruthless, disloyal, disrespectful, and violent toward its own.

The following slave-programming doctrine will hopefully change the minds of the ignorant Black people who say "Why are we still talking about slavery? That was more than 100 years ago."

In it, you will see that the condition of the Black race is due to a scientific and psychological blueprint for the perpetuation of the mental condition that allowed slavery to flourish and persist, even unto this very day.

This is a devastatingly effective blueprint for the mental and physical enslavement of the Black race!

Listen very carefully to what I am telling you here! Every negative condition the Black race suffers today – poverty, crime, violence, self-hatred, ignorance, and greed – can be traced back to this one devastatingly effective slave-programming doctrine!

LET'S MAKE A SLAVE
THE ORIGIN AND DEVELOPMENT OF A SOCIAL BEING CALLED "THE NEGRO"
by Willie Lynch

Let us make a slave. What do we need?

First of all, we need a black nigger man, a pregnant nigger woman, and her baby nigger boy. Second, we will use the same basic principle that we use in breaking a horse, combined with some more sustaining factors. We reduce them from their natural state in nature; whereas nature provides them with the natural capacity to take care of their needs and the needs of their offspring, we break that natural string of independence from them and thereby create a dependency state so that we may be able to get from them useful production for our business and pleasure.

For fear that our future generations may not understand the principle of breaking both horses and men, we lay down the art. For, if we are to sustain our basic economy we must break both of the beasts together, the nigger and the horse. We understand that short range planning in economics results in periodic economic chaos, so that, to avoid turmoil in the economy, it requires us to have breadth and depth in long range comprehensive planning, articulating both skill and sharp perception.

We lay down the following principles for long range comprehensive economic planning: Both horse and niggers are no good to the economy in the wild or natural state. Both must be broken and tied together for orderly production. For orderly futures, special and particular attention must be paid to the female

31

and the youngest offspring. Both must be crossbred to produce a variety and division of labor. Both must be taught to respond to a peculiar new language. Psychological and physical instruction of containment must be created for both.

We hold the above six cardinals as truths to be self-evident, based upon following discourse concerning the economics of breaking and tying the horse and nigger together...all inclusive of the six principles laid down above.

Note: *Neither principles alone will suffice for good economics. All principles must be employed for the orderly good of the nation. Accordingly, both a wild horse and a wild or natural nigger is dangerous even if captured, for they will have the tendency to seek their customary freedom, and, in doing so, might kill you in your sleep.*

You cannot rest. They sleep while you are awake and are awake while you are asleep. They are dangerous near the family house and it requires too much labor to watch them away from the house. Above all you cannot get them to work in this natural state.

Hence, both the horse and the nigger must be broken, that is break them from one form of mental life to another, keep the body and take the mind. In other words, break the will to resist.

Now the breaking process is the same for the horse and the nigger, only slightly varying in degrees. But as we said before, you must keep your eye focused on the female and the offspring of the horse and the nigger. A brief discourse in offspring development will shed light on the key to sound economic principle. Pay little attention to the generation of original breaking but concentrate on future generations. Therefore, if you break the female, she will break the offspring in its early years of development and, when the offspring is old enough to work, she will deliver it up to you. For her normal female protective tendencies will have been lost in the original breaking process. For example, take the case of the wild stud horse, a female horse and an already infant horse and compare the breaking process with two captured nigger males in their natural state, a pregnant nigger woman with her infant offspring. Take the stud horse, break him for limited containment. Completely break the female horse until she becomes very gentle whereas you or anybody can ride her in comfort. Breed the mare until you have the desired offspring. Then you can turn the stud to freedom until you need him again. Train the female horse whereby she will eat out of your hand, and she will train the infant horse to eat of your hand also.

When it comes to breaking the uncivilized nigger, use the same process, but vary the degree and step up the pressure so as to do a complete reversal of the mind. Take the meanest and most restless nigger, strip him of his clothes in front of the remaining niggers, the female, and the nigger infant, tar and feather him, tie each leg to a different horse faced in opposite directions, set him a fire and beat both horses to pull him apart in front of the remaining niggers. The next step is to take a bullwhip and beat the remaining nigger male to the point of death in front of the female and the infant. Don't kill him. But put the fear of God in him, for he can be useful for future breeding.

The Breaking Process of the African Woman

Take the female and run a series of tests on her to see if she will submit to your desires willingly. Test her in every way, because she is the most important factor for good economics. If she shows any signs of resistance in submitting completely to your will, do not hesitate to use the bull whip on her to extract that last bit of b_ _ _ _ out of her. Take care not to kill her, for in doing so, you spoil good economics. When in complete submission, she will train her offspring in the early years to submit to labor when they become of age. Understanding is the best thing. Therefore, we shall go deeper into this area of the subject matter concerning what we have produced here in this breaking of the female nigger.

We have reversed the relationship. In her natural uncivilized state she would have a strong dependency on the uncivilized nigger male, and she would have a limited protective dependency toward her independent male offspring and would raise female offspring to be dependent like her. Nature had provided for this type of balance. We reversed nature by burning and pulling one civilized nigger apart and bull whipping the other to the point of death- all in her presence. By her being left alone, unprotected, with the male image destroyed, the ordeal caused her to move from her psychological dependent state to a frozen independent state.

In this frozen psychological state of independence she will raise her male and female offspring in reversed roles. For fear of the young male's life she will psychologically train him to be mentally weak and dependent but physically strong. Because she has become psychologically independent, she will train her female offspring to be psychologically independent as well. What have you got? You've got the nigger woman out front and the nigger man behind and scared. This is the perfect situation for sound sleep and economics. Before the breaking process, we have to be alert and on guard at all times. Now we can sleep soundly, for out of frozen fear, his woman stands guard for us. He cannot get past her early infant slave molding process. He is a good tool, now ready to be tied to the horse at a tender age. By the time a nigger boy reaches the age of sixteen, he is soundly broken in and ready for a long life of sound and efficient work and the reproduction of a unit of good labor force.

Continually, through the breaking of uncivilized savage niggers, by throwing the nigger female savage into a frozen psychological state of independence, by killing the protective male image, and by creating a submissive dependent mind of the nigger male slave, we have created an orbiting cycle that turns on its own axis forever, unless a phenomenon occurs and re-shifts the positions of the male and female savages. We show what we mean by example. We breed two nigger males with two nigger females. Then we take the nigger males away from them and keep them moving and working. Say the nigger female bears a nigger female and the other bears a nigger male. both nigger females, being without influence of the nigger male image, frozen with an independent psychology, will raise him to be mentally dependent and weak, but physically strong...in other words, body over mind. We will mate and breed them and continue the cycle. That is good, sound, and long range comprehensive planning.

BLACK SON RISING

Warning: Possible Interloping Negatives

Earlier, we talked about the non-economic good of the horse and the nigger in their wild or natural state; we talked about the principle of breaking and tying them together for orderly production furthermore, we talked about paying particular attention to the female savage and her offspring for orderly future planning; then more recently we stated that, by reversing the positions of the male and female savages we had created an orbiting cycle that turns on its own axis forever, unless phenomenon occurred, and re-shifted the positions of the male and female savages.

Our experts warned us about the possibility of this phenomenon occurring for they say that the mind has a strong drive to correct and re-correct itself over a period of time if it can touch some substantial original historical base; and they advised us that the best way to deal with phenomenon is to shave off the brute's mental history and create a multiplicity of phenomenon or illusions so that each illusion will twirl in its own orbit, something akin to floating balls in a vacuum. This creation of a multiplicity of phenomenon or illusions entails the principles of crossbreeding the nigger and the horse as we stated above, the purpose of which is to create a diversified division of labor. The result of which is severance of the points of original beginnings for each spherical illusion. Since we feel that the subject matter may get more complicated as we proceed in laying down our economic plan concerning the purpose, reason, and effect of crossbreeding horses and niggers, we shall lay down the following definitional terms for future generations.

Orbiting cycle means a thing turning in a given pattern. Axis means upon which or around which a body turns. Phenomenon means something beyond ordinary conception and inspires awe and wonder. Multiplicity means a great number. Sphere means a globe. Crossbreeding a horse means taking a horse and breeding it with an a_ _ and you get a dumb backward a_ _, long headed mule that is not reproductive nor productive by itself. Cross-breeding niggers means taking so many drops of good white blood and putting them into as many nigger women as possible, varying the drops by the various tone that you want, and then letting them breed with each other until cycle of colors appear as you desire. What this means is this: Put the niggers and the horse in the breeding or, mix some a_ _ _ _ and some good white blood and what do you get? You got a multiplicity of colors of a_ _ backwards, unusual niggers, running, tied to backwards a_ _ long headed mules, the one productive of itself, the other sterile. (The one constant, the other dying. We keep nigger constant for other, neither knowing where the other came from and neither productive for itself, nor without each other.

    After formulating this blueprint for the psychological enslavement of the Black race, Lynch made it his life's work and passion to disseminate this doctrine throughout the United States and other pro-slavery countries around the world.

    To recount one of Lynch's historical and infamous slave-making training sessions, in 1712, Willie Lynch met with White slave and plantation owners on the banks of James River, Virginia.

Amerikkkan History

This is what he told those "distinguished" White gentlemen (i.e., White slave plantation owners) gathered on that fateful day nearly 300 years ago.

He said,

Gentlemen, I have a foolproof method for controlling your black slaves. I guarantee every one of you that if installed correctly it will control the slaves for at least 300 years, maybe even thousands. My method is simple, and any member of your family or your overseer can use it.

I have outlined a number of differences among the slaves, and I take these differences and make them bigger. The differences are age, color, intelligence, size, sex, and status on the plantation.

Now that you have a list of differences, I shall give you an outline of action. But before I do that, let me tell you that among the Blacks, distrust is stronger than trust, and envy is stronger than respect or admiration. And you must use that fact to your advantage.

Now, to maintain your control over the Blacks, you must pitch the old black slaves against the young black slaves... the dark skin slaves against the light skin slaves... the male slaves against the female slaves... and the house niggas against the field niggas.

You must also have your white servants and overseers distrust all Blacks. But it is necessary the Blacks trust and depend on us. They must love, respect, and trust only us.

Gentlemen, these methods are the keys to control. Use them. Have your wives and children use them, never miss an opportunity. If used intensely for one(1) year, the slaves themselves will remain perpetually divided, distrustful, and under your control, for generations to come.

Based on Willie Lynch's slave-making doctrine and his speech to the White plantation owners, you can begin to see how the Black race in America was psychologically conditioned into mental slaves.
You can see how the devastating effects of Willie Lynch's slave-making process are still evident to this day:

It's evident in the way we kill each other like dogs in the street.
It's evident in the way we disrespectfully talk down to each other.
It's evident in the way we talk about each other behind each other's backs.
It's evident in the way we jealously try to bring each other down.
It's evident in the way we selfishly look out for ourselves, instead of the Black race.
It's evident in the way we physically and mentally abuse and disrespect each other.
It's evident in the way we help reinforce negative Black stereotypes, and do little or nothing to uplift the Black race, but do much to help tear it down.

Yet, we're too deeply steeped in our social ignorance and slave mentality to realize *that* we even do these things to ourselves, and *why!*

35

The Willie Lynch Debate

Since the Willie Lynch letter first appeared, there has been a lot of debate and speculation as to its authenticity. You have a number of historical scholars and linguists, both Black and White, who are dismissing the letter as a fake, written in more modern times instead of in the 1700s like the letter suggests, and that a slave owner by the name of Willie Lynch never existed.

I'll be completely honest with you. I have no way of proving that Willie Lynch ever existed or that he wrote this "slave-making" letter, but there is one damn thing I know for sure that cannot be contested or debated by anybody:

Slavery existed in America and that some white man, or group of white men, somewhere decided the best way to keep Black African slaves in chains and in check was to:

♦ Drag them kicking and screaming in chains like animals from their native lands, to separate them from their base and source of ancestral strength.

♦ Brutally beat every ounce of their language and culture and history from them, to keep them from maintaining any type of cultural identity.

♦ Chain them naked on auction blocks, to be bought and sold like cattle for the profit and pleasure of White "Christian" men and their families.

♦ Rape and murder and torture the women and children in front of the males, to demonstrate the male's powerlessness to protect them.

♦ Castrate and torture and "lynch" the strong male leaders and potential resisters in front of the women and children, to kill any thoughts of future rebellion.

♦ Work them in the fields like dogs from sun up to sun down, without giving them a penny of the profits, to keep them poor and dependent upon their masters for sustenance.

♦ Use the strongest bucks as overseers, to keep the rest of the herd in check and to keep them distrustful of each other.

♦ Treat "special" slaves better than the others, to foster loyalty to the master and division amongst the slave ranks.

♦ Forbid them to learn to read and write the oppressor's language, to keep them ignorant and from gaining the knowledge necessary for their freedom.

♦ Teach them a white European version of Christianity with a blonde-haired, blue-eyed God to prove to them that God is White, and therefore all Whites must be naturally superior to Blacks.

♦ Call them derogatory and demeaning names like "nigger" and "coon" and "spade" and "jigaboo" and "porch monkey" to make them feel inferior and less than human.

♦ Teach the children of the slaves that they are too dumb and too ignorant to do anything other than manual labor on the master's plantation, to create future generations of willing slave laborers.

Amerikkkan History

You historians and linguists have completely missed the whole point of the letter. You can debate all you want but you can't debate these facts. This is what was done to our people by White men for nearly 400 years.

Who gives a damn what his name was?

Who gives a damn about whether or not he put it in a letter?

I don't need a White man or a letter to tell me what documented historical records and personal slave biographies have been telling us for years:

That the White race used psychological and physical conditioning to keep the Black race divided among itself and subservient to white slave masters, past and present!

6

SLAVERY NATION

The Long-term Effects of American Slavery on the Black Race

We have outgrown slavery, but our minds are still enslaved to the thinking of the master race. Now take the kinks out of your mind, instead of out of your hair.
- Marcus Garvey, Nationalist Leader

I freed thousands of slaves. I could have freed thousands more, if they had known they were slaves.
- Harriet Tubman, Abolitionist

I love my Black people. And we have made some extraordinary progress in terms of human and civil rights. However, the ugly truth of the matter is this:

We are still a nation of slaves, but we are too damned ignorant to realize it!

Despite heroic and monumental efforts to liberate the Black race, Black people are still both the victims and the perpetrators of a modern day slave mentality.

We've got Black people calling each other "nigga" all day long, talking about "It don't mean the same thing it used to." Nigger is a White racist word meaning, "stupid, ignorant, filthy, and lazy Blacks." It has always meant that, and will always mean that, I don't give a damn how affectionately you try to use it.

We've got Blacks selling crack and other dangerous drugs to other Blacks just so they can feed *their* families, even though they're killing *other* Black families, and destroying the Black race in the process.

We've got Blacks killing other Blacks for the opportunity to sell crack to other Blacks, just so they can buy expensive clothes and cars and jewelry, even though all this gets taken away from them when they get locked up in prison.

We've got Black drugdealers rotting away in the White man's prisons for selling drugs, even though it's the White men reaping the greatest profits, and using those profits to build the prisons the Black drugdealers are rotting in.

We've got Black gang-bangers killing thousands of other Blacks over stupid stuff like blocks and projects and neighborhoods and colors, and a bunch of other things that don't belong to them but to some rich, fat White man living off their welfare checks, their drug profits, and their self-hatred.

We've got Black "gangsta" rappers glamorizing and glorifying the gangsta lifestyle that they don't really live, but promote drugs and violence in their lyrics and videos, just to boost record sales.

We've got Black "gangsta" rappers telling our children it's okay to be ignorant and uneducated as long as they can put together useless, childish, kiddie rhymes that other ignorant Black people are willing to pay to hear.

We've got Black people going on talk shows like Jerry Springer, Riki Lake, or Maury Povich, making complete fools of themselves on national television, thereby con- firming White folks' stereotypes of Black people as lazy, ignorant, and trifling simpletons.

We've got Black men disrespecting Black women calling them hos, even though their mommas are Black women, and are the ones who are usually taking care of them.

We've got Black athletes running up and down the football fields and the basketball courts, without owning one professional sports franchise of their own, making billions of dollars for their white "mastas," who aren't putting a penny of that money back into the Black communities that the Black athletes come from.

We've got Black athletes who don't have the courage to be, or flat out refuse to be role models for our children, but they want us to go out and buy some product they endorse for their white "mastas", and we're supposed to want to buy the product simply because they endorse it.

We've got Black people spending billions of their hard-earned dollars buying clothes and products from rich, White fashion designers who don't give a damn about Blacks, but will take our Black dollars and use them to build up and invest in their own white enterprises.

We've got Black people buying a bunch of useless stuff like fashion fads, car accessories (e.g., rims), and expensive jewelry just to impress other Blacks, but they won't invest a dime in their children's college education and the computer technology they'll need to successfully compete against their White counterparts.

If it sounds like I'm venting, it's because I am!

Because I'm sick of living in a country full of Black people who are too ignorant to realize that they are being led down the path of their own self-destruction, and the people doing the leading are the same ones who created our ignorance and slave mentality, and the same ones benefiting the most from it:

The white supremacists who control the systems of institutional power in this country.

I came here today to tell you that I'm sick and tired of being sick and tired, and yet I'm sick and tired nonetheless:

I'm sick and tired of watching 100s of young Black men and women being locked up on a daily basis.

I'm sick and tired of picking up the newspaper every day and reading about more Black blood shed over stupid, petty arguments.

I'm sick and tired of going to funerals for Black children and Black teens whose lives were just starting, when they are tragically and senselessly killed by some ignorant and ruthless Black hoodlum.

I'm sick and tired of "gangsta" rappers telling Black children and Black teens it's okay to be the same kind of ignorant and ruthless Black hoodlums that are out there killing them.

I'm sick and tired of slave-minded drug dealers and gang-bangers telling our children that committing crime and violence is okay because it's the only way out of the ghetto.

I'm sick and tired of seeing Black children and teens being subjected to crime and violence because of the slave mentality that thrives in these ghettos.

I'm sick and tired of the way Black people abuse each other, and blatantly disrespect each other, and put each other down, especially in front of White people.

I'm sick and tired of the way Black people treat each other and place a priority on everything except those things that really matter, and the only things that can save us as a race: *knowledge, education, self-respect, respect for God, and respect for the Black race.*

I could go on for days, with hundreds of examples of just how ignorant and mentally enslaved we are as a race, but the bottom line is this: slavery officially ended 140 years ago; yet 140 years later, we are still bound by chains. However, the difference is that this time the chains are on our minds as well as our bodies.

Worse yet, this time we are our own slave-masters, because we are now slaves to ignorance, self-hatred, and greed; and ghettos and prisons have become our plantations.

We are still a nation of slaves!

And our slave mentality is what perpetuates the cycle of black-on-black crime and violence, because our fear, false pride, material greed, mental laziness, social ignorance, self-hatred, and misplaced anger – all the symptoms of our slave mentality – were designed to keep us dangerous to ourselves, but obedient and subservient to our White masters, past and present.

Indeed, every negative circumstance the Black race suffers today can be traced directly back to the psychological conditioning it received during its slave captivity on American soil, one effect of which has manifested itself in this deadly cycle of black-on-black crime and violence in America.

There is a famous quote from Dr. Johnnetta Cole, the first African American woman president of Spelman College, which says:

The truth is that the historical and current condition of you and yours is rooted in slavery, is shaped by it, is bound to it, and is the reality against which all else must be gauged.

I agree with Dr. Cole wholeheartedly. And today, despite the progress we've made in civil and human rights, the Black race is still entrapped by 5 separate yet strongly related forms of slavery, which I call the *Slave Matrix*:

The 5 Forms of the Slave Matrix

1. **Physical Slavery** – that which we term jails and prisons and ghettos. The purpose of physical slavery is to perpetuate a system of free or cheap labor.

2. **Psychological Slavery** – that which we term social, historical, and political ignorance; ignorance resulting from the willful mis-education of the race; and the ignorance resulting from our own mental laziness. The purpose of psychological slavery is to condition the Black race to accept their state of lack and suffering, thereby keeping the one race subservient to the other.

3. **Chemical Slavery** – that which we term drug and alcohol addiction. The purpose of chemical slavery is to pacify the race into a constant state of

mental and physical weakness so as to facilitate the process of psychological slavery.

4. **Emotional Slavery** – that which we term fear, anger, envy, apathy, cowardice, ruthlessness, and self-hatred. The purpose of emotional slavery is to instill a sense of powerlessness and hopelessness that keeps the Black race from taking a united stand against the institutions of white racism.

5. **Material Slavery** – that which we term greed and lust for material possessions. The purpose of material slavery is to lull the Black race into a false sense of achievement and prosperity by providing them with small tokens of the White man's version of "the American dream," thereby keeping the Blacks who have these tokens from rising up against the White "mastas" who bestow them.

There's no longer any question of whether or not we are a nation of slaves. The real question is this:

How do we liberate the Black race from its condition of mental slavery?

Let me say this:

You can free a man's body, but you can't free his mind. Only he can do that.

However, to be free you must think free. To think free, you must educate yourself. To educate yourself you must read. That means you have to read everything you can about your history and your heritage. Read everything you can about world history and American history.

Read everything you can about the psychology of the Black race and the psychology of the White race. And read everything you can about the American systems of institutionalized racism such as: the criminal justice system, the prison industrial complex, the economic system, the political system, the legal system, the public education system, and the mass media.

Read or die! It's that simple.

Once you understand how the Black race has been deliberately deceived and manipulated into its slave condition, you can begin to understand how we as a people can rise above that condition.

But until Black people recognize and acknowledge the fact that that they suffer from a slave mentality, and start reading and educating themselves about the root causes of their slave mentality, they are forever doomed to that slave condition, which in and of itself perpetuates the cycle of black-on-black crime and violence.

Another thing that troubles me is that a lot of people in America and around the world, including other Blacks, have a tendency to blame Black people in America for the crime, violence, poverty, and drugs that plague their neighborhoods. That's absurd!

You can't blame the Black race in America for being the victims of slavery, racism, discrimination, and racial oppression. That's like blaming a rape victim for being raped, and then condemning the rape victims for the trauma they suffer afterward.

BLACK SON RISING

It's only after years of professional and therapeutic counseling and self-healing that rape victims eventually move on with their lives, never forgetting that they were at one time a victim, but are victims no longer.

Similarly, the Black race can't be blamed for its condition. However, we have got to stop playing the part of the victim. We have got to start trying to heal ourselves of this horrendous act of human brutality that we have suffered, at the hands of people who hate the very air we breath, for no other reason than the color of our skin.

Yet, we refuse to acknowledge and move on from our pain, disguising it in fear, false pride, material greed, social ignorance, self-hatred, and misplaced anger; and by becoming the victimizers of our own people, instead of the healers of them.

And, for the record, just so that there's no misunderstanding my motives for speaking the truth (*as I understand it*): I don't hate White people. I don't hate anyone. That's a waste of my God-given energy and strength. Besides, there are good, decent, honest people in every race and ethnic group. Just like there are bad, cruel, and dishonest people in every race and ethnic group, Black, White, or other.

So, no I don't hate White people. I hate the evil that White people do. And I hate what they have done to the Black race in America.

They have taken the strongest, most noble race on the planet (*in my opinion*), and turned it into a pack of mentally weak, cowardly, ruthless, disrespectful, selfish, and materialistic house niggas and field niggas bent on keeping the status quo, and fearful of angering the white power structure that feeds them - making them dangerous only to themselves, but obedient to their White masters.

7

FATHERLESS AMERICA

An Epidemic of Fatherless Black Children

Of my father I know nothing. Slavery had no recognition of fathers, as none of families.
- **Frederick Douglass, Abolitionist**

The Black race in America has become a community of fatherless Black children. And the systematic removal of Black fathers as the head of the Black family has been the single most destructive factor in the breakdown of the Black community and the second most significant factor in the perpetuation of the cycle of black-on-black crime and violence in America.

But where have all the Black fathers gone?

There are thousands of Black fathers wasting their lives in prison for selling drugs, unable to raise their Black sons, who are now more likely to end up in prison for doing the same as their fathers.

There are thousands of Black fathers so hopelessly addicted to drugs or alcohol they can't even raise their own heads, let alone their own sons and daughters.

There are thousands of Black "deadbeat" fathers abandoning their children and not paying child support, but using their money to put new rims on their cars, or new clothes on their backs.

There are thousands of young, immature, uneducated Black teenaged boys becoming Black fathers running around making a bunch of babies that they either can't or won't take care of.

There are thousands of Black teenaged fathers unable to get jobs and support the babies they're making, because they're dropping out of school – convinced that they don't need an education – because they're going to somehow "make it" as rappers or basketball players.

This is where Black fathers are: conspicuously absent from the lives of their Black children, and especially their Black sons.

Thus the cycle of "fatherlessness" repeats itself.

And, this is exactly what is wrong with our young Black men today, and why black-on-black crime and violence is highest among young Black men who don't have positive Black father figures in their lives.

There are very few strong, noble Black fathers around to teach young Black boys the responsibilities and characteristics of manhood, because Black men have been systematically stripped of their position and responsibility as fathers, because of their drug addictions, street hustling, incarceration, and/or death.

And, in the absence of their fathers, or some other strong Black father figure teaching them, young Black boys are left to figure out for themselves what it means to be a man.

43

BLACK SON RISING

Most of the time, they learn their definition of manhood from their peers, who don't know any more than they do about what it means to be a man.

Needless to say, a lot of these young men have a badly distorted perception of what it means to be a man. Most of them get their ideas of "manhood" from violent rap videos and gangster movies like *Scarface*, or from watching the false bravado of "manliness" from athletes who strut around like lions in the fields. A lot of these young Brothers grow up thinking that to be a man, you got to act hard and tough and cool at all times, and hurt or kill anybody who disrespects you or threatens your so-called "manhood."

With this badly distorted perception of manhood, is it any wonder why these young men are out here on the streets killing each other by the thousands? They are building their whole lifestyle around this false image of men as hardcore "killas", which has been and continues to be detrimental to themselves and everyone around them.

As long as young Black men keep growing up without strong, noble Black fathers, or other strong Black male role models, this negative, destructive false perception of manhood will persist, as will the cycle of black-on-black crime and violence that results.

To some, it seems like I might be overstating the importance of having strong Black father figures in the lives of young Black boys, but just how important is it really?

Can Black boys succeed without a strong Black father figure in their lives? What are the effects of growing up fatherless?
What becomes of a young man without the proper guidance that only a strong Black man can offer?
What is the link between fatherless Black boys and the violent, criminal, and irresponsible behavior they demonstrate?

The real issue is not so much about "fatherhood" as it is about the effects of racism and racial oppression on fatherless Black boys, and what role strong Black fathers play in reversing the negative effects of racism and racial oppression.

That's the real issue.

Simply having a father in your life doesn't guarantee your chances of surviving and succeeding in this racially hostile nation, but having a strong, intelligent Black father figure who can guide you through the traps of racial oppression can certainly increase your chances.

Having an alcoholic, drug-dealing physically abusive father in the house is just as bad as having no father at all, perhaps even worse.

However, having a strong, courageous, intelligent, free-thinking, and respectable father who has successfully navigated the traps and pitfalls of racism and racial oppression and come out on top, can make all the difference in the world.

Having a strong, courageous, intelligent, free-thinking, and respectable father can mean the difference between a son who gets caught up in the "system", and one who stays out of prison, goes to college, starts his own business, and successfully raises his own family.

That's the real importance of having a strong Black father figure in the lives of Black boys.

The Effects of Racial Oppression on Black Males

In his groundbreaking research on Black male adolescent violence, the late Amos N. Wilson, Professor of Psychology at the School of New Resources, College of New Rochelle, in New York, concluded that there is strong correlation between criminal and anti-social behavior and fatherlessness.

Through his comprehensive study of adolescent Black males, Professor Wilson concluded that the absence of strong, mature, and responsible Black fathers left a void in young men's understanding of what it means to be a man, and that void was often filled with what he termed a "reactionary masculinity."

In *Understanding Black Male Adolescent Violence* (African World Infosystems, 1992), Wilson proffered that:

A goodly portion of Black male violence against other Black males is the consequence of unresolved conflicts around masculinity. The resolution of what it means to be a man is a major crisis of adolescence and young adulthood under normal circumstances, how much more the case for the Black adolescent and young adult male under conditions of oppression. . . .

These males, often misguidedly and ignorantly assuming that they are successfully defying White male authority and dominance, defying "the system," expressing their independence and "masculine prerogatives," expressing their "manhood," have been misled or misdirected into violently attacking and corrosively undermining the peace, stability, and the very viability of the African American community.

These males have been provoked by their oppressive circumstances into what we may call a "reactionary masculinity," whose presence and expression is essentially detrimental to the African American community and ironically, to their own well-being.

According to Professor Wilson, the negative and destructive characteristics (i.e., "reactionary masculinity") that are formed in response to racism and oppression, explains most of the criminal and anti-social behavior we see in adolescent Black males who don't have strong male role models in their lives to counteract the effects of racism and oppression.

As a result, these reactionary Black males [my term] in effect become the drug dealers, gang-bangers, and hustlers that populate our streets, prisons, and graveyards.

According to Professor Wilson, there are numerous negative and destructive characteristics of the "reactionary male," that are symptomatic of black-on-black crime and violence:

The reactionary Black male lacks a sense of social responsibility or social interests, and a deep and abiding African identity and consciousness; he exhibits an impoverished empathy for others.

BLACK SON RISING

The reactionary Black male tends to be opinionated and to view every social encounter as a test to his masculinity, as a struggle for power, and mistakenly identifies physicality, and crudeness, with masculinity; he views domination, insensitivity, unconcern, willingness to injure or kill, seek revenge, as essentially masculine traits.

The reactionary Black male is motivated primarily by fear, avoidance, escape, retreat from responsibility, ego-defense, and reactionary frustration; with a deep and ever-present sense of inadequacy; by an inferiority complex; and an obsessive need to appear superior.

The reactionary Black male perceives cooperation with other males submitting to the rightful authority of other males; conceding "points" to other males and relating to them, as humiliating insults to their masculinity; he mistakenly believes the mastery of knowledge, crafts, academic subject-matter, professional expertise, the actualization of intellectual potential, to be essentially feminine traits.

The reactionary Black male is a conspicuous consumer; consumer-oriented — concerned mainly with parasitically exploiting others, works merely to earn "spending money," i.e., money to spend irresponsibly; is "into" flashy clothes, cars, fads, and styles of all types.

The reactionary Black male is motivated and defined by self-alienation; exhibits an absence of self-knowledge; ignorance of his ethnic-heritage; unbounded hedonism; narcissistic drives; deep insecurities regarding the reality of his masculinity and of his masculine courage.

The reactionary Black male lacks self-control, discipline, persistence, and high frustration tolerance; lacks long-term goals and commitment to pro-social values.

This is the effect that racism and racial oppression can have on Black boys who grow up without that necessary influence to negate their effects:

They become self-destructive, self-centered, ruthless, and dangerous street thugs and hoodlums bent on hurting everything and everyone who opposes them, or threatens their so-called "manhood."

The bottom line is this:

Physically, any boy can grow up to be a man, but someone has to teach him what it means to be one. Someone has to tell him that money, guns, and drugs won't make him a man, but that knowledge, discipline, and responsibility will. Someone has to challenge the false, destructive ideas about manhood that will lead him to a life of crime, prison, and violence - and replace them with positive and constructive ideas that will lead him to a life of social and economic prosperity.

This is where that strong, intelligent, free-thinking, and respectable Black father figure comes into play, because that's his responsibility to teach these things to Black boys.

And most of the Black fathers I know, even the ones who are in their son's life, don't teach their sons what they really need to know about being a decent, honest, and responsible man or the real reasons why they should avoid the criminal lifestyle altogether.

Be honest. How many of you so-called strong, intelligent Black men out there have actually sat down with your sons, or some other young Back boy who didn't have a father, and said to them:

Son, let me tell you what it means to be a man, and more importantly what it means to be a Black man in America:

Son, Black men don't disrespect women, especially Black women.

That means you don't cheat on them, physically or mentally abuse them, or call them disrespectful names. Women should be treated with respect at all times, and any man who puts his hands on a woman is a coward himself.

How would you like it if someone called your mother or sister a ho? How would you like it if some punk beat up on your mother or sister?

Son, Black men support their children physically, emotionally, and financially.

A man who doesn't provide for and support his children is the worst kind of coward there is. If you think you're man enough to lie down with a woman, then be man enough to stand up and take responsibility for that baby you thought you were man enough to make.

Son, Black men don't make excuses for their actions or their behavior.

Real men take responsibility for everything they do and accept the consequences for their failures and mistakes. Blaming others for your failures and mistakes is a sign of fear, weakness, and immaturity.

Son, Black men don't lie to protect themselves from being punished for the consequences of their actions.

Liars are cowards who are too scared to tell the truth and face the consequences of their actions. If you're man enough to do the crime, be man enough to do the time.

You can't be a "bad boy" one minute, and then a punk the next. If you did it, say you did it, and take your punishment like a man.

Son, Black men don't physically abuse their mind and body with drugs or alcohol.

BLACK SON RISING

Drug and alcohol abusers are people who are too weak and too scared to face their troubles with a clear mind and a strong spirit, and drugs and alcohol destroy both.

Son, Black men don't sell deadly drugs like crack and heroin to their own people.

Crack and heroin destroy Black children, families, and communities, and selling it gives the law the right to take away your freedom, your respect, and your manhood.

Son, Black men don't commit crime to put money in their pockets.

Crime is for people who are either too weak, or too greedy, or too stupid to get what they want the legal way. If you want money, you have to earn it the honest way. No matter how hard you have to work for it. That way the law can't take it from you once you get it.

That's where we keep making our mistake. This is exactly what is wrong with our young Black boys and men today. No one is telling these young Black men what real men are and what real men do. And in the absence of someone telling them, they are left to figure it out for themselves, or they learn their concept of manhood from their peers, and the streets.

Do you think if a strong Black father figure or role model had sat down with you as a young boy and told you these things, that maybe your life might be different now?

Is it possible that you might not be in prison right now for the 3rd time, back to back, for doing same stupid stuff you got locked up for the 1st and 2nd time?

Is it possible that you might not have a bunch of children running around that you can't or won't take care of?

Is it possible that you might not be hustling on the streets right now because you dropped out of school and don't know how to do nothing else?

Is it possible that you might have thought twice about taking that young brother's life over a dime bag of crack that you had no business selling to him anyway?

Is it possible that you might not be standing in front of some White judge that don't give a damn about you, begging and pleading for mercy, talking about "Please give me another chance, Your Honor"?

I know that there are no guarantees in life, and that people do what they want to do no matter what you tell them or who's in their life, but isn't it possible that just hearing someone you look up to say these things could have changed the way you think and act and conduct yourself?

Isn't it possible that we just might be able to break this cycle of black-on-black crime and violence if we start telling Black boys what it means to be a man, *before* they become one?

I want to remind you that one of the keys to keeping the Black race down and subservient to the White race is to remove strong, intelligent Black father figures from the lives of Black boys and Black families, so that young Black men grow up without the skills, tools, and knowledge they need to succeed and survive within this racially hostile nation.

This is not a new or recent concept. This particular practice, along with other methods used to break down the structure of the Black family, has its historical roots in the brutality and racism of American slavery.

48

8

MAMA'S BOY

The Challenge Single Black Mothers Face When Raising Black Sons

Black women raise their daughters and love their sons.
- **Jawanza Kunjufu**

Black mothers have been forced to assume the duties of the surrogate father and the head of the household, due to the absence of strong Black men from the Black family dynamic. With so many Black men in prison, or dead from street violence, Black women have had to step up to the plate, take up the slack of absentee fathers, and hold the Black family together, practically single-handed. Despite the fact that they have become the head of the house by default, the question is:

Can Black mothers successfully raise Black sons by themselves?

That's a very complicated question, with an even more complicated answer, but the short and simple answer is:

No, they can not!

First, for the record, let me just say that nobody on this planet loves Black women more than I do. I worship the ground they walk on, and I have always considered women in general, and Black women in particular, to be stronger, more courageous, and more intelligent than men. All you have to do is read the chapter, *Protecting the Black Queen,* to see how much I truly adore and admire Black women.

However, despite their strength, their courage, and their intelligence, Black women are not without their major flaws, faults, and weaknesses, because many of them have fallen victim to the same type of ignorance and slave mentality that fosters ignorance, irresponsibility, and disrespect among Black men.

I've seen too many Black women calling other Black women "hos" in front of their Black *sons*, and then they wonder where Black *men* get it from.

I've seen too many Black women in the clubs shaking their butts and dancing to songs that refer to them as "hos," talking about "They not referring to me." (*So, it's okay if they call your Black Sisters hos?*) And then they wonder why Black men have no respect for Black women.

I've seen too many Black women down at Family Court talking to their girlfriends about how their son's father is "useless, lazy, and no good" in front of their sons, and then they wonder why Black boys don't respect Black men.

I've seen too many Black women raising their Black daughters to be strong, responsible, and independent, but raising their Black sons to be lazy, dependent, and irresponsible, and then they turn around and complain that Black men ain't worth a damn.

BLACK SON RISING

I've seen too many Black women prostituting themselves in front of their sons, by sleeping around with a bunch of sorry Brothers just to get some new designer outfit, or handbags, or jewelry.

I've seen too many young Black girls running around competing with each other to see who can get pregnant the quickest, because they think that having babies is the only thing Black women are good for.

I've seen too many young Black girls walking around in school and in the streets in clothing more for a strip club or a brothel, with their breasts and butt on display for everybody to see, because they don't have enough self-respect to entice men with their minds, instead of their bodies.

I've seen too many Black teenaged girls dropping babies like Black rabbits, and raising Black boys to be ignorant, lazy, and irresponsible Black sons who end up becoming drug dealers, street hustlers, or gang-bangers, because these girls (not women) haven't learned enough about life yet to teach some other child how to live it.

I've seen too many young Black welfare mothers without a pot to piss in or a window to throw it out of, buying their kids $150 sneakers from Nike and Reebok, just to keep up with the latest fashion fads worn by Black athletes and entertainers, and then complain that they don't have the money to send their kids to college.

I've seen too many Black women who will buy their sons every video game and rap album in the store, but won't buy them a book or inspire them to listen to any success or motivational tapes, and then wonder why their sons don't value or respect knowledge and education.

I've seen too many Black mothers dressing their sons, or allowing their sons to be dressed, in the latest ghetto fashions and gangsta attire like oversized pants, and gold chains, and skullcaps, just so their sons can look hip and fit into the "cool" crowd, because they don't have enough common sense or financial sense to put that money they're spending on clothes into savings or investment accounts.

And all of this stupid stuff that Black women and Black girls are doing is contributing to the ignorance and irresponsibility that gives rise to black-on-black crime and violence.

I hate to say it, and I am going to anger a lot of Black women with this statement, but the truth of the matter is that most of the ignorant and irresponsible behavior of Black men is coming from our Black women!

You think I'm lying? Think about it for a minute:

All behavior is learned behavior. That means everything you do you learned from somewhere or somebody. Statistically, Black women are the primary caregivers in the Black family, because Black men are nowhere to be found. That means some Black woman, either your mother or your grandmother, is the one who is raising you. That means she is the one who is responsible for what you learn, see, hear, and do. That means all of your behavior is the result of things you learned from the environment she directly or indirectly created.

If you are a parent, then you know that children watch everything you say and do, and then incorporate your behavior into their own.

Therefore, if Black men "ain't nothing," it's because some Black woman raised him that way.

50

Black men learn to call women "hos" from hearing their mommas call other Black women "hos" or from hearing other Black men call their mommas "hos."

Black men learn to cheat on Black women from watching their mommas cheat on their husbands or boyfriends, or from their fathers who cheat on their wives or girlfriends with women who know the man has a wife or a girlfriend.

Black men learn to disrespect women from watching their mommas being disrespected by some ignorant and irresponsible Black man that their mommas let disrespect them just so that Black man will take care of some of her bills, or take care of some of her other "needs."

Black men learn to mentally and physically abuse women from watching their mommas live with, stay with, and have sex with Black men who are mentally and physically abusive, simply because they so-call "love" these men.

Black men learn to become violent and ruthless drug dealers and hustlers from watching their mommas lay up with violent and ruthless Black drug dealers and street hustlers, simply because that drug dealer can pay the rent.

Black men learn to be lazy, unemployed, and irresponsible from watching their mommas shack up with lazy , unemployed, and irresponsible men who do nothing but sit around the house and get high while that Sister is out busting her butt to make ends meet.

And it doesn't matter if you are telling your child don't do this and don't do that. I don't care if you tell your son not to disrespect women, or not to call women "hos," or not to hit women, or not to get involved in drugs or gangs or crime:

Children watch and do what you *do*, not what you say to do!

The sad part is, you may not be one of these Black women who's doing this in front of their sons. You could be a really classy, intelligent, and responsible mother.

But guess what? Your son goes to school where he is surrounded by other powerful influences outside your home. He hangs out with his peers and friends before, during, and after school. He spends more time with his peers than he does with you, because for the most part your are out there busting your butt at work to make ends meet.

He could be learning his ignorant and irresponsible behavior from some other boy whose mother is the kind of ignorant, trifling, and irresponsible parent we just talked about.

Either way, that still means that somewhere, somebody's momma is teaching their son some really bad and nasty and harmful behavior, and then their son turns around and teaches your son, and then your son turns around and teaches somebody else's son, or his own children when he has them.

Do you want your son, or your daughter, hanging out with friends who think it's okay for a man to disrespect Black women or call them hos; or who think it's okay for Black people to sell drugs and kill other Blacks; or who think it's okay for a Black man to lay up under women while the woman does all the work; or who think it's okay for a Black man or woman to run around making a bunch of babies; or who think it's okay for a Black man to be lazy, uneducated, and unemployed?

Do you really want your son or daughter to learn this kind of backward slave mentality?

Do you see how this cycle of ignorance, irresponsibility, and disrespect perpetuates itself, over and over again?

That's why as a parent, it's very important that you find out who your children are hanging out with, and what kind of behavior they are learning from them, because they could be learning *"everything they think they know"* about life from someone other than you.

Raising the Black Male Child

The words I expressed in the previous section may seem cold and unappreciative of the issues that Black women have to deal with in trying to hold together the Black family while raising difficult Black sons .

It's not that I don't appreciate their efforts and their hardships, but the fact remains that nearly 75% of all the Black men in prison come from single parent homes where the mother or grandmother is the primary caregiver.

The majority of Black boys who join gangs or become juvenile offenders don't have a father, or any other strong Black father figure in the household, or any other responsible adult around to supervise and guide them.

The majority of the Black teens out there hanging out on the corners all hours of the day and night come from households where the mother is the only disciplinarian.

The majority of the Black juvenile offenders in juvenile detention centers come from backgrounds where the mother is either working too hard or too busy chasing her own life to give them the kind of quality time they need to keep them out of trouble.

What does this tell you?

That tells me that Black women can not, or have not been able to, successfully raise or control their Blacks sons.

Have any Black women successfully raised Black sons? Of course they have. There is always the exception to the rule. There are hundreds of Black women in single parent homes who are raising Black sons to be successful lawyers, doctors, businessmen, educators, etc.

I have talked with and interviewed hundreds of Black women who have successfully raised Black sons. You know what they tell me? They tell me that even though their son's father was absent from their lives, there was still some strong Black influential role model present like a grandfather or an uncle, who was able to teach their son the characteristics and responsibilities of manhood.

And that's the difference. There has got to be some sort of strong Black male present in the lives of Black boys to show them and teach them what it means to be a man. It doesn't necessarily have to be the boy's father, but it does have to be a man because a man is the natural vehicle through which the concepts of manhood are to be transmitted.

Obviously any woman can tell her son what it means to be a man, but it takes a man to demonstrate those qualities before any son will embrace and apply them. Boys have to see it first to live it.

There are three (3) basic reasons why Black women are generally incapable of successfully raising Black sons by themselves, and why at some point in time the Black mother will lose all control of her son's behavior, and her effectiveness as his parent.

Three Reasons Why Black Mothers Can't Successfully Raise Black Sons:

1. **Black women coddle their sons.**

There is an old saying, "Women raise their daughters, but they coddle their sons." And it's true. First of all, it is the most natural thing in the world for a mother to love, nurture, and protect her children. However, mothers tend to take this natural tendency to the extreme when it comes to their sons. For some unknown reason that even the psychologists don't understand, women are far more protective of their sons. Women expect their daughters to be as strong and as independent as they are, but they don't set or enforce the same standard for their sons.

If the daughter falls down and scrapes her knee, the mother will tell her to get up and brush herself off, and "stop that crying." But, if the son falls down, the mother will run to his aide, kiss his "boo boo," and hug and rock her "poor baby" until he stops crying.

When she comes of age, the daughter in the house usually has to do all the cooking, cleaning, ironing, and grocery shopping for the whole house, because that's "women's work." If the girls are doing all the housework, what are the boys doing? Usually, absolutely nothing! As a result they become spoiled and pampered from the special treatment they get from their mothers. That's why boys never learn how to be independent or how to do for themselves.

This tendency of Black mothers to coddle their sons makes the sons weak, lazy, dependent, irresponsible, and disrespectful of women. Yet women refuse to see it that way.

2. **At puberty, Black sons begin to lose all fear or respect for their mother's authority.**

Psychologically and physiologically something happens to boys when they reach puberty, and their male hormones start to kick in. They start "smelling themselves," and start *thinking* that they have become men. In fact, that's exactly what they are becoming: *young men.* The problem is if there is no other male around to challenge their new sense of manhood, or if the other males in the home are perceived to be weaker, the stronger male becomes very aggressive and starts assuming the role as "the man of the house."

Anthropologists refer to this phenomenon as the "Alpha Male" syndrome.

That means that in the absence of a strong Black father figure in the house to keep him in check, sooner or later that Black son will begin

exerting his authority over the only person in the household who threatens his "manhood": *his mother.*

3. **Black women do not truly understand men, or what it means to be a man.**

Women can only speculate on how the male mind works. Therefore they cannot pass on to their sons how to think and act like a man, because they don't have that knowledge to pass on, themselves. There are simply some things that girls must learn from women, and that boys must learn from men.

This is not a macho thing. This is not about teaching boys how to be tough and hard and unemotional. This is about connecting with Black boys in a way that's non-threatening, informative, and meaningful, and that teaches them the qualities and characteristics of "manhood" from a man's point of view, while leaving their dignity and sense of growing "manhood" intact.

And only a man can do that.

The bottom line is this:

Generally speaking, women have done an outstanding job in picking up the slack in raising Black children and holding together the so-called Black family, due to Black men's failures as fathers, leaders, and mates. Black women truly are the backbone of the Black family.

However, without a Black man in the house to lead it, there is no Black family!

Every backbone needs a head at the top. The problem is Black women are undermining the ability of Black boys to become the natural head of the family, because they are behaving in ways, and teaching their sons to behave in ways, that are counterproductive to the development of strong, independent, responsible, loyal, and successful Black fathers, leaders, and mates.

And thus the cycle of ignorance and irresponsibility of Black men, and the abuse and disrespect toward Black women, and the crime and violence in Black communities, repeats itself from one generation to the next!

9

READ OR DIE

The Consequences of Black Illiteracy

We are the only racial group within the United States ever forbidden by law to read and write.

- **Alice Childress, Writer**

To be free, you must think free. To think free, you must educate yourself. To educate yourself, you must read.

The White race has been systematically oppressing the Black race with its laws, its public policies, and its capitalist marketing strategies, all of which can be found in their written doctrine. Everything the White race does to oppress people of color they put into writing first.

That's why reading enables us to break free from our ignorance and our slave mentality, because it gives us the ability to gain knowledge for ourselves, and to learn how the lies, half-truths, and deceptions of the White race have been used to keep us enslaved and oppressed as a people.

Don't ever forget that it wasn't that long ago that we were forbidden, by White law, to read or to write. White lawmakers who supported the institution of slavery knew that a slave's ability to read naturally led to questions about his slave condition, and ultimately to freedom.

Think of it this way:

If White racist law makers thought it was important enough to keep Blacks from reading and writing by putting this rule into law, then inhibiting Black people's ability to read and learn must have been absolutely crucial to our continued enslavement. Why else would you forbid someone from learning to read and write?

My question is, "Now that we are legally able to read, why do so many Black men refuse to pick up a book and learn about something other than hustling?"

The fact that the law once barred us from reading, should be reason enough for us to want to read everything we can get our hands on, and educate ourselves about the methods and strategies and psychology of our oppressor!

Yet, instead of reading about our Black history and heritage, and the history and psychology of the White race (our oppressors), we would rather play or watch basketball, or play childish video games, or play cards and dice, or hangout on street corners instead of libraries or bookstores, none of which can teach us anything about how to survive and succeed in this racially hostile nation.

And our refusal to place any value on knowledge is evident in the way we live.

BLACK SON RISING

How many people know that Baltimore, Maryland, has the highest high-school dropout rates in the country for Black males, with nearly 76% of Black males in the city dropping out before finishing high school? These are the same young men working in the underground economy (drug game) that leads to only one of two places: *prison or death.*

Most of the Black men in my Life Skills class at the prison are barely literate, and most of them never finished high school. In fact, 75% of my students don't have high-school diplomas or GEDs, and most of them have never held a legitimate job of any kind, because no one will hire them without a diploma or GED.

Yet, knowing this, Black men are still dropping out of school like flies.

Our failure to read and learn and value knowledge is keeping us ignorant, uneducated, unemployed and unemployable, and vulnerable to racial oppression; and it is perpetuating the conditions that cause us to live in poverty, rot in prisons, and die on the streets like dogs.

All because we would rather play kids' games, and bury our heads in the sand pretending that we don't care, instead of picking up a book and trying to rise above our ignorance.

Below is a conversation between a Black businessman and a White Republican that highlights the need for African Americans to read more so that they can gain the knowledge they need to survive and succeed in this racially hostile nation:

Introduction: I am a fairly well-educated Black Democrat with a degree in business management. I own a lucrative real estate business and a beautiful home in Prince George's County, one of the most prosperous Black counties in the nation. I try to stay abreast of what's happening in other Black communities around the nation. I confess that a lot of what I see greatly troubles me because it's a lot of negativity about crime, violence, poverty, and drugs.

One of my business associates is a White Republican. From time to time, we have some interesting conversations about American politics, but we never had a discussion about Black people in general before this. So up until now, I never knew how he felt about African Americans.

I will share with you a very disturbing conversation I had recently with this White Republican.

This White republican and I were talking about the recent presidential elections (*if you can call that scam an election*), and I happened to mention that I was proud of P. Diddy's efforts to rouse Black voters with his Vote or Die campaign.

The White Republican smirked and shook his head in amusement, and that began one of the most interesting and enlightening conversations I ever had with a White person.

Black Businessman: What's so funny?

White Republican: Vote or Die? The slogan should have been "Read or Die."

Black Businessman: What does that mean?

White Republican: Come on now, you've got to be able to read first before you can vote. And everybody knows Blacks don't read.

Read or Die

Black Businessman: (*Outraged, I stood up over him with balled fists*) What did you say to me?

White Republican: Hold on, hold on now, I'm not trying to offend you. I'm not talking about the handful of intelligent Blacks like yourself. I'm talking about your average, unemployed, or under-employed blue-collar worker drones, who can barely read a newspaper.

Black Businessman: I don't give a damn who you're talking about, that's a pretty f—ked up and racist thing to say.

White Republican: Wait! Stop thinking like a Black Democrat for a second, and just hear me out, okay?

(*Instead of punching him his face like I wanted to, I decided to wait to hear just how he was gonna justify it, and then I was going to punch him in his face. However, what he said next really shook me up.*)

White Republican: Listen, American history has proven time and time again that as far as the welfare of the Black race is concerned, it doesn't really matter who's in office. The White power structure in this country will still continue to contain and control the lives of Black people as long as they refuse to read.

Black Businessman: Man, what the hell does reading have to do with who's running the country?

White Republican: Think about it. Every measure we use to control Black people's lives, we put in writing first. We put it in our laws, we put it in our history books, in our public policies, our business tactics, and our marketing strategies. Everything is right there in *black* and *white*, for anybody who cares enough to go looking for it.

Black Businessman: Wait a minute, wait a minute. You're forgetting about one thing. There are more Black business owners, and more Black college students, today than there has been in any other time in history. You can't tell me these Black entrepreneurs and Black college students aren't reading.

White Republican: Oh, sure. They're reading. They're reading what we tell them to read and when to read it, and even then they only read just enough to get by and make a passing grade. Very few of them actually read for the purpose of gaining knowledge for knowledge's sake.

Black Businessman: Hold on, now. You're discounting the efforts of an awful lot of successful Black people. How are they becoming successful without being able to read?

White Republican: You still don't get it do you? The success of a handful of Blacks is meaningless without the success of the race as a whole. That's the point the Black race keeps missing. However, I'll tell you one thing: White people haven't missed it, the Asians haven't missed it, and the Latinos are starting to get the point, too. The only ones that haven't figured it out yet are the Blacks.

BLACK SON RISING

Black Businessman: Man, that's wrong!

White Republican: Hey, man, the truth hurts. But don't kill the messenger. You know the Black race as a whole presents an interesting study in contradictions.

Black Businessman: In what way?

White Republican: Historically, Black people are the strongest race on the planet. They have suffered more and survived under more adversity than any other race on the planet. Yet, they have 3 inherent weaknesses that keep them from achieving any significant degree of success as a race.

Black Businessman: Such as.

White Republican: If you think about with it some objectivity, you will see that the Black race has 3 crippling weaknesses. And as long as they have these weaknesses, the White race, and any other race for that matter, will be able to contain them and control them indefinitely.

Your 1st weakness is "ignorance." And, by "your" I mean Black people in general. Ignorance continues to be the primary weapon of containment of Blacks.

A great man once said, "The best way to hide something from Black people is to put it in a book."

We now live in the Information Age. Blacks have the opportunity to read any book on any subject in the world, yet they refuse to read. There are millions of books readily available at Borders, Barnes & Noble, and Amazon.com., not to mention their own Black bookstores.

A lot of these Black bookstores offer books on how to reach economic equality with Whites, but very few of them bother to go in the store, let alone buy a book from it. Go in any mall that has a Black bookstore, and you'll see for yourself that Blacks are in every store and shop but the one they need to be in.

Do you agree or disagree?

Black Businessman: I'm withholding my comments until I hear everything you've got to say. What's our 2nd so-called "weakness"?

White Republican: Okay, then. Your 2nd weakness is greed. Greed is another powerful weapon of containment of the Black race. Blacks, since the abolition of slavery, have had tremendous monetary spending power at their disposal. Yet, last year alone, they spent 15 billion dollars during Christmas, out of their 800 billion dollars in total yearly income.

Any of us can use them as our target market, for any business venture we care to dream up. It doesn't matter how ridiculous it is, or how insulting it is to their race, they'll buy into it anyway.

Being primarily a consumer people, they function totally by greed. They continually want more, with little thought for saving or investing. And, most of the Brothers I know, would rather buy a new car with flashy rims than invest in starting a business.

Isn't it ironic that Black people buy sneakers by the thousands, yet there's not one Black sneaker manufacturer in the entire country?

Let's not even talk about fashion. Some Blacks even neglect their own children just to have the latest Tommy, or FUBU, or whatever's popular with the hip-hop crowd. And they still think that having a Mercedes and a big house gives them some kind of "status," or that they have achieved the American Dream.

I'm sorry man, but Black people are so stupid! The vast majority of them are still living in poverty because their greed holds them back from collectively making better communities.

And, thanks to BET, and other Black media organizations, White-owned companies like Tommy and Nike and Reebok, are making a killing off of Black people.

What kills me about Blacks is that Tommy Hilfiger came right out and said he doesn't want their money, yet Black people spend more money on Tommy than ever before! They're still showing off their Tommy "gear" to each other, while we're building better communities with the profits from our businesses that we market to them.

Shall I go on?

Black Businessman: Go ahead–don't stop now.

White Republican: Your 3rd weakness is selfishness. Your selfishness, ingrained in your minds through slavery, is one of the major ways White people can continue to contain Blacks.

One of your own people, the highly respected Black philosopher, W. E. B. Dubois, said that there was a natural division in the Black culture between Black achievers and Black underachievers. He called the Black achievers the "Talented Tenth."

He said that the talented 10% of the Black population has always achieved some measure of success. However, he also said that the "talented tenth" was responsible for guiding, and making life better, for the other 90%.

However, instead of making improvements for the Black race as a whole, the "talented tenth" created another class, a Black bourgeois class that looks down their noses at their own people, or only aids them when it's to their own benefit. And, even when they do render aid, they do it in such a condescending manner so as to make the recipients feel inferior.

I hate to say it, but Blacks will never achieve what White people, or Asians, or Latinos have. Their selfishness does not allow them to be able to work together on any project or endeavor of substance. When they do get together, their selfishness lets their egos get in the way of the goal.

And your so-called "community" organizations seem to only want to promote their name without making any real change in their communities.

You have all of these uppity, bourgeois Blacks who are content to sit in conferences and conventions in *our* hotels, and talk about what they will do, while they award plaques to the best speakers, not the best doers. And, they still don't see that Together Each Achieves More (TEAM)! They still don't understand that what little they do possess doesn't make them better than the other Blacks who have nothing.

In fact, most of these bourgeois Blacks are but one or two paychecks away from poverty themselves. Because the only jobs they do have are under the control of our pens, in our offices, and our boardrooms.

No, my friend, Blacks pose absolutely no threat whatsoever to the White power structure in America, or in the world. We will continue to contain and control the lives of Black people, as long as they refuse to read, continue to buy merchandise we market, and keep thinking they are "helping" their communities by paying dues to organizations which do little more than hold expensive conventions, in our hotels.

Conclusion: I sat there and absorbed everything he had to say, and a lot of what was said deeply disturbed me, because there was an element of truth to it. So, I did the only thing I could do under the circumstances: I got up, thanked him for his honesty, and then went to the local library to sign up for the volunteer adult literacy program to teach African Americans how to read.

The message from the above dialogue should be crystal clear:

If you want to know who enslaved the Back race, then read.
If you want to know why the Black race was enslaved, then read
If you want to know what keeps the Black race enslaved, then read.
If you want to know what will free the Black race, then read.
If you want to know what's killing the Black race, then read.
If you want to know what will save the Black race, then read.
If you want to know how to survive in this racially hostile white nation, then read.

In other words, if you want to live, then read.

Read or die! It's that simple.

10

BLACK FACES/WHITE MEDIA

The media's the most powerful entity on earth. They have the power to make the innocent guilty and to make the guilty innocent, and that's power. Because they control the minds of the masses.
- **Malcolm X**

The mass media is one of the most powerful systems of institutionalized racism in the country. It has been, and continues to be, one of the biggest creators and enforcers of negative and destructive stereotypes of Blacks.

Hate is a powerful word, and I try never to use it or feel it toward anything in the universe, but this is the one time that I think that the word "hate" is totally appropriate, because hatred is the only word that adequately expresses my absolute disgust with the mass media.

Why do I hate the mass media so much?

I hate the mass media so much:

Because every time you turn on the television, or pick up a newspaper, or watch a movie, all you see is oceans of White faces of White people doing wonderful "white" things that are totally irrelevant to Black life, as though Black people don't even exist on the planet.

And the little bit of airtime, print-time, or screen-time we do get, we are being depicted as useless, lazy, ignorant, and uneducated parasites; and as ruthless and dangerous dope fiends, drug dealers, criminals, thugs, and hoodlums.

You know what else I hate about the mass media?

I hate the fact that 99.9% of the television programs on hundreds of different cable and satellite channels are nothing but programs about, by, and for White people. My friend and I once sat in front of the television and tried to find something "Black" to watch. She has direct TV with 800 channels. We literally flipped through all 800 channels without finding one Black television program, unless it was Black men playing some sports.

I hate the fact that the only time Black men are given any significant airtime is when we are running up and down basketball courts or football fields for sports franchises that "they" own. The sports channel is the only place you will ever hear a White man giving a Black man a compliment, and it's usually, "Wow, look at how fast he runs" or "Boy, look at how high he jumps."

But let that Black athlete do something other than jump up and down on white courts, and watch how quickly the compliments turn to insults and watch how quickly it becomes a major news scandal, covered in every major news outlet on the planet. Yet White athletes can punch out head coaches or referees, and rape or assault women, and all of a sudden all the major news outlets get amnesia.

61

BLACK SON RISING

I hate the fact that the only time you see Black people in the news is when we have robbed somebody, shot somebody, or when we're getting locked up for selling drugs.

Have you noticed that whenever the TV news anchor talks about Black criminals they say "a <u>Black</u> man robbed a bank," but when they talk about white criminals they don't say "a <u>White</u> man robbed a bank"; instead they say "a man robbed a bank"? What happened to the "<u>white</u>" part of that report?

Have you also noticed that when TV news anchors interview Black people on the street, they go out of their way to find the most ignorant, inarticulate Black person they can find to give comments?

Why are there no dark-skinned news anchors, but only light-skinned ones who apparently have passed some kind of the brown bag test to get the job?

I hate the fact that the only time you see Black people on TV commercials is when we are dancing for a chicken, rapping for soda, or balling for sneakers. Because that's all we know how to do. Right?

I hate the fact the my son and other Black children have no Black superheroes to look up to, and can only relate to white superheroes like Superman, Batman, and Spiderman. Why are all the superheroes White? What's wrong, Black people can't be superheroes?

I hate the fact that they cancelled the one good Black television drama, *Soul Food.*

I hate the fact that there are so few good Black movies like Boomerang, The Best Man, and Deliver Us From Eva.

I hate the fact that the only time you get to see Black people in television dramas is when we are playing a sidekick or comic relief to some white lead character. The only time you see Blacks as lead characters on a television program is when we're playing in some unrealistic, stereotyped sitcom about Black life, like *The Parkers* or *Eve.*

I hate the fact that just about every Black sitcom on television, including *The Parkers, Half and Half, Eve, Love Inc,* and *One on One,* has a central White character. Yet, all the top White sitcoms, including *Friends, Will and Grace, Charmed,* and *Seinfeld,* don't have a central Black character. What are they trying to say "that White people can live without Black people in their lives, but Black people can't live without Whites"?

I hate the fact that TV talk shows like *Maury Povitch* and *Jerry Springer* purposely go out of their way to get the most trifling Black people they can find to showcase their ignorance on national television. It breaks my heart to see that there are Black people who are ignorant enough to go on these shows, and air their dirty laundry in front of Whites.

I hate the fact that the only time you see Black women on television or film is when they are shaking their butts for the camera in some rap video, or snapping their neck or swirling their heads as some ghetto queen, or flipping their hair around like some stuck-up, white-washed, valley-girl-talking house negress.

I hate the fact that 99.9% of the movies that are in the theatre are movies about White folks saving the world, or some kind-hearted White person saving Black children from the ghetto, or some Black woman falling in love with a White man.

I guess White folks are the only ones who can save the world and our Black children.

Halle Berry got her start in Black films, but she didn't get any recognition as a serious actress until she started playing roles as the love interest of a White man. She got the Oscar nod of approval for playing the part of a welfare mother who had sex with a poor white trash correctional officer, in the film *Monsters Ball*. Yet Denzel Washington didn't get an Oscar for playing the role of the greatest Black man in American history in the film *Malcolm X*.

Have you noticed that they advertise White films in Black neighborhoods, but don't advertise Black films in White neighborhoods, unless it's a film that reinforces negative Black stereotypes?

I hate the fact that every time NBC, CBS, or ABC broadcast some "extraordinary" human interest story, it's always about some White person performing some monumental act of charity for Black people. Are you trying to tell me that Black people don't do charitable work for themselves, or charitable works for White folks?

I could go on and on for days about how much and why I hate the media, but what good would it do? What will it change?

The real question is, "Am I making a big deal over nothing?"

Am I blowing this thing way out of proportion?

Does it make any difference how we are viewed in the minds of Whites?

Does it really make a difference what we do on TV and films as long as we're there?

The answer is:

It is a big deal.

I'm not blowing this thing out of proportion.

It does matter how we are portrayed in television, movies, and the news. Why?

Because our Black children and teens are watching and listening to and influenced by the media; and what they are seeing and hearing and learning is that "White people are wonderful and Black people ain't' nothing!"

On any given day, on almost any given channel, or any given film, or any given newspaper, our Black children and teens are bombarded with the media-savvy message that says:

"White people are intelligent, hard-working, courageous, respectful, generous, kind, fun-loving, adventurous, and serious-minded individuals; and that Black people are lazy, ignorant, simple-minded, backward, drug-dealing, gang-banging, ruthless, treacherous, disrespectful, and dangerous playas, pimps, and hustlers, or white-washed, wanna-be-like white house niggas and field niggas."

It's the same message White people have been bombarding Black people with for the past 400 years in this country that says:

"If you're White, you're all right. If you're Black, get back, nigga!"

That's the message, and it's strong and loud and clear!

Absolutely nothing has changed in this country in the way White people see and think about Black people, and the way Black people in turn see and think about themselves.

Therein lies the seriousness and dangerousness of mass media:

The media can and does negatively influence White people's attitudes and behaviors toward Blacks, and it can and does negatively influence Black people's attitudes and behaviors toward themselves.

Most independent research conducted on mass media portrayals of Blacks has proven this.

But we don't need a research study to tell us what we already know.

BLACK SON RISING

All we have to do is look at our firsthand experiences with the way other people deal with us and behave toward us, and the way we deal with and behave toward each other, to know that this is true.

Media Depiction of Blacks

How many times have you walked into a department store or convenient store and had the store clerk or owner follow you around the store?

They were following you because they think all Black people steal.

Where did they get that perception?

How many people think that all or most White people are really smart, or that White people are a lot smarter than Black people?

Where did they get that perception?

How many times have you heard a Black person say, "I want a White or Jewish lawyer, because they are better than the Black ones"?

Where did they get that perception?

These negative perceptions of Blacks aren't just limited to the U.S.; they are international.

When I went to Kenya and Tanzania and Morocco in Africa, the Africans there were very surprised to see a Black American, because they didn't think Black Americans traveled to Africa.

When I had conversations with them about Black people in the U.S., they told me that they thought that all the Black men in America were drugdealers and gang-bangers, and that all the Black women were strippers and video dancers, or welfare mothers.

Where did they get this perception?

From European and American news and television programs that are broadcast into their country.

European and American news agencies all over the world depict Blacks as violent and dangerous criminals, thugs, gangstas, and hoodlums. The few times Blacks receive any news coverage at all, it's usually about poverty, famine, welfare, crime, drugs, or civil unrest.

When the news media covers Blacks being accused of a crime, the Blacks are more likely to be shown in dangerous-looking mug shots, or they are being physically restrained by the police officer (usually a White one), while looking wild or crazy or pathetic.

I don't know about you, but I have yet to see one White person in a news story about crime or drugs or violence, that showed the white person being physically restrained by cops and thrown to the ground like an animal. The perception of the news viewer becomes that Blacks deserve to be physically restrained because they are more dangerous than White people.

The media is a particularly dangerous influence on our Black children.

Our little Black girls don't want to play with the Black dolls. They want to play with the White ones like Barbie. Why? Because the white doll is "prettier" and has "nicer" hair. I actually heard a little Black girl tell her mother that in a toy store, while shopping for Christmas presents.

When you turn on the television on Saturday, which is "kid's day," how many cartoons are there which feature Black superheroes?

Zero. There are a hundred different superhero cartoons on a hundred different channels, yet not one of them has a Black superhero.

One Christmas, I had some friends and their children over for dinner. After dinner, I tried to get their kids to watch some movie about a Black superhero.

They didn't want to watch the Black superhero movie; they wanted to watch the White superhero movie instead. When I asked them why, they said, "There's no such thing as a Black superhero, that's stupid." And they were serious.

That blew my mind, but it is typical of Black children's reaction to the idea of a Black superhero.

Then there is our Black children's perception about Africa.

I conducted a lecture one day at a predominantly Black middle school, and I was telling the kids about my trip to Africa. They were all shocked, because they couldn't believe that I had gotten out of Africa without being bitten by some wild animal or getting sick from some deadly disease.

Their perception was that all Africans are poor, starving, and disease-ridden, and that everybody in Africa was running around half naked and getting eaten alive by wild animals roaming free in African villages.

When I asked them where they had gotten their notions about Africa and Africans, they all said they learned about Africa from watching television programs and movies about Africa, including the old Tarzan movies, and more recently the Ace Ventura movie with Jim Carey.

Both of those movies, which were made 50 years apart, still depict African men as barefoot, spear-chucking cannibals and savages who run around chasing "innocent" and "harmless" White people through the jungle. And African women are shown as some "Great White hunter's" concubine, or as half-naked slave girls with 2 or 3 babies strapped to their backs who do nothing but lounge around poorly constructed straw-thatched villages.

That's a hell of an image to project to a kid who doesn't know any better and isn't told anything different by a responsible adult, to refute these negative, false images.

Then there is the whole thug and gangsta image our Black children are bombarded with on a daily basis.

BET, once owned by Robert Johnson, but sold to a White CEO, and MTV are notorious for broadcasting music videos which depict Blacks as drug-dealing, gun-toting, gang-banging, back-stabbing murderers and thieves who "pimp" women and kill other "niggas" for fun and drugs.

This is what Black kids and teens are watching and building a lifestyle around.

So that now, Black children and teens want to grow up to be rappers, entertainers, and athletes instead of doctors, teachers, lawyers, and entrepreneurs, because their perception is that all Black people know how to do is fill their grills with gold teeth, sport chains the size of hubcaps around their necks, spit violent and childish rap lyrics, gyrate their hips on stage, or shoot hoops in $200 sneakers their parents can't afford.

What's wrong with this picture?

Why are we letting our children be inundated with this kind of negative imagery?

Studies have shown that Black children are more susceptible to the dangers of media influence, because they watch more unsupervised television and film than other children, and they see a disproportionate number of negative images of Blacks, and a disproportionate number of positive images of Whites.

It's the combination of these factors that makes the media so dangerous to our Black children, because together they can create a much more negative and destructive image of themselves than of their White counterparts. They are more at risk to the effects of violence in the media, and their self-esteem is more likely to suffer from the negative stereotypes they see of themselves in the media.

BLACK SON RISING

Therefore, if the media continue to depict Black people in such a negative light; if Black children are more susceptible to media influence; and if a higher exposure to violent television leads to aggressive behavior and lower self-esteem, then the media is setting up our Black children for failure and subjecting them to a dangerous, self-fulfilling prophecy.

The mass media has focused only on the negative aspects of Black community life (i.e., drugs, crime, violence, poverty, unemployment, and welfare) instead of the positive aspects of Black community life (i.e., college, business, family, and fun) because that's what the white racist power structure wants the media to focus on.

They own the media and they decide what issues are important and what issues are irrelevant; they decide who gets airtime and who doesn't; they decide who is beautiful and who is ugly; they decide who the good guys and bad guys are (the good guys are typically White and the bad guys are typically Black); and they decide when, where, how, and by whom these images will be projected.

That's a lot power for *anyone* to have. The problem is that this power rests largely in the hands of white supremacists who use that power to deliberately mislead people and distort the image of Blacks to promote their racist agenda.

That's what makes the mass media so dangerous, and that's why I hate it.

The World's 10 Biggest Media Companies and What They Own

10 Companies Control 90% of the Information and Entertainment You Receive:

[Source: Young African Americans Against Media Stereotypes (YAAAMS) at www.YAAAMS.com]

1. **Time Warner**
    Owns:
    Time, Inc., which publishes 24 magazines, including *Time, Sports Illustrated, People, Fortune,* and *Life.*
    Warner Music Group, including Warner Brothers, Atlantic, Interscope, and Elektra Records.
    Warner Brothers studios owns part of the Warner Brothers Television Network.
    Time Warner is the largest owner of cable systems in the U.S., as well as owning such cable channels as CNN, HBO, and Cinemax.

2. **Walt Disney Company**
    Owns:
    Walt Disney, Miramax, Castle Rock, Touchstone, Hollywood, and Buena Vista Film Studios.
    ABC TV and radio.
    Disney theme parks, stores, sports teams, record labels, and book publishing houses.
    Part of Lifetime, A&E, and History cable channels.
    Has interest in European TV networks.

3. **Bertelsmann**
    Owns:
    Music companies RCA and Arista.
    Publishing houses, including Bantam and Doubleday.
    Extensive European TV and radio holdings.

4. **Viacom**
    Owns:
    Paramount Pictures.
    Blockbuster Video.
    MTV, Nickelodeon, and other cable channels.
    UPN TV network.
    Publishing houses, including Simon & Schuster and Pocket Books.

5. **News Corporation (Headed by Rupert Murdoch)**
    Owns:
    20th Century Fox.
    Fox broadcasting network, the Fox News cable channel.
    25 magazines including *TV Guide* and *The Weekly Standard.*
    132 newspapers including the *New York Post* and the *London Times.*
    HarperCollins books.

6. **Sony**
    Owns:
    Sony Worldwide/SW Radio.
    Sony Pictures.
    Columbia Tri-Star Pictures and Columbia Records.

7. **Tele-Communications, Inc.**
    Owns:
    TCI cable systems.
    Liberty Media and MacNeil/Lehrer Productions.
    Has interests in many cable channels including Discovery Channel, E!,
    Home Shopping Network, QVC, Court TV and Black Entertainment TV.

8. **Universal (Seagram - Subsidiary of the Seagram beverage company)**
    Owns:
    Universal Pictures.
    Universal Records.
    Half-owner of USA Networks.

9. **PolyGram (Phillips - Parent company is a Dutch electronics firm)**
    Owns:
    PolyGram music and films.

10. **NBC (General Electric parent company produces consumer electronics,
    as well as being a major manufacturer of military hardware and nuclear
    power equipment)**
    Owns:
    NBC TV network, CNBC, MSNBC, and is part owner of the History
    Channel.

11

BEARING FALSE WITNESS

If the truth is that ugly - which it is - then we do have to be careful about the way that we tell the truth. But to somehow say that telling the truth should be avoided because people may respond badly to the truth seems bizarre to me.
- **Chuck Skoro, Deacon, St. Paul's Catholic Church**

One of the most powerful and effective forms of mental slavery is religious slavery – that being the willful and deliberate promotion of false ideas about the origins and character of a particular religion, for the "soul" purpose of subjugating a people to the will of the religious authorities.

I tread cautiously here, because one of the most sensitive and touchy subjects in the world is people's religion and spiritual belief systems. People grow up surrounded by religious practices and traditions that they take very seriously, and become deeply offended when you challenge their long-held preconceived notions about religion and God.

So I'm stepping out on a limb here, but I truly believe that people need to know the truth regardless of how they might react.

As you learned in the chapter *Stolen Legacy,* the Black race has been deceived, manipulated, and "mis-educated" into believing a lot of false information about world history in general, and African history in particular, in order to keep us enslaved.

However, nothing has been more dangerous or devastating to the Black race, nor more effective in keeping us enslaved, than the mental, emotional, and spiritual conditioning we received through the institution of white racist Europeanized Christianity.

European Christianity has effectively removed and/or hidden any traces of the African origins of not only Christianity, but all the major world religions, thereby keeping the people of African descent in the "dark" about their significant contributions to religion – which is the study of man's true spiritual relationship to his Creator.

This willful and deliberate hiding of the true color origins of Christianity was carried out for the express purpose of convincing the African, and his descendants, that he is inferior to Whites.

For if God is white, and the religions of God were developed by White men, then logic dictates that white people must be superior to all the other races of color, correct?

It is through the "heathen" doctrine of the white European Roman Catholic Church, which held that those who were not believers in the "one true Christian Church" were obviously inferior beings and "less than human." It was during this period of white Church history that Blacks began to be depicted throughout the world as an uncivilized, savage, and sub-human species.

This is the kind of false, backward religious slave training the Black race has been subjected to for more than 2000 years, creating within us a sense of worthlessness because we are obviously "less than human."

This religious slave indoctrination has been very effective in perpetuating our mental, emotional, and spiritual bondage.

To this day, I still see Black people worshiping a blond-haired, blue-eyed image of Jesus (Yashua) despite the fact that he was a Palestinian (Middle Eastern) Jew.

That means he was a man of color.

He wasn't Black, but he damn sure wasn't White either.

How important is it what color or race Jesus was? It's only important to the extent that one race would use his color and race to justify their superiority over another.

Ask yourself this: Would White people accept a Black Jesus? No they wouldn't. How do I know that? Because they can't and haven't accepted the brown one.

It's unfortunate, but most Black people in this country have swallowed this purely Eurocentric and racist version of Christianity, one which bears very little resemblance to "true" Christianity and its central figures like, Jesus (Yashua), Moses, and Abraham. And we have swallowed this false, Europeanized concept of Christianity, hook, line, and sinker.

That's because, in general, Black people have a bad habit of believing and accepting whatever anyone tells them without bothering to verify and corroborate the facts for themselves.

This is one of the things that keep us enslaved as a race. That, and the fact that we are generally too lazy to search for the truth.

Anybody can walk into our homes, sell us a bunch of half-truths and flat out deliberate lies, that we accept as the "truth" and fight tooth and nail to defend, without conducting one shred of independent research of our own, before it becomes our "gospel."

And God forbid someone should come along to point out, with hardcore facts, mind you, the glaring errors and falsehoods in what they have been "led" (*as in led into bondage*) to believe.

What is the typical reaction of so-called "Christians" when you challenge anything they have blindly accepted as "truth"?

Anger, hostility, resentment, and rage! And sometimes physical violence!

The ones who defend their beliefs the loudest, and most violently, are usually the ones who have done the least amount of independent biblical research, and don't know the difference between "faith" and "belief."

You can have "faith" that there is a God, but your "beliefs" are ideas that you have been "taught" (or mistaught) to believe about what God is and what He looks like.

Most "Christians" have been mistaught to believe in the image of a White God.

Most "Christians" simply parrot what they "mislearned" in Sunday school when they were 12 years old, and haven't learned anything of any significance since.

Any intelligent, well-read, sincerely truth-seeking Christian would freely admit to the numerous historical discrepancies in the European version of the origins and true philosophy of the "Yashua (Jesus) movement," which came to be known throughout the world as Christianity.

What is it that blocks otherwise intelligent Black people from looking objectively at Christianity or its origins?

What are they afraid of?

Is it the truth? Or is it the confirmation of their ignorance that the truth will reveal to them?

A wise man once said that "the recognition and admission of one's ignorance is the beginning of wisdom."

BLACK SON RISING

I think Black people prefer to remain ignorant of the truth, or even loathe to look for it, because it requires them to admit that they have been wrong most of their lives and that they allowed themselves to be conned into believing something that isn't entirely true.

I think it is sad that most Black Christians have no real understanding of what it means to be a Christian, or what the true origins of Christianity are.

So why pick on Christianity and Christians?

Why not point out the historical fallacies in the origins of Islam or Judaism, or some other world religion?

Because Christianity, at least the white racist Europeanized version of it, has a firm foothold in the hearts and minds of the Black family, Black community, and the Black church, and it has done infinitely more harm to them than good.

It was through the European version of Christianity that white supremacists tried to justify the enslavement of Blacks.

It was through the European version of Christianity that white so-called "Christian" missionaries paved the way for the colonization of African nations.

It was through the European version of Christianity that many of the slaves were convinced to turn the other cheek, and wait for their freedom and salvation in heaven.

It was through the European version of Christianity that Blacks were taught to worship the image of a blond-haired, blue-eyed, merciful white God who took pity on us "heathen" savages, and saved us from our lowly existences.

It was through the European version of Christianity that Blacks eventually became docile, harmless chattel property.

The reason Black people are in America today, instead of their native African homeland, can be attributed to the massive slave trading business of the European so-called "Christians."

The reason why Africa is in such an awful condition today is because it was ravaged of its wealth and resources by European so-called "Christians."

The reason most Black people do not know who they are, or what their history is, and turn their noses up at anything "African," is because of European so-called "Christians."

This whole white supremacist process of using Christianity to categorize people into "separate and unequal classes," began with Pope Julius II who signed a document known as a "Papal Bull," dividing the world amongst his two most powerful Christian countries, Portugal and Spain.

Prior to the 16th century, Spain signed a contract with the Portuguese called "Asiento," allowing them a monopoly in the carrying and selling of Africans across the Atlantic, until the English joined in the fun, followed by the French and the Dutch.

Slavery in the United States, carried out by the European so-called "Christians" in the name of Christianity, ushered in the worst form of slavery in world history; "chattel slavery." In other words, Africans were not considered human but rather property or animals, with absolutely no type of human rights at all. This was justified through the misinterpretation of Bible stories, particularly about African people being cursed, and turned black, and forced to live for all eternity as slaves of other races.

It is for all of these reasons that I address Christians and Christianity, because the legacy of European Christianity and "Christians" and their false doctrine of white supremacy, based on religious lies and half-truths, are still evident to this day.

First, let's set the record straight: I am not a biblical scholar or theologian. I do not presume or pretend to know everything about Christianity or any other world religion for that matter.

However, I can read, and I do research the historical context of most religions to gain a better understanding of how they were developed. The information that I am sharing with you comes from hundreds of different sources, too many to annotate in this volume. What I have learned, and what I am still learning is mind-blowing, and would be considered sacrilegious to your average, uninformed lay Christian.

I do not put forth any of this information as the absolute truth, for there is but one entity that knows the absolute truth about all things in heaven and on earth, and that's God Almighty Himself.

However, there is significant historical evidence, if you bother to look for it, that contradicts much of what most so-called Christians have been misled to believe about God, Christianity, Jesus the Christ (*the word Christ being a title, not his last name*), and the infallibility of the so-called "Holy" Bible.

There is not enough room in this book to detail all of the significant biblical findings that many scholars have spent their entire lives researching in an effort to come up with a more accurate account of the historical bible. However, I will recount to you some of what I have learned so far.

Most Christians, Black and White, have no idea, nor are they likely to care, after thousands of years of racial oppression and false teachings, that their sacred Old Testaments are the creations of Black Africans, specifically Black African Egyptians of North Africa. Looking at a map of the world will help you understand how, through the geographic proximity of Egypt and Israel, Judaism (the predecessor of Christianity) could have originated in the African continent and migrated north into the Asiatic continent, where Israel sits.

The so-called "Bibles" we use today are the result of a period of hundreds of revisions and translations that cover approximately 2,500 years.

Yet each of the "biblical" revisions has its roots in a much more ancient religious text that was developed by African people. These earlier religious texts are in fact the basis of Judaism, Christianity, Islam, and Hinduism.

The very first "Bible" (*or scroll*) on record produced by man that paid divine respect to our Creator was written in hieroglyphics, by the inhabitants of the Nile Valley, and was based on the Egyptian Mystery Systems. The title of this religious text was *The Egyptian Book of Coming Forth by Day and by Night*, commonly referred to as *The Egyptian Book of the Dead*.

Following is what I have learned regarding the historical development of Christianity and the Bible:

This "original" bible was produced more than 3500 years before the Old Testament, and more than 4300 years before the New Testament. *The Egyptian Book of Coming Forth by Day and by Night* (*Egyptian Book of the Dead*), the original bible, was written in hieroglyphics by Black Egyptian high priests to honor their Creator 3500 years before Moses' five books were "written."

Moses, an African of Qamt (Kemet, or Egypt), the so-called "father" of the first five books of the Old Testament, used the ancient African knowledge he learned from the Egyptian Mystery Systems to teach the Hebrew descendants of Abraham about man's relationship to God, and how they should worship him. The Hebrew people, once slaves of the Egyptians, took Moses' teachings and later converted them into what would become known as the Pentateuch, or Old Testament, or Holy Torah.

Abraham (*Abram*), a Hebrew Semite (*meaning half Black, half White*), was born in Chaldea, an Asiatic nation under African rule, to parents who were Sun Worshipers. Abraham and his family were driven by famine into Kemet (Egypt), in North Africa.

Moses (*Mos*) was born in Africa and raised in Kemet as a high priest in the Egyptian Mystery Systems as taught via the *Egyptian Book of the Dead*. He spearheaded a revolt against Ramses II and led the Hebrew descendants of Abraham out of Kemet into the land which eventually became known as Israel.

The Pentateuch (*Five Books of Moses, Holy Torah, Old Testament*) as taught by Moses to the Hebrew "slaves," with the Hebrew distortions of their experience in Egypt, was placed into circulation and became the basis of Judaism. The Septuagint version of the Pentateuch was written in the Greek language, by seventy-two African Hebrew rabbis and scholars, in Alexandria, Egypt. It was a compilation of forty-five books called the Alexandrian Canon, and was used by the earliest Greek and Latin churches.

In A.D. 331, Emperor Constantine commissioned and financed a new version of the Bible. It was at this point that crucial alterations were made. A year after the Council of Nicea, Constantine ordered all works that challenged his version of "religious truth" to be destroyed. Constantine never converted to Christianity. He was actually baptized when he was on his deathbed, completely unaware of the fact.

Your contemporary "Bible" is only a small selection of numerous scriptural works. It has been drastically edited and revised to fit the agenda of the powerful and power-hungry church clergy. During the Council of Nicea, Constantine instructed a priest by the name of Eusebius to compile a "uniform" collection of writings from a collection of manuscripts from several hundred sources, with the instruction "make them to astound!"

This was the first Christian New Testament. Constantine decreed that these were to be considered the "words of God." The New Testament was also to be bound with the Old Testament to give the appearance of combining the two religions. Constantine then ordered that anyone possessing the earlier manuscripts should be beheaded instantly. He also sent Joseph of Tiberias to Jerusalem to construct a small temple over the site of a cave that was to be referred to as the birthplace of Jesus. He offered bribes for influential people to accept the new creed.

Constantine issued edicts forbidding other Christian sects that did not conform to his new version of Christianity, from hold meetings, and many were put to death because they refused to accept his altered doctrine. It should be noted that Constantine drowned his wife in boiling water and killed his son.

The Roman Catholic Church inherited Roman cruelty and lust for power, because no other Christian sects beside the Roman Church were tolerated.

The denial of Roman Catholic authority met with tragic consequences for anyone who dared to oppose it. In 1208 Pope Innocent III ordered the extermination of over 30,000 Christian Cathars who opposed the Roman Catholic Church, including children, women, and the elderly, who were brutally massacred over a number of years. Those who escaped the sword were burned alive and subjected to other horrible deaths.

In A.D. 1607, a committee of 47 men took two years and nine months to "rewrite" the Roman Catholic Bible, which was then called the King James Bible. The committee removed seven books from the Roman Catholic version of the Bible. King James chose Sir Francis Bacon to edit the manuscripts.

The so-called "authorized King James" version that most Christians claim as "the one, and only true Bible" is one of the very latest versions of the "Holy Bible." There have been dozens of other versions of the Bible that existed long before the King James version. The KJV only became the most popular version, because Britain used its military power to force everyone under its rule to use that particular version. King James, himself a pedophile, was the first to proclaim his version as the "official Bible of the Church of England and the one and only, true and Holy Bible."

This is a very, very brief account of the origins of Christianity and the Christian Bible, but as you can see, it was men's lust for religious power that took the original African teachings found in the *Egyptian Book of the Dead* and altered the text, over hundreds of years and dozens of revisions, to fit their own agendas.

The bottom line is this: I am not trying to offend anyone's Christian sensibilities, or debunk Christianity as a false religion, for truthfully, although I do not consider myself a Christian by any traditional sense of the term, I do believe that Yashua ben Yosef (Jesus the son of Joseph) was in fact the physical incarnation of our Creator.

What I am asking Black Christians to bear in mind is that everything you think you know about Christianity was taught to you by your parents.

Everything your parents know about Christianity was taught to them by your grandparents.

Everything your grandparents know about Christianity was taught to them by your great grandparents.

And everything your great grandparents know about Christianity was taught to them by their White racist slave masters.

Question: Why on earth would a slave master enslave you on one hand, and then teach you the true and correct knowledge of God on the other?

Answer: He wouldn't and he hasn't. That means that everything you believe about your religion and God was passed down to you from one generation to the next by a white supremacist who has done everything in his power to keep you and your people enslaved.

Is that really someone from whom you should be getting your knowledge about God?

Stop thinking like a slave for five minutes and look at the *logic* of what I'm asking you to do.

I am asking you to open your eyes, your mind, and your heart to the very real possibility that you have been willfully lied to about your Christian beliefs.

BLACK SON RISING

I'm asking you to use the intelligence that God gave you to help you discern fact from fiction, and history from "his story."

I'm asking you to take the time to research your Bible, and your religion, before accepting everything someone tells you as "gospel."

I'm asking you to stop letting people who don't have your best interest at heart (i.e., white supremacists) define the images and the doctrine you use to establish and build a relationship with God.

I'm asking you to take the chains off your mind and remove the bonds of religious slavery that have been placed on you and your people to keep them obedient and subservient to the "white god" of the "master race."

Publisher Addendum

CHRISTIAN RESPONSE TO ATHEIST HISTORIANS AND MUSLIMS
by Dr. Jawanza Kunjufu

1. The Old Testament is filled with African history.

2. Ancient history begins after the Flood (4000 B.C.). One of Noah's sons, Ham, had four sons: Cush (Ethiopia), Mizraim (Egypt), Phut (Libya), and Canaan (Isreal). The curse was placed on Canaan not Ham.

3. The river in the Garden of Eden (Pishon) is the Nile River.

4. The word Egypt and its derivatives are used 750 times in the Old Testament. The word Ethiopia and its derivatives are used 64 times. Greece is only stated 4 times in the Old Testament and Rome is not mentioned at all.

5. The major tenets of Christianity (i.e., monotheism, life after death, libation, water as a sign of purification, and moral truths) have their origins in Africa. King Akhenaton advocated the belief in one God in 1379 B.C. The building of the Pyramids, temples, tombs, and mumification, illustrated a belief in the afterlife. The libation, sacrifice, pouring of the blood shows an acknowledgment. At the temple of Karnak, near Thebes, water was used as a form of purification. The Ten Commandments are very similar to the negative confessions.

6. Three of the greatest interpreters of scriptures were St. Augustine, St. Cyrian, and Tertullian, all Africans.

7. Africans were introduced to Christianity long before slavery in America, as described in Acts 8:26-40. (An Ethiopian eunuch was worshipping God, reading the Book of Isaiah, and baptized in the name of Jesus Christ.)

8. Moses, an Egyptian (Exodus 2:19) (1250 B.C. -1200 B.C.) rescued some Ethiopians, including Zipporah who became his wife. He is given the Ten Commandments, in Africa, as other Africans were given the Negative Confessions. There are no European Jews until the 7th century A.D.

74

9. King David, Bathsheba, and their son Solomon were Hittites who were Hamitic. Jesus Christ who came to Earth in the flesh possessing "feet like unto fine brass as if burned in a furnace," and with hair "like wool," can be traced through this family lineage on Joseph and Mary's side.

10. There was slavery perpetuated by Egyptians, Arab Muslims, Israelites, and Roman Christians. Muslim slavery preceded Christian slavery.

11. Prophet Muhammad was born in the 6th century A.D. How is this the original religion of Africans? He did not die for our sins and did not say he was coming back.

12. Christianity is **not** a weak, passive religion. Jesus Christ was a liberator as described in Luke 4:18-21 and Isaiah 58. Most of the 265 slave revolts were led by Christian ministers.

13. There are three types of churches—entertainment, containment, and liberation.

14. Many religions and the Old Testament are based on the law—an eye for an eye and a tooth for a tooth. If this continues we'll have a war-torn society with everyone blind and toothless. With the New Testament and Jesus Christ—Grace wins over the law.

15. After all is said and done, it is not about **scholarship** or **history**, but a **relationship** with Jesus, that He is real; He died for our sins; and those that believe will have everlasting life. We conclude with Jesus asking the last question from Matthew 16: 13-15:

16. Who do the people (atheist historians, Muslims, etc.) say I AM? The most important question follows: Who do you say I AM?

For additional information read the Bible and the works of James Cone, Cain Felder, and Walter McCray.

PART II

THE EFFECTS

Black-on-black crime is the result of self-hatred. Self-hatred is the result of our oppression. We can't get back at the folks who oppress us so we attack ourselves.
- **Joseph Lowery, Civil Rights Activist**

12

MURDER INK

Who taught you to hate the texture of your hair? Who taught you how to hate the color of your skin? Who taught you how to hate yourself?
- **Malcolm X, Nationalist Leader**

In 2005, Baltimore, Maryland, was named the third most dangerous city in the country behind Detroit, Michigan, and Camden, New Jersey. Baltimore finished the year with 263 murders. Ninety-five percent of the homicides were of Black men. Ninety percent of the homicides were carried out using a handgun.

Preliminary investigations into the homicides led police officials to believe that most of these men were killed by other Black men.

This is an absolute tragedy!

The homicide rate in Baltimore skyrocketed in the months of June, July, and August, the summer months, which are typically the most dangerous months of the year in the inner city.

As you read these police homicide blotters, try to picture these victims as they might have appeared to their families and friends before their lives were taken from them, and think of the enormous sense of loss their loved ones continue to suffer to this day.

These victims were father, son, brother, or husband. Or they were somebody's mother, daughter, sister, or wife. Someone loved them. Someone needed them. Someone wanted them.

Someone waited for them to come home, but they didn't. And now they are gone. Forever.

Why?

Because the Black man's fear, false pride, material greed, social ignorance, self-hatred, and misplaced anger is what now dictates and drives his behavior, and as a result he has become his own worst enemy.

Please review each one of these homicides so that you can fully appreciate the senselessness of these tragedies, and how readily handguns are available and in use in the Black community, and how serious this epidemic of black-on-black crime and violence is in the inner city.

I wrote this chapter for those individuals who think that I am exaggerating or making a big deal about the rate of black-on-black violence in Black communities. If you can read this chapter and still think that Black people in America are really progressing, then there is something seriously wrong with your mind.

After you are finished reading the police blotters, please observe a moment of silence to pray for the safekeeping of those deceased, and to pray condolences for the grieving families who are forced to live with the tragic and senseless loss of their loved ones.

BLACK SON RISING

I offer my deepest, most sincere condolences to the families and friends of the deceased, and for them I too cry out with my whole heart.

(Source: Baltimore City Police Blotter)

Wednesday, Aug. 17
1:37 a.m. Tavon Granger, a 20-year-old African American man, was standing with a group of people at the corner of Pall Mall Road and Loyola Southway near Park Heights when someone pulled out a handgun. Granger saw the gun and ran, but the person chased him, fired, and hit Granger, who fell to the ground. The shooter continued firing as he lay there. Granger was taken to Sinai Hospital, where he died a half-hour later.

Saturday, Aug. 20
2:58 p.m. That afternoon, Harry Johnson, a 34-year-old African American man, left his mother's house in the 3000 block of Ascension Street in Cherry Hill. He was walking to his car when a man approached him. The two talked. Johnson answered his cell phone, and the other man pulled out a gun and shot him repeatedly in the head.

Monday, Aug. 8
3:10 a.m. George Buggs, a 31-year-old African American man, was stabbed in the neck at his home in the 3000 block of Grayson Street near Gwynns Falls Park. When police officers arrived, a medieval-style knife was sticking out of his neck. He was pronounced dead five minutes later.

Tuesday, Aug. 9
4:15 a.m. The next morning, less than a mile away in the 2400 block of Winchester Street, police were met by the mother of Donnie Foster, a 26-year-old African American man. The woman told the officers that her son had been shot. They found him lying dead in the doorway of a bedroom in the apartment. He had suffered several gunshot wounds.

Sunday, Aug. 14
12:17 a.m. Also in Lakeland, police found Jerome Hooks, a 24-year-old African American man, lying on the sidewalk in the 2600 block of Wegworth Lane. The area around him was riddled with casings. He had been shot in the head and was taken to the Maryland Shock Trauma Center, where he died at 12:59 a.m. Hooks lived in the 2700 block of Wegworth Lane. This was the fourth homicide in Lakeland this year.

Monday, Aug. 1
2:25 a.m. Police officers found Craig Crowder, a 34-year-old African American man from East Baltimore, lying in the middle of the 2300 block of West Baltimore Street. He was standing outside when several men drove up in a station wagon and shot him repeatedly. Crowder was taken to Maryland Shock Trauma Center but died shortly after he arrived.

Tuesday, Aug. 2
1:12 p.m. Darrell Winston, a 21-year-old African American man, got into a physical altercation with a woman in the 600 block of North Curley Street. Jene Foreman, a 15-year-old African American male from Essex, tried to get Winston

to let the woman go. Winston and Foreman argued, then Foreman allegedly produced a gun and shot Winston several times. Winston was taken to Johns Hopkins Hospital, where he died less than half an hour later. The next day, Foreman was shot a few blocks away from where he argued with Winston, in the 700 block of Kenwood Avenue. He was also taken to Hopkins and survived. He was served with a warrant there on Aug. 5, charging him as an adult with first-degree murder.

Thursday, Aug. 4
2:20 a.m. Police found Gary Robinson, a 28-year-old African American man, lying in front of a building in the 500 block of Orchard Street in Seton Hill near the intersection of Martin Luther King Boulevard and Route 40. He had been shot in the head and died at Shock Trauma at 11:30 a.m.

Friday, Aug. 5
12:30 a.m. Police drove into the 600 block of Ashburton Street just off Edmondson Avenue in West Baltimore and saw Thomas Mason, a 39-year-old African American man, lying in the middle of the street. He had been shot several times and died at Shock Trauma half an hour later.

Saturday, Aug. 6
2:50 a.m. Theodore Ross, a 21-year-old African American man, was at a party in the 3800 block of Cedarhurst Road near B'nai Israel cemetery in Northeast Baltimore. Four men crashed the party and asked for food. They got into an argument with Ross and moved the argument outside to the front yard. One of the men pulled out a gun and shot Ross, who made it as far as the doorway before collapsing. He was taken to Johns Hopkins Bayview Medical Center and died at 3:35 a.m.

Sunday, Aug. 7
6:50 p.m. Paul Talley, an 18-year-old African American man, was shot in the head several times as he sat in the driver's seat of a maroon Ford Taurus in a parking lot in the 800 block of East 30th Street in Greater Waverly. He died at 7:20 p.m. at Hopkins Hospital. He was about two blocks from home. Talley is the fourth person to be murdered in Greater Waverly this year.

Tuesday, July 26
10:35 p.m. David Howard, a 19-year-old African American man from Parkville, was found sitting in a red Cadillac Deville in the 2600 block of Norland Road near the Baltimore-Washington Parkway. There were bullet holes through the window. Howard had been shot in the head and neck. He was taken to Maryland Shock Trauma Center, where he died at 12:40 a.m. the next day. In May, a man was murdered a block away from the location where Howard was shot.

Wednesday, July 27
5:30 a.m. Five hours after Howard died, another man was found shot to death in a car. Police officers found Ernest Pope, a 53-year-old African American man, slumped over in the driver's seat of an Isuzu Rodeo parked behind the 3800 block of Elmora Avenue in Belair-Edison. Pope had left his house that morning to go to work. When he got into his car and started it, a man shot him in the head and walked away. Pope was pronounced dead at the scene.

Thursday, July 28
1:25 p.m. Police officers were flagged down by a person who said there was a man lying in the middle of the street bleeding. They found Robert Montgomery,

a 22-year-old African American man, dead in the 1000 block of Tunbridge Road near Chinquapin Middle School in North Baltimore. He had been shot in the head and killed.

Sunday, July 31
7:20 p.m. An unidentified man was found dead in an apartment complex in the 2400 block of Bridgehampton Drive near the Parkway Crossing Shopping Center in Northeast Baltimore. He, too, had been shot in the head, making him at least the 58th homicide victim this year to die that way.

Tuesday, July 19
7:54 p.m. Dennis Wilson, a 60-year-old African American man, was at his job as the evening shift supervisor at a juice factory in Northwest Baltimore near Reisterstown Road Plaza, when Levi White, a 49-year-old African American man and former employee of the factory, entered the building through the back door. He was carrying a shotgun. White walked up to Wilson, hit him in the face, and then shot him. White then walked out the front door. When the police officers arrived, they told White to drop his weapon. Instead, he pointed his gun at the officers, who shot him in the chest. Wilson was pronounced dead by medics at the factory at 8:20 p.m. White died at Sinai Hospital at 2:33 a.m. the next day.

Wednesday, July 20
2:15 a.m. Police got a call for a shooting in the 200 block of East 22nd Street in the Barclay neighborhood. Upon arrival, they found Dante Jordan, a 26-year-old African American man from the 1800 block of St. Paul Street, lying in the street two blocks from Lovely Lane Methodist Church. He had been shot. He died at Johns Hopkins Hospital half an hour later. Jordan was the third person murdered in Barclay this year.

Friday, July 22
12:56 a.m. A group of women got into a fight outside an apartment building in the 4800 block of Lorelly Avenue near Herring Run Park in Frankford. During the fight, someone pulled out a knife and stabbed Angel Simms, a 23-year-old African American woman who lived at the apartment building, in the neck. Simms was taken to Johns Hopkins Bayview Medical Center but died shortly after she arrived.

Saturday, July 23
1:40 a.m. The next night in Curtis Bay, Damont Adams, a 23-year-old African American man from the Barclay neighborhood, was sitting on the steps in front of a house in the 1600 block of Hazel Street. A man approached him and started shooting at him. The victim ran inside of the house next door and collapsed. He had been shot in the torso and was pronounced dead by medics 20 minutes later.

Sunday, July 24
3:17 a.m. Police got a call for another shooting in Northeast Baltimore. According to the call, a juvenile had been shot in the 4100 block of Eierman Avenue in Arcadia near Herring Run Park. When they got there they did not find a juvenile. Instead, they found Anthony Jackson, a 26-year-old African-American man who lived less than a block away, lying in the street. He had been shot in the back of the head. Police later found a 16-year-old African American girl in a nearby house who had been shot in the left arm. Both were taken to Hopkins Hospital. The girl was in stable condition. Jackson died half an hour later.

Wednesday, July 13
3:41 a.m. A four-door Chrysler New Yorker was found parked in the first block of North Culver Street near Saint Joseph Monastery in Southwest Baltimore. The door was open, the headlights were on, and the radio was blaring. Inside the car Keith Butler, a 23-year-old African American man, lay on his back, bleeding. He had been shot in the head, and was pronounced dead on the scene.

Thursday, July 14
11:15 p.m. Eugene Carr, a 23-year-old African American man, was riding a bike in the 2800 block of Prospect Street in West Baltimore's Mosher neighborhood. A man approached him and shot him in the head. He was taken to Shock Trauma and pronounced dead at 11:51 p.m.

Friday, July 15
6:55 a.m. Police got a call for a shooting in the first block of Benkert Street, just two blocks from where Keith Butler was killed two days earlier. When they arrived, Desean Dorsey, a 28-year-old African American man, had already been pronounced dead by medics. He died from a gunshot to the head.

Saturday, July 16
10:39 p.m. Damon Wilder, a 21-year-old African American man, was sitting on a stoop in the 400 block of Whitridge Avenue, a small street off Barclay Street between 27th and 28th streets. A man walked up to him, shot him repeatedly, and left. A three-year-old boy who was nearby was hit by bullet fragments, but survived. Wilder was pronounced dead at the scene.

Sunday, July 3
2:11 p.m. On Sunday afternoon Marvin Raines, an 18-year-old African American man, was shot repeatedly on his front porch in the 2800 block of Spelman Road in Cherry Hill. He was taken to Harbor Hospital and pronounced dead at 2:36 p.m.

Monday, July 4
10:16 p.m. Carl Griffin, a 44-year-old African American man from the Middle East neighborhood, was shot in the head in the 1400 block of Exeter Hall Avenue, about four blocks south of the former site of Memorial Stadium. He was pronounced dead on the scene.

Thursday, July 7
6:10 p.m. Police officers in West Baltimore heard several gunshots coming from the 1500 block of Poplar Grove Avenue. When they got there they found Jamie Parker, a 27-year-old African American man, lying in the street unconscious. He had been shot repeatedly and was pronounced dead on the scene. Four other people have been shot to death this year within a two-block radius of where Parker was found.

Friday, June 24
6:56 p.m. Charles Harris, a 43-year-old African American man, was found unconscious in the 1800 block of East Preston Street in the Broadway East neighborhood. He was taken to Shock Trauma and pronounced dead at 4:30 p.m. the next day. This week, his death was ruled a homicide due to blunt-force trauma to the head.

BLACK SON RISING

Monday, June 27
4:37 p.m. A person taking photos in the 1700 block of Boyd Street in Union Square near the H.L. Mencken House saw a body lying on the ground. Samuel Umstead, a 39-year-old Caucasian man from the neighborhood, had been shot. He was taken to Shock Trauma and pronounced dead half an hour later.

Wednesday, June 29
6:40 p.m. Police officers found Michael Guy, a 20-year-old African American man, lying in the middle of the 2500 block of Lauretta Avenue in West Baltimore. He had been shot repeatedly and was taken to Shock Trauma where he was pronounced dead at 7:15 p.m.

Thursday, June 23
10:52 p.m. An hour after Orrison was shot, Brian Sampson, an 18-year-old African American man, was in the 1200 block of West Lexington Street in Poppleton near Franklin Square. An unknown man started shooting at him. Sampson tried to run but was shot several times and collapsed in the 1100 block of Lexington. He was taken to Shock Trauma and pronounced dead at 2:26 a.m.

Saturday, June 25
1:27 a.m. Jerrod Hamlett, a 22-year-old African American man, and another man were shot in the 4000 block of Oswego Court in Northwest Baltimore. Hamlett was shot in the chest and pronounced dead at Sinai Hospital at 1:55 a.m. The other victim was shot in the back but survived. A juvenile has been arrested for the crime.

Sunday, June 26
3:21 a.m. Caprilla Jackson, an African American woman, was found lying in her backyard in the 1300 block of Pentridge Road near Morgan State University. She had been celebrating her 31st birthday earlier. Jackson had been shot repeatedly and was pronounced dead on the scene. Jackson was the 17th homicide in the Northern police district this year. There were 17 murders in the Northern district during all of 2004.

Tuesday, June 14
1:20 a.m. Antoine Williams, a 25-year-old African American man, was sitting on a porch near his home in the 600 block of North Potomac Street in East Baltimore's Ellwood Park/Monument neighborhood. An unknown person came out of a nearby alley and started shooting at him. Williams tried to run but collapsed in front of a house. He was taken to Johns Hopkins Hospital and pronounced dead at 1:50 a.m. This is the sixth homicide in that neighborhood this year. Ellwood Park/Monument is approximately five blocks square.

Thursday, June 16
4:35 a.m. Jerry Evans, a 23-year-old African American man, was in the 1100 block of McAleer Court in Oldtown when a man walked up to him and started shooting. Evans was hit in the head and body and taken to Hopkins Hospital in cardiac arrest. Doctors there could not revive him.

Friday, June 17
12:13 a.m. Baltimore police officers got a call for a shooting in the rear of the 2000 block of Belair Road near Clifton Park. When they got there they found

Anthony Boyce, a 19-year-old African American man. He had been shot. He was taken to Hopkins Hospital and pronounced dead half an hour later.

Saturday, June 18
12:41 a.m. Twelve hours later, Troy Barnett, a 30-year-old African American man, was found lying on his own kitchen floor shot in the 1500 block of Holbrook Street in Oliver near the Greenmount Cemetery. He was taken to Hopkins Hospital and pronounced dead shortly after he arrived. This is the fourth homicide in Oliver this year and the second in the last 30 days.

Sunday, June 19
10:43 p.m. An unknown man was found shot in the head at the tennis court in Hanlon Park in the 2700 block of North Longwood Street. He was pronounced dead at the scene.

Monday, June 6
1:26 a.m. Baltimore police officers received a call for a shooting in the 4900 block of Queensberry Lane in Central Park Heights. When they arrived they found Kevin Dozier, a 19-year-old African American man, who had been shot repeatedly in the torso. There was a 20-yard blood trail leading to his body. Dozier was taken to Sinai Hospital and pronounced dead 15 minutes later.

Tuesday, June 7
12:46 p.m. Police officers found Bobby Anderson, a 35-year-old African American man, lying on the floor inside a building in the 5400 block of Park Heights Avenue near Pimlico. He had been shot in the head. Anderson was taken to Sinai and listed in critical condition, but he died at 11:15 p.m. the next day.

Wednesday, June 8
3:04 p.m. Antonio Fox, a 20-year-old African American man, was found lying on the ground in the 900 block of North Chester Street in Middle East. He had been shot in the stomach. He was taken to Hopkins Hospital and pronounced dead three and a half hours later. Fox was the 76th African American man shot to death this year.

TRY TO UNDERSTAND
by Susan R. George Shipman

Last night while I was trying to sleep,
My son's voice I did hear
I opened my eyes and looked around,
But he did not then appear.

He said: "Mom you've got to listen,
You've got to understand
God didn't take me from you, mom,
He only took my hand.

"When I called out in pain that night,
The instant that I died,
He reached down and took my hand,
And pulled me to His side.
He pulled me up and saved me

BLACK SON RISING

From the misery and the pain.
My body was hurt so badly inside,
I could never be the same.
"My search is really over now,
I've found happiness within,
All the answers to my empty dreams
And all that might have been.
"I love you all and miss you so,
And I'll always be nearby.
My body's gone forever,
But my spirit will never die!

"And so, you must all go on now,
Live one day at a time.
Just try to understand-
God did not take me from you,
He only took my hand."

A PRAYER FOR THE GRIEVING

He will swallow up death in victory; and the Lord God will wipe away tears from all faces.
- Isaiah 25:8

Father, right now, standing at the grave of the one I love, I cannot be consoled by any ordinary words. I am capable of weeping only for my unbearable loss; all I can feel is despair and anger that my loved one has been ripped from my life because of stupid, senseless, needless violence.

I am in complete and utter shock at this tragic waste of human life; and I am stumbling through my miserable life, while others desperately try in vain to comfort me and ease my pain. Lord, I cannot be comforted by their efforts alone, and my pain will not end without You.

How empty my life seems without my loved one, Lord. You brought us together for a time, and filled our lives with both good times and bad times. Lord, I thank You for the time You allowed us to spend together, and I will cherish these memories forever, even though it may hurt my heart to do so.

Father, I pray that You keep my loved one safe in Your loving arms, and please don't let him suffer anymore than he already has.

Father, I pray that You fill my emptiness with Your healing love, and make me whole in You as You fill me with Your healing Spirit.

I pray these things in the name of the Almighty Father, the Most-High, the Supreme Creator of all that exists.

Amen

13

BOYZ N THE HOOD

How Angry Young Black Men Contribute to
the Cycle of Black-on-Black Crime and Violence in America

There is nothing more frightful than ignorance in action.
- **Goethe**

Black ghettos - with their stifling poverty, their climate of hopelessness, and their deplorable living conditions - have produced a lot of angry, hostile, and ruthless young Black men, who are both the victims and the perpetrators of Black-on-Black crime and violence.

As a result, we've got thousands of young Black men running around the streets thinking that their violent, criminal, and irresponsible behavior is some kind of ghetto birthright – that somehow just being born into an environment of drugs, and crime, and violence is automatic justification for their involvement in drugs, and crime, and violence.

What you Brothers don't realize is that it's not your ghetto living conditions that give rise to your violent and criminal behavior. Instead:

It's your ignorance, your slave mentality, and your false perception of manhood that allow you to *justify* your violent and criminal behavior!

It's your ignorance, your slave mentality, and your false perception of manhood that perpetuates the cycle of black-on-black crime and violence!

Black-on-black crime and violence ain't no joke! This thing is deadly serious! Let me tell what I know and see and hear is going on in Black communities, every single day, as a result of your ignorance, slave mentality, and false perception of manhood.

Every single day, I hear in the news about some poor grieving Black mother whose son or daughter has been murdered, because some Black thug or gangsta was ignorant enough to *think* he was being a "man" by taking somebody's life.

Every single day, and every single night, I listen to ambulance and police sirens screaming up and down my streets, all hours of the day and night, only to find out later on that another Black person has been shot, stabbed, or killed.

Every single day, I look outside my window and see 12- or 13-year-old Black boys on bicycles selling dope, because some slave-minded street hustler or gangsta rapper is teaching them that's the only life and "work" available to young Black men and boys.

BLACK SON RISING

Every single day, I drive through my neighborhood and see a bunch of unemployed and uneducated Brothers hanging out on street corners all hours of the day and night, because they're still too stupid to realize, after all this time, that the only thing waiting for them on that corner is *prison or death.*

Every single day, I see some young Sister waiting at the bus stop with two or three fatherless Black children she has to raise by herself, because the father of the children has abandoned them, or he's either *dead or in prison.*

Every single day, I walk through the prison yard and see hundreds of Black grandfathers, fathers, sons, brothers, and uncles locked-down behind barbed wire fences like caged animals, because there are two things you can always count on:

1. **Some Brother will be stupid enough to sell drugs on the same corner where he just witnessed another Brother arrested the day before.**
2. **Some Brother will be ruthless enough to kill another Brother for the right to sell drugs on that same corner.**

Can you see how your ignorance and slave mentality is perpetuating this cycle of black-on-black crime and violence? Let's break this thing down point by point!

First Point:

Taking somebody's life does not make you a man. In fact, the exact opposite is true, because any coward can pull a trigger, and any fool can take a life, but a real man shows mercy and compassion even to those who have wronged him.

The truth is:

Cowards pull triggers!

The truth is:

Cowards are quick to violence, and violence is the tool of the ignorant, but the only thing more dangerous than an ignorant coward, is a Black man who doesn't know he is one.

Second Point:

For the record, you have every right to be angry and hostile and resentful. After all that has been done to Black men and Black people in this country, and after all we still suffer, who could blame you?

But you have absolutely no right whatsoever to direct your anger, hostility, and resentment toward your own people. Some of you "boyz" *think* that just because you grew up in a rough neighborhood and in a poor family, that your violent and criminal behavior is somehow justified.

You think you are fighting back against the "system" by selling drugs and hustling for a living, instead of working for "da white man," right?
Wrong!
I've got news for you:

You're not fighting the "system"; you're helping the "system" to destroy the Black race!

And, personally, I am ashamed of you!

Your violent and criminal behaviors are the actions of a coward!

And Black people by nature are not cowards! We have suffered more, endured more, and survived more than any other people on this planet; not by cowardly deeds, but by courage, discipline, strength, and compassion for our fellow man.

You are a disgrace to every Black man and woman who strives, through legitimate pursuits, to take 2 steps forward, because every cowardly act you do takes us 10 steps backward.

And frankly, I'm sick of all the excuses you use to justify your behavior.

I'd have more respect for you if you just came right out and admitted that you were scared, and weak, and ignorant, instead of hiding behind this so-called "thug" and "gangsta" image – which is just another way of saying that you don't have what it takes to compete against the White man.

Oh sure, you'll compete against him on the basketball court or the football field, where you have a distinct physical advantage. But what about the business court or the science field, where your mental skills are more important than how high you can jump, or how fast you can run up and down white-owned courts and fields.

Or you'll compete against him in the drug game or the rap game, where the only thing you have to count is how many rocks you sell, or how many "niggas" you kill, or how many hos you done "pimped."

And for all of you brothers blaming racism for your behavior and your failures: find another excuse! That excuse simply won't work any more! Being a victim of racism and oppression does not give you the right to disregard the law!

Peddling that chemical slavery to your own people does not end racism!
Killing and victimizing your own people does not end racism!
Rotting your life away in prison for peddling that chemical slavery, or killing your own people, does not end racism!

In fact, you're doing everything the "system" wants you to do, because that gives them the excuse to put you where they want you anyway: *in graves or in prisons*!

Find another excuse! You are not the only ones who have ever been oppressed or discriminated against. Thousands of Black men and women, before you and since you, have succeeded despite the barriers of racism, discrimination, poverty, and other social injustices.

You tell the thousands of successful Black doctors, lawyers, educators, scientists, corporate executives, business owners, artists, and entertainers that racism and discrimination can't be overcome!

BLACK SON RISING

The difference between these successful Black men and women and you so-called "thugs" and "gangstas" and "hustlers" is that they had the strength, the courage, and the discipline to endure the hardships that success demands.

And you don't, yet!

Hopefully, one day you will open up your mind and your eyes to the truth about how your ignorance, your slave mentality, and your false perception of manhood are helping the white power structure in this country to destroy the Black family and the Black community.

Maybe by then, you'll get up off your excuses and your ignorance and start finding ways to uplift the Black community instead of helping the white power structure tear it down.

Third Point:

There are no guarantees in life, except one:

YOU WILL PAY FOR YOUR ACTIONS!

I don't give a damn who you are, or what you've been through, or how you try to justify your behavior. I can promise you one thing in life:

Sooner or later, somewhere or somehow, you are going to pay for the consequences of your actions. And the longer it takes to pay, the worse it's going to be!

There is a universal and unbreakable cosmic law that says, "You reap what you sow."

That means that no evil deed goes unpunished forever!

If you earn your money, power, or "respect" by destroying other people's lives, or causing other people misery and pain, eventually your life, or the life of someone you love, will be destroyed!

The real tragedy is that most of the time, the payback doesn't affect you directly, but somebody you really care about like your mom, or your best friend, or your girl, or your kids for that matter.

Don't take my word for it. Ask anybody who has been around long enough to see the law of reaping and sowing in action. Ask them how painful it was when their "chickens came home to roost."

You think it's okay to sell drugs just to make money?

You think it's all right to steal?

You think it's cool to drop out of school and hang out on corners all day?

You think it's brave to be banging with other Brothers over drugs or women or hoods?

You think it makes you a man to murder someone else's son or daughter?

You can keep doing all this stupid, ignorant, and irresponsible stuff if you want to, but the law of reaping and sowing is inescapable, and it will catch up to you when you least expect it!

It might not happen today, next week, or even next year, but it's coming!

That's a guarantee! You can take it to the bank and draw interest on it!

14

MENACE II SOCIETY

Black Gangs, the KKK, and the Politics of Black Racial Genocide

Hated by whites and being an organic part of the culture that hated him, the black man grew in turn to hate in himself that which others hated in him.
- **Richard Wright, Novelist**

There are a lot of ruthless and dangerous young Black men in ghettos and hoods all over this country, but no one is more ruthless or more dangerous than Black gang-(slave) bangers. They are by far the worst example of the kind of dangerous slave mentality that exists in adolescent Black males.

What makes them especially dangerous?

First of all, they prey on Black people who are weak and defenseless.

They peddle chemical slavery to their own people just to put money in their pockets.

They kill other young Black men who might have the potential to be the next Malcolm X, or Martin Luther King, Jr., or some other great leader who might uplift the Black race to greater heights of success and prosperity.

They brag about the number of Black people they have killed, as if they're proud to be "nigger killers" like the KKK.

They terrorize the neighborhoods they claim to be protecting, and the honest, hard-working Black people that live in them.

Worst of all, despite how hardcore they claim to be, they won't lift a finger against the white oppressors who are creating the conditions that give rise to the Black ghettos upon which they prey.

All of these factors together make them a pack of ignorant, cowardly, drug-dealing, gun-toting, gang-banging, back-stabbing, race-betraying murderers of their own people!

These slave-bangers, as I call them, are killing other Blacks by the thousands, and calling themselves "street soldiers" like they're some kind of ghetto heroes – yet they're too ignorant to realize that they are not fighting, nor are they defeating the white power structure they claim they hate; instead, they're assisting the white power structure, and white supremacist groups like the KKK, in their efforts to destroy the Black race.

And they're doing a better job of killing each other than the KKK ever has!

BLACK SON RISING

Most of the black-on-black violence committed by Black gangs is over stupid things like drug turfs, territorial disputes, gang initiation rites, or revenge motives.

These so-called "street soldiers" are not noble and courageous street rebels protecting their neighborhoods from crime and violence.

Nor are they socially conscious Black freedom fighters trying to revive the Black Power movement, like Ray Washington and the original founders of the Crips (*originally known as the Baby Cribs*).

How many of you know that the original Crips, originally called Baby Cribs, was created by Ray Washington as a model of the Black Panthers?

How many of you know that the original Crips were feeding poor children and the homeless, and were protecting their neighborhoods from criminals and drug dealers?

And now, instead of protecting their people, these young Black slave-bangers of today are victimizing their own people. They are no better than the KKK or any other white supremacist group that hates Blacks.

And what are they fighting each other for?

They're fighting over drugs, and the right to sell them to their own people.

That's why I call them slave-bangers! Because they're fighting and killing each other to sell their White "mastas" new cotton (i.e., crack and heroin), inside the White "masta's" new plantations (i.e., Black ghettos and prisons).

And the KKK loves them for it.

Don't take my word for it, hear it from the horse's mouth.

In the year 2000, the KKK sent a letter to the *New York Post,* thanking Black gang-bangers for killing as many Blacks as they have.

This is what the letter stated:

The Ku Klux Klan would like to take this time to salute and congratulate all you nigger gang-bangers for the slaughter of over 4,000 black people since 1975. You are doing a marvelous job.

Keep killing each other for nothing. The streets are still not yours, niggers...they are ours. You are killing each other for our property.

You are killing what could be future black doctors, lawyers and business-men that we won't have to compete with. And the good thing about it is that you are killing the youth. So we won't have to worry about you niggers in the generation to come.

We would further like to thank all the judges who have over sentenced those niggers to prison. We are winning again. Pretty soon, we will be able to go back to raping your women and enslaving your children. Because all the nigger men will be dead or locked up.

So, thank you nigger gang-bangers...keep up the good work. We love to read about drive-by shootings. We love to hear how many niggers get killed over the weekends. We can tolerate the niggers with jungle fever (for now) because that further breaks down the race.

Menace II Society

To all nigger gang-bangers across the world: we don't have to love all you niggers, but we can appreciate you nigger gang-bangers. You are doing a wonderful job in eliminating the black race. Without the men... your women cannot reproduce... unless of course, we do it for them. Then we will have successfully eliminated the black race, thanks to your help and commitment to killing each other.

And, finally, we want to add special thank you to the nigger drug dealers for selling our product to your own people.

Thanks to your efforts, you have helped us chemically enslave millions of black people. And, the profits we make from the drugs you sell for us, are being used to build prisons to warehouse the rest of you niggers.

It's amazing, but you niggers are doing a better job of killing each other, than we ever have.

So, thank you from the bottom of our hearts. White Power!

There is a strong message in this letter. And in case you missed it, the message is this:

Wake up Black man, you're working for the Klan!

Every time you kill, or sell crack to, another Black man or woman, you are doing the job of the KKK for them, but your disease, mental slavery, and your fear, false pride, material greed, mental laziness, social ignorance, self-hatred, and misplaced anger, clouds your mind and keeps you from seeing the truth about your race-betraying actions.

Why is all your violent and criminal behavior directed toward other Blacks, in poor Black neighborhoods? Why are you victimizing the already victimized? It's double jeopardy.

If you're Black and living in the ghetto, you are first victimized by the oppressive white power structure that creates and perpetuates the ghetto by withholding the means to escape the ghetto (i.e., gainful employment), and then you're victimized by the ruthless Black predators who are created by the conditions that persist in the ghetto.

Now, I'm not condoning any kind of violence against anybody, Black or White. However, if you slave-bangers are that angry at the white power structure that keeps you confined in ghettos through poverty and unemployment, then why are you not out in rich, white neighborhoods, killing White folks, and selling these deadly drugs to young White kids, instead of victimizing your own people?

The answer is:

You Black slave-bangers are scared to death of the white power structure of this country!

This is the same white power structure that feeds your ignorance, and violence, and greed, by supplying you with the guns and the drugs you are using to destroy your own neighborhoods.

How many Black gun manufacturers are there in the U.S.? None! Not one! That means that the gun you are using to kill your Black Brother was made with white hands, and most of these gun stores that sell the guns are owned and operated by white supremacists.

Why are you destroying your own neighborhoods and the Black people who live in them?

Admit it, you street-tough, hardcore killers are scared to death of the white power structure, and you know that the white power structure doesn't give a damn about how many niggas you kill. You slave-bangers know that the minute you start entering rich, white neighborhoods, and killing White folks, you will incur the full wrath of the white power structure's machinery of war.

That scares the hell out of you and keeps you in check!

As proof of this fact, look at South Central Los Angeles, home to the infamous Crips and the Bloods, two of the most ruthless and notorious Black gangs in existence, just minutes away from rich, white Beverly Hills.

If the Crips and Bloods want to bang so bad, and take out their anger on the people who are oppressing them, then why don't they bang in Beverly Hills, and bang with the heads of the major white corporations that have been denying them the job opportunities that keep them in poor ghettos and force them to join gangs and deal drugs in the first place?

Wouldn't that be more constructive and effective than brutalizing and victimizing their own people who are just as oppressed as they are, by the same damned oppressor?

Look, obviously I'm not suggesting or condoning the idea of Black gangs going into Beverly Hills, or any other rich, white neighborhoods and wreaking havoc by killing innocent White people.

I don't condone or advocate violence, period, because violence is the tool of the ignorant man who doesn't know how to beat the system without resorting to it.

So don't take what I say and try to use it to justify destroying White neighborhoods.

I'm merely trying to illustrate a point here.

My point is that the poor Black people living in the ghetto have it just as bad as you Black gang members, so why take your anger, frustration, and vengeance out on them?

They're not responsible for your condition, and they don't deserve to be treated worse than they already are, especially by their own people.

So why not take up your grievances with the system that created the negative conditions that the majority of Black people live under.

Personally, I feel that you have every right to be angry at racism, poverty, and injustice, and a system of government that perpetuates oppression.

I'm angry too, and I want to strike out at something or somebody, just as bad as you do, maybe even more!

But how are you helping the situation by further victimizing the victims of racism, poverty, and injustice like yourselves?

Instead of using your gang's strength to destroy your neighborhoods, why don't you use that strength to build them up?

There is strength in numbers.

You've got strength and you've got the numbers. All you need now is a positive, constructive worthwhile purpose in which to channel your strength and numbers.

I believe that what you really want is for someone to recognize you as valid and important human beings. I think you are tired of being ignored by mainstream society, and that you want to be treated with the same respect that other people seem to get who have money and power. I think most of you are just afraid to stand on your own two feet, for fear of being rejected or bullied by all the "cool" people who are smoking weed, getting high, getting laid, and disobeying the authority figures that just about everybody hates.

I don't blame you for wanting to belong to something bigger and more important than yourselves, which gives you the sense of "family" that you probably are not getting at home from your own family. I understand what that feels like.

However, at some point in your life you are going to have to stand on your own two feet and walk the path of a man, instead of a child.

That means you are going to have to put away your childish ways (*i.e., getting high and hanging out*), and start assuming the responsibilities of manhood.

That means you are going to have to take a leadership role, instead of being a follower who does all the dumb things you see everybody else doing.

That's mean you are going to have to get up the courage and discipline to walk away from ignorance and stupidity, even if it means standing alone.

That means you are going to have to start building and protecting your family, your home, and your community, instead of tearing them down, because that's what "real men" do.

The truth is:

Boyz want to destroy things. Men want to build things.
Boyz want to play all day. Men want to work to earn their keep.
Boyz want to hurt and tease people whom they think are weaker. Men want to protect the innocent and defend the weak.

Therefore, if you insist on being a gang, be a gang of men.

Instead of colors, hand signals, and other gang symbols, adopt the symbols of manhood: *strength, courage, intelligence, discipline, honor, dignity,* and *self-respect.*
Instead of being united for destructive and childish purposes, be united for constructive and manly purposes.

Consider how much good you could do if you were to officially organize your gangs into nonprofit community service organizations with the power and numerical strength to clean up your neighborhoods by building parks and recreation centers, rehabbing low-income housing, providing transportation to the elderly, forming landscaping and block beautification teams, holding neighborhood unity rallies, and developing your own community policing units.

What would happen if you made that the focus of your gang activity, instead of all the same stupid, destructive things that all the other gangs do?

How "bad" would your a_ _ be then?

I'm challenging all of you Black gang-bangers to stop taking the easy way out of life, stop being the pawns of the white power structure and hate groups like the KKK, stop playing up to the negative stereotypes that White people hold of all us Black men, and start showing these "monkeys" how dangerous we can be when we become united for our common greater benefit, not theirs.

15

NIGGAS WITH ATTITUDES

The Slave Rappers of the Music Industry

Nothing in the world is more dangerous than sincere ignorance and conscientious stupidity.
- **Reverend Dr. Martin Luther King, Jr.**

Chris Rock once said in one of his live stage performances, "There's two kinds of Black people: Blacks and niggas." The niggas are the ones out here killing each other for nothing.

I say, "There's rap, and then there's gangsta rap," which I call "gangsta crap," and the ignorant so-called "gangsta rappers" whom I call "slave rappers."

Personally, I love rap and hip-hop, and the talented young brothers and sisters who very creatively chronicle the struggles of the hood life in their lyrics and music, with brothers like Tupac, Chuck D and Public Enemy, KRS One, and Kanye West, to name a few.

However, it's one thing to talk about the drugs, crime, and violence that are affecting Black communities, it's another thing to brag about it and glorify it and promote it, just to boost record sales for record companies owned by rich, fat middle-aged White men.

And that's exactly what these ignorant Black "slave rappers" do!

Listen to any gangsta rap album and then count the number of references to "niggas" selling drugs, and killing other Blacks, then compare that to what you read or hear in the news every day, and then tell me *"it's just a song"* and that there's no connection between the violence in our streets and the violence in the music.

These slave rappers have become one of the white power structure's most effective tools in its efforts to kill young Black men and keep young Black minds mentally enslaved.

Through gangsta rap, white record company executives have already success-fully entrapped and destroyed the minds of at least 2 generations of Black teens and Black children.

If you don't believe me, then let me ask you a few questions:

When did it become cool to be a "pimp"?
When did it become cool or hip to murder somebody else's son or daughter?
When did being a drug dealer make you a hero or a role model?

Now, let me answer those questions:

It became cool and popular to be a drug-dealing, gun-toting, nigga-killing, woman-hating pimp, when "gangsta" rappers started glamorizing

95

the so-called street life and pimp mentality through their music, videos, and lyrics.

It became cool when young people started seeing "thugs" and "gangstas" seemingly living the life that just about every young person, Black or White, longs for: *a life of big money, expensive cars, fancy jewelry, fame, and popularity.*

And these are the words and images that our youth are bombarded with through the powerful medium of gangsta rap music.

Through powerful video images, and slamming dance beats, and very clever lyrics, gangsta rap tells Black children and Black teens that it's okay to be ruthless, disrespectful, uneducated Black gangstas because by doing so, they can enjoy some kind of plush fantasy lifestyle, filled with drugs, guns, cars, women, and famous celebrities. And, to some extent this is actually true.

The downside to that is that now, instead of wanting to grow up to become doctors, lawyers, educators, and other professionals, Black children and teens want to grow up to be pot-smoking, drug-dealing, gun-toting gangsta rappers.

Gangsta rappers are notorious for, and pride themselves on, their willingness to say anything they want to say out their mouths, at anytime, without the slightest consideration for who they might offend.

I respect their fearlessness and their artistic integrity (*or is it ignorance?*).

Well, if they can do it, so can I.

So, now it's my turn.

In the proud tradition of gangsta rap, I get to say whatever I want to say, and to whomever I want to say it, and I don't give a damn who I offend, but don't get mad at me.

So, indulge me for a brief moment while I assert my Fourth Amendment rights of freedom of speech, and tell these ignorant Black slave rappers exactly what I think of them.

Let me start out by saying this:

With the exception of Tupac Shakur most of these Black slave rappers are a bunch of mindless, spineless children sitting around making up nursery rhymes that boast of their already over-inflated false male egos, because they're too damned ignorant, or too damned "crunked" out to do anything else.

I listen to gangsta rap and gangsta rappers all day long, to analyze the content of their lyrics. I've made it my personal mission to try to find some redeeming quality, or some profound life-changing truth, in the messages they put forth.

However, all I ever hear them talking about is the same old tired, *slave-minded hood drama about popping gats, and how they're going to kill this nigga or that nigga, or pimp this* ho, or how they're going to smoke this blunt and snort that coke, like that's the only thing Black people in the hood know how to do.

They never rap about the hard-working single Black mothers who bust their butts every day to make an honest living so they can provide these ignorant Black fools with a home, a bed, and a meal.

They never rap about the thousands of young Black teens who do get up every morning, and go to school, and graduate from high school, in the same hoods these Black gangsters live in. Yet, according to the gangstas all hood life is so full of misery and pain and hopelessness, that you don't have a choice but to become a drug-dealing, gun-toting hoodlum.

They never rap about how these same Black teenagers become the responsible adults who are holding down halfway decent jobs, and going to work every day, and who are usually the people supporting them.

And, what about the thousands of Black college students who come from the hood, and go on to become successful Black professionals in all different kinds of career fields?

What the hell is that – luck?

No! All you ever hear about from these miserable Black slave rappers, is the negative stuff that happens in the hood, things they usually have a hand in creating.

And, frankly I'm sick of hearing the same old lame excuse that gangsta rappers throw out every time somebody criticizes their lyrics, which is "we just singing about how it is."

If I had a dollar for every time some ignorant Black drug-dealing, gun-toting, wanna-be gangsta rapper said, "I'm just singing about how it is," I'd be a millionaire by now.

Here's a news flash, you ignorant music prostitutes:

Stuff is the way it is because you keep it going that way. Because if you didn't, you wouldn't have anything else to rap about!

That's what makes most of these gangsta rappers a bunch of damn cowards! Because they're always talking about how bad it is, when in reality what they really mean to say is:

"I've got a f-cked up attitude about life, I'm too damned lazy to do something positive with my time and energy, and I want to take you down with me, because misery loves company."

That's really what they're trying to say. And, I would have more respect for them if they just came out and said that up front, instead of trying to convince everybody else that everything in the hood is as jacked up as they are.

Their biggest claim to fame is their willingness to take another Black man's life over some drugs, or screwing somebody else's woman, like that somehow makes them a man.

What kind of slave-minded niggas are these?

Taking another man's life, or selling drugs to your own people, or screwing another man's woman doesn't make you a man. That makes you a ruthless, back-stabbing coward and hoodlum.

The truth is:

Cowards pull triggers!

After all we've been through, what's a Black man doing talking about killing another Black man, anyway? Don't we have enough cowards in white hoods (*i.e., KKK*) trying to kill our people and put us back in chains.

That don't make you a man.

Real men throw fists, not bullets, and even then only in self-defense.

BLACK SON RISING

You don't see Mike Tyson or Evander Holyfield pulling gats on brothers, do you? If somebody messes with Mike Tyson, he just knocks them out, period.

And bragging about what you "gonna do" don't make you a man either.

And, what about that "one less nigga" y'all keep bragging about smoking? Don't that brother have a mother and a family who loves him just as much as your mother and your family loves you?

So, how would you feel if the "one less nigga" in the world, was your son or daughter, or someone you love, or one of your "boyz"?

That would piss you off wouldn't it?

Well, you need to think about that the next time you brag about killing some other Black man? That's *somebody's* Black son or father or brother, even if it ain't yours!

More importantly, that's exactly what the KKK and the white racist power structure in this country wants your dumb Black self to do anyway, kill other Blacks so they don't have to.

Here's a question:

If things are as bad in the hood as you say, then why don't you so-called gangstas try doing something positive and constructive to change it, instead of capitalizing on the misery of the brothers and sisters who look up to you as some kind of ghetto heroes.

You slave rappers aint nobody's heroes! You're just a bunch of whiny little punks, crying about, "my life is too hard, so I got to kill somebody, smoke some weed, and sell drugs to my own people, to make me feel like a man."

Ah, poor baby! You want somebody to hug you?

That's too damn bad!

Suck it up and take it like a man, and stop crying. I can't stand a crybaby! There're millions of other people in the world who have it a whole lot worse than you do.

You ain't nobody's heroes!

You want to know who the real heroes are?

They are men like Marcus Garvey, Malcolm X, and Martin Luther King, Jr.,

Nobody hated racism, discrimination, and oppression, more than Malcolm X and the Black Muslims of the Nation of Islam, but you never heard Malcolm running around talking about killing niggas, or smoking weed to hide from his problems, or pimping hos.

You don't hear Louis Farrakhan talking about "pushing weight" and getting "crunked" up.

And which one of you Niggas with Attitudes has done more for Black people than Brothers Marcus, Malcolm, Martin, or Farrakhan?

There's not one single person or one single organization in this country that has done more to get Black men off the streets, off of drugs, and out of prison, than the Nation of Islam.

Yet, instead of getting behind the NOI and supporting their efforts to make things better in Black neighborhoods, you ignorant slave rappers would rather help the White man destroy them by convincing other Blacks to become the same kind of back-stabbing, race-betrayers that you are, by killing your own people and peddling the white man's poison to them.

You don't have to agree with the NOI's religious beliefs, but you do have to respect their efforts to uplift and liberate the Black race from its mental and physical bondage, unlike you whiny, crybaby, do-nothing slave rappers.

Niggas with Attitudes

And, I challenge all of you slave rappers to show me one positive change you've made in your neighborhoods since you made it big.

Because all I see is you driving around in big, expensive cars, in fur coats and diamond rings, strapped from head to foot, because you're scared you are going to get jacked by the same kind of ruthless Brothers y'all claim to be.

Every time I watch gangsta rap videos, I become furious at how dangerously ignorant these young slave rappers are. Every word out of their mouth brags about killing other Black men, and buying and selling or using drugs, like it's a badge of honor to be a low-life drug dealer.

Sometimes I get so furious that all I can think about is how I want to line all these slave rappers up, and bash their damn skulls in with a baseball bat.

Yet, when I finally calm down, and analyze what I see and hear in conjunction with what I know about the psychological conditioning of the Black race, it occurs to me that being angry with somebody just because they are ignorant, is the same as being angry at somebody just because they have cancer or some other deadly disease.

A person with cancer didn't ask to get cancer, they just got it somehow. Similarly, these ignorant young slave rappers didn't ask to be ignorant, they just are.

The treatment for these ignorant Brothers should be the same as that of a cancer patient, which is: first tell them that they have cancer, and then show them what the cancer will do to their bodies if left untreated, and then prescribe a rigorous treatment methodology to remove the cancerous cells from the body.

Similarly, someone has to tell these young Brothers that they are woefully ignorant and that their ignorance makes them dangerous to themselves and others; show them the crime and violence that their ignorance has and will continue to produce; and them show them how to remove their ignorance by teaching them about the process by which they became ignorant.

And that's exactly what I am trying to do.

I'm telling you brothers that you suffer from a dangerous form of cancer called ignorance that is the result of your slave mentality and your false sense of manhood.

Your cancerous ignorance perpetuates this cycle of black-on-black crime and violence.

Here's what I need you to do to remove this cancerous ignorance from your minds:

1.	Instead of rapping about "how it is," why don't you try rapping about how "things" should or could be if young Black men were to start making knowledge and education, not hustling, their priority in life.

2.	Grow up, stop bragging about being a childish, ruthless, cowardly, race-betraying hoodlum, and start acting like a damn man.

3.	Stop "pimping" women and start treating these Black queens with the respect with which you want your mothers and daughters to be treated.

4.	Put down the glocks and the gats, pick up a book, and make knowledge and education your weapons of choice.

5.　　Stop promoting drugs and violence just so you can put money in your pockets, and start promoting things that can save us as a race:

knowledge, education, self-respect, and respect for the Black race.

It's very unfortunate, but you Black slave rappers are role models whether you like it or not. For reasons I still don't completely understand, these young Black men and women listening to your music look up to you.

And, now you use your clever lyrics, and slamming beats, and powerful music videos to convince them that it's cool to be a drug-dealing, gun-toting, cowardly, and ruthless Black hoodlum.

Now that you've got their undivided attention, "flip the script" on them!

That's what Tupac had planned to do before he was gunned down by the same kind of ruthless hoodlum that you brothers keep bragging about.

Use your clever lyrics and music videos to tell them how cool it is to go to college and become a school teacher or college professor or a business owner?

Tell them how cool it is to treat all their Black brothers and sisters with the love and respect due to every man and woman?

Tell them that the only weapon they ever have to carry is their mind and the knowledge they need to fill it?

If you say it, they will listen. If you sing it, they will dance to it. If you promote it, they will believe it and start building a lifestyle around it. A lifestyle that will lead to social and economic prosperity, instead of crime, violence, prison, and/or death.

Be a real ghetto hero, instead of a ghetto slave!

Use that God-given talent to help eliminate the problems plaguing the Black community.

Use that talent to help free your community from the clutches of poverty and drugs and crime and violence.

Use that talent to stand up and be counted as a strong, courageous protector and leader of the Black community, instead of a drug-dealing, dope-smoking, lyrical prostitute for your white music industry pimps.

16

CRACKENOMICS

The Cocaine Investment Agency and the Economic Legacy of Crack

We have a generation enslaving itself to drugs, young men and women doing to our race what slavery couldn't.
- Lucille Clifton, Poet

There is a new Ku Klux Klan out there called Killer Crack and Cocaine, and the new lynch mob is sweeping all through the black neighborhood.
- Joseph Lowery, Civil Rights Activist

From the mid 1980s into the late 1990s crack cocaine turned tens of thousands of Black men, women, and teens into strung-out, slack-jawed, zombie-eyed crack fiends, and destroyed the lives of thousands of Black families for generations to come.

There has been a lot of controversy, speculation, and debate regarding the means by which this crack menace has entered Black communities.

Well, you can stop wondering, debating, and speculating, because it has been proven that the proliferation of crack cocaine in Black neighborhoods was facilitated by the Central Intelligence Agency, also known as the CIA (*which I call the Cocaine Investment Agency*) – a white agency, run by a white government, built by white men.

There is extensive, conclusive evidence of the CIA's involvement in and silent approval of the cocaine drug trade, in numerous investigations conducted by journalists and members of Congress, most notably by the recently deceased (*or murdered?*) journalist and author Gary Webb, and Congresswoman Maxine Waters, respectively.

Gary Webb, a highly respected journalist for the *San Jose Mercury News,* blew the lid off the crack cocaine and CIA conspiracy in his book, *Dark Alliance*: *The CIA, the Contras, and the Crack Cocaine Explosion.*

Gary Webb died recently, allegedly by committing suicide (he had two gunshot wounds to his head), after being publicly humiliated and discredited by several major news organizations whose allegiances are suspect at best.

Yet, despite their best efforts to discredit Webb's findings, the hardcore evidence is overwhelming and undeniable, and is upheld by numerous respected journalists who now corroborate his facts.

As a result of his findings, and amid strong allegations of a CIA and crack connection by respected members of several news organizations, the U.S. Department of Justice, under then Attorney General Janet Reno, launched a full scale investigation whose conclusions have never been publicly reported to this day.

"My investigation into the allegations of CIA-Contra drug dealing has led me to an undeniable conclusion: that U.S. intelligence and law enforcement agencies knew about drug trafficking in South Central Los Angeles and throughout the U.S. and let the dealing go on without taking any actions against it.

BLACK SON RISING

"Robert Parry and Brian Barger first broke the shocking story of Contra involvement in drug trafficking in 1985, at the height of the Contra war against Nicaragua. As a result of this story's revelations, Senator John Kerry conducted a two year Senate probe into the allegations and published the sub-committee's devastating findings in an 1,166-page report in 1989.

"Remarkably, the Committee's findings went virtually unreported when they were released.

"Then, in August, 1996, Gary Webb published his explosive series in the *San Jose Mercury News.* It resulted in a firestorm of anger and outrage in the Black community and throughout the nation. Here was evidence that while the nation was being told of a national "war on drugs" by the Reagan Administration, our anti-drug intelligence apparatus was *actually aiding the drug* **lord**s in getting their deadly product into the U.S.

"Quite unexpectedly, on April 30, 1998, I obtained a secret 1982 Memorandum of Under-standing between the CIA and the Department of Justice, that *allowed drug trafficking by CIA assets, agents, and contractors to go unreported to federal law enforcement agencies*. I also received correspondence between then Attorney General William French Smith and the head of the CIA, William Casey, that spelled out *their intent to protect drug traffickers* on the CIA payroll from being reported to federal law enforcement."

These and other similar documents and investigations are just the tip of the iceberg, but the facts speak for themselves, and the evidence is overwhelming:

The CIA, a white agency, run by white men, backed by a white government, brought cocaine and crack into Black neighborhoods!

So for all you ignorant young brothers out there peddling this chemical slavery to your own people, claiming that you sell drugs because the white man won't give you a job, think again.

The white man has given you a job, fool – you work for the CIA!

Crack cocaine has single-handedly accomplished what centuries of American slavery attempted to do, but couldn't: which is to *create a legal, economic system of physical slavery (prison) – using psychological slavery (ignorance), emotional slavery (self-hatred), and material slavery (greed) – to get Blacks to kill each other for the sake of selling and buying the illegal product of chemical slavery (crack) – whose distribution was facilitated by an agency (the CIA) of the white racist power structure.*

As a former federal law enforcement officer, I can honestly tell you with absolute certainty that everybody and their mother is making money hand over fist in the drug trade and the criminal justice system that supports it, including: the drug kingpins (*with the help of the CIA*), the judges, the lawyers, the cops, the border guards, the corrections officers, and the government officials who are taking kickbacks to allow the drug trade to flourish.

Everybody that is, except the low-level Black street hustlers who are doing all the work, taking all the risks, getting paid the least, and suffering the greatest consequences.

Crackenomics

This so-called "game" that all of you ignorant pawns keep playing and losing, is the most perfect system of economic slavery ever devised.

Listen and learn:

THE DRUG GAME

The Object of the Game:
The winner is the individual or group that can make the biggest profit, while locking up as many people of color as can fit into as many prisons as can be built, with the profits made from selling the winner's product.

The Players:
1. The White CIA
2. The White Drug Lords
3. The White Cops
4. The White Prosecutor
5. The White Defense Attorney
6. The White Judge
7. The Black Man – the street hustler (i.e., the loser)

The Product: Drugs
1. Cocaine
2. Crack
3. Heroin
4. Marijuana
5. Crystal Meth

The Rules:
1. The CIA helps the drug lords bring crack into Black neighborhoods for the Black man to sell. The Black man sells the crack, destroying the lives of thousands of other Black people, but the drug lords and the CIA make the biggest profit.

2. Then, the white cops arrest the Black man for selling the crack that the drug lords brought into Black neighborhoods with the assistance of the CIA.

3. Next, the white defense attorney defends the Black man against the white prosecutor who wants to "persecute" the Black man for distributing the crack that the drug lords sold to him with the assistance of the CIA.

4. Finally, the Black man ends up in front of a white judge, who sentences the Black man to 10 years, in the prisons that the white government builds, with the profits they make from drug seizures of the crack the Black man sold for the drug lords with the assistance of the CIA.
Game over! You lose, Black man! Once again the white man wins it all! Any questions, fool?
It's an absolutely brilliant economic system of drug distribution that takes full advantage of the social ignorance, material greed, and slave mentality of the Black race.

CRACK FACTS

☑ Crack cocaine is the only drug for which the first offense of simple possession can trigger a federal mandatory minimum sentence. Possession of 5 grams of crack will trigger a 5 year mandatory minimum sentence.

☑ In 1986, before mandatory minimums for crack offenses became effective, the average federal drug offense sentences for Blacks were only 11% higher than sentences for whites.

Four years later, following the implementation of harsher drug sentencing laws, the average federal drug offense sentences for Blacks were 49% higher than sentences for whites.

☑ The U.S. Sentencing Commission found that nearly 90% of the offenders convicted in federal court for crack cocaine distribution were Black while the majority of crack cocaine users were White.

☑ In federal court today, low-level crack dealers and first-time offenders sentenced for trafficking of crack cocaine receive an average sentence of 10 years. According to the U.S. Sentencing Commission, only 5.5% of all federal crack defendants are high-level dealers.

What do all these crack facts and statistics tell you?

The message should be loud and clear to all of you ignorant Black drug dealers who think you're "playing" the system by selling drugs for a living, instead of working for "da white man," who by the way owns the drugs that you are selling to your own people.

For all you "playas" in the "game" who still don't get it, the message is this:

You're playing a dangerous game you can't possibly win, and you're the ones getting played!

You don't even know what the rules of the game are, because the only one losing is you! And, what are you paying with? Your freedom, your respect, your manhood, and your life!

Don't be a fool! Every time you step out on that corner to peddle that chemical slavery to your own people, you put your life and your freedom at risk. And, for what? Just so you can sport some gold and diamond jewelry, and push the latest "Lex"?

Who have you helped with your crack pipes and heroin needles? No one! Not even yourself! All you've done is temporarily lined your own pockets with dirty, dishonest money!

However, won't you feel stupid when all of these things are taken away from you, and you're left with nothing to show for your greed and stupidity, but "lock-down."

And, to all you hustlers talking about, "I'm just trying to feed my family," Find another excuse! That lame "feed my family" excuse is just as played out as you are.

Don't get me wrong. You have the right to do whatever it takes to survive on the streets, and to feed your families – even if it means committing a crime to do it. However, committing a crime to feed your family should be your absolute last resort, not the first.

You do whatever it takes.

However, you do not have the right to destroy someone else's life, or someone else's family, just so you can feed yours.

Personally, I'd have more respect for you if you went out and robbed a bank to feed your family, instead of selling this crack or heroin to other Blacks. *Why*?

Because that Black mother to whom you just sold crack or heroin: she has a child at home, a child who needs his mother to be able to get up in the morning and go to work, so she can feed that child.

How much work can she do strung out on crack or heroin?

How is she going to feed her child, when all she can think about is that next crack high?

And, what happens to that child when he becomes a ward of the state, and gets passed around from one foster home to the next; because thanks to you, his mother is now a bone-thin, unemployed, burnt-out, crack whore.

You and I both know that's what a powerful addiction to crack turns beautiful, intelligent Black women into, in less than a month.

Yet, you think it's okay to sell crack to Black people, don't you? Because, if *you* don't sell it to them somebody else will, and if they didn't buy it, you couldn't sell it, right?

Wrong!

That's your ignorance, your greed, and your slave mentality speaking to you, and allowing you to justify your actions.

The truth of the matter is this:

If you're selling crack or heroin to other Blacks, you are a cold-blooded, race-betraying murderer of your own people!

I don't care how hard you try to justify it, selling a deadly drug like crack or heroin to your own people is the same as putting a gun in their mouths, and blowing their brains out the back of their heads.

The only difference is that when you blow someone's brains out, they die almost instantly. But with crack and heroin, they die a long, slow, painful, and demoralizing death, destroying their children and their families in the process.

Either way you look at it, the end result is the same: *the destruction of another Black family.*

And guess who's sitting back laughing at us as we peddle that chemical slavery to our own people?

The good ole' hood-wearing, cross-burning, nigger-hating KKK, that's who!

They love watching us do each other. The good thing about the KKK is that at least you know whose side they're on. They come right out and tell you they "hate dirty, filthy niggers, and the only good nigger is a dead one."

You don't have to like their opinions of Blacks, but you can appreciate their honesty.

BLACK SON RISING

What I can't appreciate is you Black crack and heroin dealers smiling in our faces, calling us "Brother," acting like you're down with the struggle in your Malcolm X caps and MLK t-shirts; meanwhile stabbing us in the back the whole time by selling drugs to the same people you claim to be down with.

Truth be told: I'd rather be killed by a White man in a hood, than by a Black man in a skull cap selling crack.

I expect the White man to do me harm, but being betrayed by own people is too hard a pill to swallow.

17

PLANTATIONS TO PRISONS

The Prison Industrial Complex and the Legalized System of
Modern Day Slavery

It frightens me that our young black men have a better chance of going to jail than of going to college.
- Johnnie J. Cochran, Lawyer

The American prison system, also known as the Prison Industrial Complex (PIC), is one of the most powerful systems of institutionalized racism in the country; and prison is now the new legalized system of modern day slavery, designed to warehouse Black men in prison plantations, and to use them as cheap slave labor for white-owned private corporations.

Black Prison Statistics
(Source: The November Coalition, 2004)

☑ Of the 246,100 state prison inmates serving time for drug offenses, more than 135,000 of them were Black, and only 57,300 were White.

☑ Among the more than 2 million offenders incarcerated an estimated 596,400 were black males between ages 20 and 39.

☑ Among persons convicted of drug felonies in state courts, whites were less likely than African Americans to be sent to prison. Thirty-three percent (33%) of convicted white defendants received a prison sentence, while 51% of African American defendants received prison sentences.

☑ The U.S. had more Black men (between the ages of 20 and 29) under the control of the nation's criminal justice system than the total number in college.

☑ 1.46 million black men out of a total voting population of 10.4 million have lost their right to vote due to felony convictions.

☑ One in three Black men between the ages of 20 and 29 years old is under correctional supervision or control.

You can always count on the white racist power structure in this country to find yet another way to make a dollar off of Black people's misery. In the United States, more than 1.2 million of our Black fathers, sons, mothers, and daughters, are locked-down in hundreds of federal, state, and local prisons which are owned, operated, and funded by the Prison Industrial Complex, which is nothing more than a very profitable, multi-billion-dollar slave industry, run by some of the biggest, privately owned corporations in the country.

BLACK SON RISING

The sole purpose of the Prison Industrial Complex is to use a mass prison population of poor people, mostly Black, to make billions of dollars:

1. By charging prisoners rent and fees for being in prison;
2. By allowing privately owned corporations to build and operate new profit-making correctional facilities;
3. By setting up these "correctional corporations" to compete with "free" labor;
4. And by exploiting cheap prison slave labor in "factories behind fences."

For years, people have been misled to believe that prisoners are living a "country club" lifestyle in prison where they are getting three hot meals a day, watching cable TV all day long, getting free college degrees, and living a better life than the average person on the street, all at the taxpayer's expense.

I've been to dozens of different prisons all over the country, and not one of them, at least not the ones where Blacks are warehoused, meet this false perception of prisons as country clubs for people too lazy to work for a living.

Most of the prisons I've been to are rundown, stinking hellholes with cold filthy cement 4x4 boxes for cells, that are full of poor Black men and women, most of whom committed crimes in the first place because they couldn't find legitimate jobs on the street to pay for their own rent, let alone pay the *state's* rent just to be in prison.

That's the craziest statement I ever heard of in my life, "You have to pay to be in prison."

That's why if you're Black, you need to stay the hell away from the criminal (in)justice system, which is another one of the most powerful systems of institutionalized racism in this country.

Because if you're Black standing on the corner slinging rock, or smack, or meth, you will go to prison.

If you're Black walking around illegally strapped with an unregistered handgun or ammunition, you will go to prison.

And if you're Black robbing people, or jacking people for their cars, or selling weed, or getting high out in public, or doing any of the other stupid things that Black men keep getting locked up for, you will go to prison, because you are 7 times more likely to get arrested, convicted, and imprisoned than some white boy who's doing the exact same things you do.

Who do you think they keep building all of these prisons for? It damn sure "ain't" for no White folks!

How many more Brothers have to get locked up before you finally wake up and smell the coffee?

The criminal (in)justice system and the Prison Industrial which, which I call the "evil twin sisters," were designed to entrap and warehouse Black men so that they can't compete for jobs and other opportunities that are reserved for white men and their children and families.

And once they got you where they want you, the only question left is, "What do we do with these niggas now that we got em back on the plantation?"

Simple:

Put them niggas to work.

After all, "The only thing better than a dead nigga, is a live nigga who's making me a lot of money." Right?

Wake up Black man, prison is modern day slavery, and correctional facilities are modern day slave plantations:

The prisoners are slaves, the warden is the slave master, the guards are the overseers, and the jobs you have are the products that you slave over. In prison you make 25 cents an hour for doing the same thing you would earn $10 an hour for, out on the street.

These prisons have dozens of lucrative contracts with major corporations to build products for the consumer on the outside. You make the sofas, chairs, desks, nightstands, and other products for 25 cents an hour. Then the corporations turn around and sell them in stores for hundreds of dollars, and kick back a large percentage of the profits back to the prison.

If that "ain't" slavery, I don't know what is!

You Brothers need to wake up and get off the damned plantation!

This whole concept of creating private corporations to run the prison system began in 1980, with the Corrections Corporation of America (CCA). And now 26 years later, CCA has spread to 32 states and several other countries. It trades on the New York and U.S. stock exchanges, and has made its investors billions of dollars in profits.

CCA comes in and takes over a prison, by promising local government and state officials that it can save them millions of dollars by running the prison as an efficient "business." There is no proof that these private corporations run the prisons any better than the government agencies, but there is proof that they cut the wages of prison guards, and drastically reduce spending on critical prisoner services, meals, and medicines.

Smelling potential profits in the corrections industry, other corporations, like Wackenhut Correctional Services, have entered the fray like sharks feeding on a bloody carcass. The contracts shared between all of these corporations are worth an estimated $4 billion.

Another corporate shark of the Prison Industrial Complex is UNICOR, which is run by Federal Prison Industries. UNICOR, based in almost all federal prisons, makes everything from guided missile parts to clothing and furniture for the military and federal agencies. It makes $100-$500 million in sales and $30-$50 million in profits each year. In contrast, the prisoners make about $1-$2 per hour.

For years, federal law had forbidden prison workers from competing with free labor, but this has now been changed. Prison labor is being used to not only undermine free labor but to drive other companies out of business. The state prisons have now formed similar companies to run their prison businesses.

Finally, "factories behind fences," which allow a company to hire or rent a team of prisoners, is becoming commonplace. Some of the largest U.S. companies — Microsoft, TWA, Sears Roebuck, and others — are using prisoners as customer service agents, seamstresses, airline reservation agents, assemblers, and other workers. This even includes the creation of unique brands of prison products, such as "Prison Blues" denim jeans, made exclusively in prison workshops.

Although the 13th Amendment to the U.S. Constitution outlaws plantation-based "slavery," prison-based slavery is acceptable because the slaves (prisoners) do not belong to a plantation owner, but to the state. Therefore, instead of being sold like you would be on a plantation, you are merely being "rented out" by your prison-warden pimp, and put out to field for the prison-corporation johns.

Behind the Fence

In terms of reputations in the community, prison inmates get a pretty bad rap. Most people would rather take a mentally insane person into their homes than an ex-offender. That's because many people believe that "prison is just a school for criminals, and those who go to prison come out worse criminals than what they were before they went in."

To some extent that's true, because if you take any group of people, strip them of their privacy and possessions, expose them to constant threats of physical violence and sexual assault, put them in overcrowded filthy prison cells, deprive them of any kind of meaningful job or educational opportunities, what do you get?

A bunch of angry, hostile, resentful, violent, and non-rehabilitated throw-away members of society who are more intent than ever on getting even with the society that put them behind bars like animals to begin with.

So yeah, you are going to find some of the most hardcore killers and criminals behind prison walls. Prison is a dangerous, cutthroat, dog-eat-dog environment where "survival of the fittest" is the only rule of the land.

However, what very few people know, and what "they" usually don't tell you is that there are a lot of intelligent and talented Brothers behind bars, and that not every Black man in prison is lazy, ignorant, and uneducated.

Don't forget that one of the most brilliant Black men in history, Malcolm X, learned most of what he knew in prison.

There are a lot of correctional educators working in prisons around the country. These are my professional colleagues and I respect what they do, but a lot of them go into prison with the preconceived notion that they automatically know more than the inmates, simply because that person is locked up behind bars.

It is a huge and potentially dangerous mistake to make that assumption!

As of the writing of this book, I have personally taught over 500 inmates behind the fence. Ninety-five percent of them were Black men. Most of these Brothers were highly intelligent, incredibly talented in many different areas, and extremely knowledgeable and insightful about life in general.

I honestly believe that I have learned just as much from my prison students as they have learned from me.

These men are, first and foremost, human beings, and I think we often forget that.

I once asked my prison students to tell me about their lives and the personal experiences that led them to prison, and what happened to them after they got to prison. What I heard was both shocking and amazing. I was blown away by the shear tragedy of some of their stories. A lot of these men have been subjected to the worst kind of violence, and mental and physical abuse you can imagine.

Make no mistake. I'm not condoning the crimes these men have committed. Nor am I trying to provide them a convenient excuse for their behavior. Many of these men have hurt a lot of people, and permanently damaged a lot of lives, families, and communities, as a result of their fear, false pride, material greed, social ignorance, self-hatred, and misplaced anger.

However, I want people to refrain from so quickly passing judgment on any man or his actions, until you have walked in that man's shoes.

Until we have lived that man's life, none of us can say for sure what we would do if given the same set of circumstances. Some of us think we are better than these inmates, simply because we are not in prison, or because we haven't sold drugs, or haven't taken someone else's life, but the truth is at any given moment:

A hero can become a coward, a wise man can become a fool, and a prince can become a pauper, all in the blink of an eye.

Conversely, a coward can suddenly perform a monumental act of bravery, a person once considered a fool can say something or do something incredibly wise, and the poorest man on the planet can become filthy rich overnight.

My point is, don't be so quick to write people off as lost causes simply because they have made some serious errors in judgment, and are now paying for those errors with their freedom, their respect, and in many cases, their manhood.

One thing we know about human nature is that people tend to model their environment.

In other words, we do what we see done around us every day. That means that if criminals had lived in environments where everybody was succeeding, and going to college, and owning their own homes and businesses, and living drug-free/crime-free lives, then that's what they would have been doing as well. Instead, most criminals, at least the poor Black ones who make up 60% of the prison population, lived in neighborhoods infested with poverty, unemployment, welfare, high dropout rates in school, drugs, crime, and violence.

If this is what they saw every day, what else would you expect them to do?

Can people raised in these environments avoid the destructive lifestyle present in these environments? Of course they can. But are they likely to? No, they are not, and the proof is in the pudding. More people concede to that negative lifestyle than don't, because most people don't have the knowledge and strength of character to overcome the pain, misery, apathy, and sense of hopelessness that are characteristic of these environments.

Therein lies the problem: the environment itself doesn't teach the people living there the kind of knowledge they need to figure a realistic way out of it; nor does it foster the kind of strength of character necessary to break free even if they had the knowledge. Therefore, the cycle just goes on, and on, and on, with no foreseeable end in sight, feeding more and more people into these factories of despair.

Question: What would you do if your mother was a drug addict, and your father was in prison most of your life, and you were raised in a household where no one valued strength, courage, or intelligence? Where, or better yet, *who* would you be right now, if that had been your life?

"Judge not, lest ye be judged, and found wanting!"

Putting the Bars Behind You

As I mentioned previously, I teach job readiness skills to inmates at the prison in Baltimore, MD. Every day I get four or five guys in my class who have six or seven arrests but no convictions. They thought that having several arrests but no convictions wasn't going to keep them from getting a job.

What they didn't realize or care about at the time they were running around doing the stupid stuff that got them arrested, is that most employers run background checks and that they won't touch a person with more than two arrests, because that shows a "pattern of consistent criminal behavior."

Who the hell wants to hire somebody with a "pattern of consistent criminal behavior"?

Would you?

So what happens when these Brothers try to go straight and get a legitimate job? Well, it should come as no surprise that none of these Brothers has been able to get even a low-wage job at McDonalds, because of their extensive arrest records.

It's not just jobs either. There are consequences in housing and education assistance too.

Most states have a law that requires public housing units to run criminal background checks on all of its applicants. Guess what? If you have a felony conviction for drugs or violence, or if you have an extensive arrest record, you can be denied public housing.

If you have a felony conviction, there's a federal law that prohibits you from getting student loans and grants.

Not to mention the fact that you are now disenfranchised. In other words, you are no longer eligible to vote in state or federal elections.

So now what?

You can't get a job! You can't get housing! You can't get an education! You can't vote!

You can't do anything! All because you thought you were being hip, and cool, and slick, while you were running around sticking people up, or peddling chemicals for a living instead of staying in school.

There are two important lessons here for you to learn. What are they?

1.   **If you get locked up, you will keep paying the consequences, over and over and over!**

2.   **Don't do things to get locked up!**

18

TRUTH B TOLD

I'm just another Black man,
But I came here with a message today.
The message is truth and truth be told,
There's a message in this "game" you play.

The truth is I'm dropping knowledge,
On you brothers who think you're men,
Cause you're packing heat, and selling drugs,
And driving the latest Benz.

This truth is for you gangstas,
And you soldiers, and bangers, and thugs,
Popping Glocks and Macs, killing blocks and Blacks,
And slinging that slavery you call drugs.

This truth is for you "playas"
And you pimps, and hustlers, and "boyz"
Caught up in the white man's game, that I call the "shame"
Cause ya'll "niggas" are getting played like toys.

Now the truth will probably offend you,
So you're welcome to leave or to stay.
But this truth will be taught, whether you stay or not,
And I'm gonna say what I came to say.

The truth is:
A lot of you brothers are dying
From guns, and violence, and drugs.
And you're more likely to die, in the blink of an eye
By the hands of one of your thugs.

Now I'm tired of being silent, so I'm calling a spade a spade.
Statistics will show what you Brothas don't know;
There's only player in this game getting paid.

The truth is:
White men are building prisons
With the profits from the drugs that you sell,
That white boys out there living the life
While you dying in a prison cell.

How long is it gonna take till you realize
You're playing a game you can't win.
The deck is stacked, your brothers get whacked
While this white man keeps raking it in.

BLACK SON RISING

Why don't you brothers wake up
And smell the coffee that's in the pot.
Where was that white man when you were locked down
And your brother was getting shot?

The truth is:
You're playing a game you keep losing.
But you pay with your freedom and life.
And now you giving that a_ _ to some Boyz from the Hood
Who want you for their punk and their wife.

How could you be so stupid?
To keep playing this dangerous "game,"
When all you see, are people like you and me,
On lock-down for doing the same.

The truth is:
I'm sick of all the excuses,
And all the bulls_ _ _ that you brothers will sell.
I've heard every excuse, from poverty to abuse,
For why you're Black a_ _ is sitting up in jail.

After 400 years of slavery,
No Black man should be bound up in chains.
"The truth of the matter, your brothas getting skinny, while your pockets getting fatter"
Now you're the cause of our misery and pain.

The truth is:
I don't see no white man
With a knife or gun to your head.
Yet y'all blame "da man" for your failures and faults,
But the fault is yours, instead.

Because can't nobody make you
Deal blow, and smack, and crack.
And, you're brothers are the ones who are dying
From the Macs and Glocks that *you* pack.

The truth is:
The KKK is just laughing,
Because your a_ _ is too dumb to read
The writing on the wall,
Which says, "We're losing it all
To ignorance, and violence, and greed."

Why don't you brothas' stop pretending,
That ya'll so bad instead of scared,
And admit that you're only playing "games" ,
Because you're afraid instead of feared.
Why don't you brothers be honest,

Truth B Told

And say your fear has made you weak,
And now you've lost the strength to be a man,
So you live like a dog on the streets.
Now, there's no shame in admitting
That you're scared, and weak, and lost.
But there's a price *we* pay, when you fail to weigh
The consequences and the costs.

Now, how would you like your gravestone to read?
"Here lies a nigga too dumb
To realize for sure, that death's the cure
For living the way of the gun.
He could have gone on to college,
But he chose the streets instead,
And now here he lies 6 feet under,
Too cold, too still, and too dead."

The truth is:
I don't know you and you don't know me,
But there's one thing I know for certain:
This so-called "game" you play, costs too many lives,
And your people are the ones that you're hurting.

You know, Black people boast that they're stronger than most,
And their strength is the source of their pride.

Yet, our strength is wasted
In means streets and dark places
And on brothers too ready to die.

But where's the strength in that?
Packing Glocks and Macs,
And popping every damn brother you meet.

Where's the pride in that?
Slinging rock and crack,
And dying like a dog in the street.

People have argued and debates are still raging
About the "African American plight."
It seems they say, we've lost our way,
And we have no leaders in sight.

But who needs leaders when the lives we lead
Are the results of the choices we make.
We could learn to read, make knowledge our creed,
And stop wasting the lives that we take.

But because of our choices,
We have lost our power to be the masters of our fate.
Now some other "masta" is cracking the whip,
And pimping us through our greed and hate.

115

BLACK SON RISING

The truth is:
As men of color you have 2 choices only,
and these are the choices you face:
You can act like a man, or you can act like a coward,
and live out your life in disgrace.

To be a man means taking a stand
Against ignorance, self-hatred, and greed,
Through honest pursuits, not killing your roots
Ty peddling crack, and heroin, and weed.

To be a coward is the easy way out.
It means you quit before you try,
It means you pick up a gun instead of a book,
And cause your people to suffer and to die.

Now, if my words seem harsh, and a bit too cold,
I say them with love and respect.
But the truth can hurt and truth be told,
You're now the cause and the effect.

But just who am I to tell you
What you should or should not do?
I am a Black son, and a Black father,
And a Black man just like you.

That's why I'm dropping this knowledge,
So you Brothas can understand.
This so-called "game" you play, starts with the letters KKK,
And was designed by the *Ku Klux Klan*!

PART III

THE SOLUTION

I believe that it would be almost impossible to find anywhere in America a black man who has lived further down in the mud of human society than I have; or a black man who has been any more ignorant than I have; or a black man who has suffered more anguish during his life than I have. But it is only after the deepest darkness that the greatest joy can come; it is only after slavery and prison that the sweetest appreciation of freedom can come.
- **Malcolm X, Nationalist Leader**

19

SURVIVING WHITE AMERICA

The Keys to Surviving in the Racially Hostile Nation
Known as "America"

The day has arrived that you will have to help yourselves or suffer the worst.
- **Elijah Muhammad, Nation of Islam Leader**

With its numerous systems of institutionalized racism, America is a very dangerous place to live for all people of color, but it is a particularly dangerous place to live for Black men.

That's because the laws and policies of this country - written by White men, for White men - were designed to rob Black men of their freedom, their respect, and their manhood.

The real power in this land is in the law.

It is through the law that slavery was allowed to flourish and persist.

It is through the law that Black men and women were allowed to be treated as sub-humans and chattel property.

It is through the law that Black people were forbidden to learn to read and write.

It is through the law that Black people were prohibited from attending the same schools, or drinking from the same water fountains, as Whites.

It is through the law that lynching of Blacks was a legally accepted form of discipline.

It is through the law that the penalties for crack, a predominantly Black drug of choice, are 5 times worse than the penalties for cocaine, a predominantly White drug of choice.

It is through the law that 60% of the prison population is made up of Black men.

And it is through the power of the law, that the white power structure continues to rob Black men of their freedom, their respect, and their manhood.

The power in this land is in the law!

And as long as white people are the ones making the laws, they're the ones holding all the power.

We as Black men have to stop giving them that power!

That means to survive in White America, we have to stop giving the law makers, and the law enforcers, the excuse to put us where they want us anyway: *in graves or in prisons.*

That means to survive in White America, we have to break free from our ignorance, our slave mentality, and our false sense of manhood, to escape the traps and pitfalls that the white power structure has created for our demise.

That means to survive in White America, we have to stop making excuses for our negative, destructive behavior, and start finding positive, constructive solutions to break this cycle of Black-on-Black crime and violence.

Understanding this, we must find a way to convince Black men that the only way they are going to survive in White America, is if they:

§ Stop aspiring to become thugs, pimps, gangsters, and hustlers, and start striving to become responsible, respectful, mentally liberated, and highly educated protectors of the Black family and Black community.

§ Stop making babies they can't or won't take care of, and start becoming responsible fathers to the babies they have made.

§ Stop blaming racism, and other excuses for failing, and start finding reasons and ways to succeed.

§ Put down the guns, trade their anger for knowledge, and start making knowledge and education their weapons of choice.

§ Stop waging war on their brothers, and start waging war on their real enemies: *fear, ignorance,* and *self-hatred.*

§ Stop perpetuating the modern day version of slavery called *prison*, and start earning their money, power, and respect through lawful measures "the system" can't touch.

§ Put away the crack pipes, the heroin needles, and the liquor bottles, and start getting high on God and Life.

If we are to survive in this racially hostile nation, we have to liberate Black men from their ignorance and their slave mentality – and teach them to become strong, courageous, responsible, and self-educated protectors of the Black race – instead of drug-dealing, gun-toting, gang-banging murderers of their own people.

We have to convince Black men to learn and apply The Rules of Survival for African American Men!

The Rules of Survival for African American Men

1. Put down that 40 ounce and that 5th, which "they" brought into your neighborhoods to cloud your mind and keep you weak.

Obviously, no one can make you drink or become an alcoholic, but the people who keep building liquor stores in poor neighborhoods are counting on you being too drunk and too weak to face your realities with a clear mind and a strong spirit. And alcohol destroys both! Wake up! You are being pacified. As long as you stay intoxicated, you won't have the mental or physical strength to rise above your circumstances.

Ask yourself this: Who benefits the most from your continued mental and physical weakness? And why are there more liquor stores in our cities than bookstores?

2. Stop peddling that chemical slavery to your own people.

Brothers are always talking about, "What else can I do? Ain't no White man gonna give me no job." The White man has given you a job, fool! Whose drugs do you think you're pushing? How many Black men do you know that own ships and planes? And when's the last time you saw cocaine plants growing in Baltimore, New York, or D.C.?

The truth is cocaine and crack was brought into Black neighborhoods by the CIA – a white agency working for a white government built by white men. So you tell me, who do you think you're working for?

3. Stop making excuses for peddling that chemical slavery to your own people.

Brothers are always talking about, "I'm just trying to feed my family." How much family are you feeding from a prison cell? How many children are you raising from the grave?

Don't be a fool! You are playing a dangerous game you can't possibly win. You don't even know what the rules are, because the only one losing is you! And what are you paying with? Your freedom, your respect, and your manhood, because every time you step out on that corner to peddle that chemical slavery to your own people, you put your life and your freedom at risk. And for what? Just so you can put some bling on your wrist, or some rims on your ride, or some "Tims" on your feet.

Who have you helped with your crack and your heroin? No one! Not even yourself! All you've done is temporarily line your own pockets with dirty, dishonest money! But won't you feel stupid when all of these things are taken away from you, and you're left with nothing to show for your greed and stupidity but "lock-down."

4. Stop blaming racism for everything you don't have but want in life.

Brothers always talking about, "Da white man be keeping a Brother down." The only thing keeping you down is your own mind, which lacks the strength and discipline to strive for what you could achieve if you spent as much time in the books as you spent in the streets.

How do I now this about you? Because thousands of Black men before you, and since you, have succeeded despite the challenges of racism, poverty, and other social barriers.

Racism is forever. Discrimination is here to stay, but if you let any man tell you what you can and can't have because of the color of your skin, that's your fault, not theirs!

5. Channel that infamous "Black anger" into something positive for a change.

What is it that you're angry about anyway: racism, oppression, or injustice? Or is it that you feel powerless against these things? It's your powerlessness that's making you angry! However, it's your anger, unfocused, that's keeping you powerless!

If you're angry at racism, use that anger to get you through law school and become a civil rights attorney! If you're angry at oppression, use that anger to find ways to fight the systems of oppression in ways that uplift the Black race! If you're angry at injustice, use that anger to organize other people who feel the same way you do, and become a politician or an activist! If you took that same "Black anger" and used it to do some good for a change, you would be unstoppable!

Personally, I believe that Black men choose to cling to their anger, because to let go of it requires them to admit that they are afraid.

6. Put down the guns, pick up a book, and trade your anger for knowledge, which is more powerful than any weapon you can possess.

Having a gun doesn't make you a man. Any coward can pull a gun, and any boy can pull a trigger; and a gun makes you powerful only as long as you possess it. But what happens when it's taken away or runs out of bullets? Where is your power then?

Prisons are full of men who thought they were powerful while they had guns in their hands. These same men are some inmates' punk, right now. However, knowledge, with its infinite possibilities, is the true source of power! And once gained, can never be taken away!

Question: Who is more powerful: the man who owns a gun, or the man with the knowledge to make them?

7. Stop taking lives that don't belong to you!

The only life you own is your own! What gives you the right to decide who lives or who dies? You're not God! You're not even a man! In fact, you're just a coward! Because cowards are quick to violence, and violence is the tool of the ignorant, and the only thing more dangerous than an ignorant coward, is the Black man that doesn't know he is one.

Cowards are ruthless, but real men show mercy and compassion even to those who wronged them.

8. Start treating everyone you meet with courtesy and respect.

Just who are you to judge? What have you done that makes you better than anybody else? Why should anybody respect you, if you don't even respect yourself? You have to give respect to get it! You have to earn respect before you can demand it! You want somebody to respect you? Then start respecting yourself.

You want somebody to give you the respect you think you deserve, then start doing something to earn it!

Like selling knowledge, instead of selling crack.
Like building up the Black community, instead of tearing it down.
Like becoming knowledgeable about something, instead of ignorant about everything.

9. Stop calling other Black men "nigga."

Nigga is a white racist word meaning ignorant, filthy, lazy Black. It has always meant that and will always mean that, and I don't give damn how harmless you think it is.
Nigga is what the slave-masters called us as we picked his cotton.
Nigga is what the overseers called us as he whipped the skin off our backs.
Nigga is what the lynch mobs called us as we swung from a tree.
Nigga is what they still call us behind our backs, while playing golf at the country   clubs.
Nigga is what you are, every time you call another Black man by that name.

Racism systematically verifies itself anytime the slave can only be free by imitating his master.
- **H. Rap Brown, Activist**

10. Stop making babies you can't or won't take care of.

Making babies does not make you a man! In fact, any 13-year-old boy can do it. However, if you think you're man enough to lay down with a woman, then be man enough to stand up with her and take responsibility for that child you thought you were man enough to make.

Every time you make a baby and then abandon it, that's one more fatherless Black child that is likely to become a victim or perpetrator of black-on-black crime and violence.

11. Give up the thug and gangsta image.

A thug is not a man! Real men don't brag about being hoodlums!
A thug is what they call you when you lack the courage, intelligence, and discipline to compete against White men.
A thug is what they call you, when you sell your integrity for a fast, dishonest dollar.
A thug is what they call you, when you no longer possess the dignity to be anything other than just another Black crime statistic.
A thug is what they call you, when what they really mean is: loser!

We have enough thugs and gangstas and hustlers. In fact prisons are full of them. What we need right now are more intelligent, free-thinking Black men to lead us into social and economic prosperity. The only place a thug can lead you to is the path of self-destruction.

12. Stop spreading fear and hatred in your own neighborhoods!

Who are you scaring and hurting anyway, besides your own people? White men aren't afraid of you Black thugs and gangstas. They know you're no threat to them. Black-on-Black crime statistics prove that. Ain't no White man afraid of you running around looking all "thugged" out. That just makes it that much easier for him to identify you as one less "nigga" to compete against for a job.

You want to scare a White man, get a college degree, buy your own home, and start your own legitimate business! You want to scare a White man, start doing things to unite the Black race, instead of terrorizing it. The White man's greatest fear is *racial unity*! That scares the hell out of them!

13. Stop lying to cover up your mistakes.

Everyone makes mistakes! Be man enough to admit to yours. The worst mistake you can make is not admitting that you've made one, and then blaming something or someone else for what you've done. If you think you're man enough to murder, steal, and deal drugs, then be man enough to face the consequences of your actions when you get caught.

You can't act like a "Bad Boy" one minute, and then a punk the next. If you did it, say you did it, and take your punishment like a man!

14. Stop accepting failure as a natural condition of your environment, just because it's what other people expect you to do!

A lot of people, even other Blacks, are expecting Black men to fail because of the negative environments we live in. But an environment is where you are, it's not who you are. Just because there is failure *around* you, that doesn't mean it has to be *in* you. There's no question that your environment influences your life! However, no environment is more powerful than your power to choose!

You choose to hang out on corners!
You choose to sell drugs to your own people!
You choose to weaken your mind with drugs and alcohol!
You choose to abandon your children!
You choose to take another man's life!
You choose! Not your parents! Not your teachers! Not your boyz! Not your hood!
You choose! And your choices will determine whether you live like a man, or whether you live like a slave.

So instead of becoming a product of your environment, start becoming a living example of what all Black men can accomplish when they decide to stop acting like thugs, gangstas, and hustlers, and start acting like men!

20

BLUEPRINT FOR REVOLUTION

We need a revolution inside of our minds.
- **John Henrik Clarke, Historian**

We have been beaten, kidnapped, tortured, raped, robbed, deceived, manipulated, and castrated; and most of this occurred *after* American slavery ended 140 years ago.

Since our involuntary arrival on the shores of this racially hostile nation, we have suffered more and endured more than any other race on this planet, and all at the hands of our white oppressors, for no other reason than the color of our skin.

Enough is enough!
It's time we take back our freedom!
It's time we take back our dignity!
It's time we take back our manhood!

It's time for a revolution!

But wait!
Who are we fighting?
Who is the enemy?
Which specific White man can we point to that is responsible for the black-on-black murders we commit, or the drugs we sell, or the pain we inflict on our own people?
The revolution is not about Black people fighting against Whites!

White people are no longer the ones we have to defeat. We are.
White people are no longer the ones keeping us enslaved. We are.
White people are no longer our greatest enemies. We are.

Through our own fear, false pride, material greed, mental laziness, social ignorance, self-hatred, and misplaced anger, we have become in fact our own worst enemies:

We are the ones killing each other by the thousands, not the White man.
We are the ones selling dangerous drugs to each other, not the White man.
We are the ones wreaking havoc on our communities, not the White man.

The white man no longer has to lift a finger against us. He has trained and conditioned us so effectively to hate, fear, and disrespect each other that all he has to do now is sit back and watch us destroy ourselves, and laugh.

BLACK SON RISING

And he will never, ever admit to his responsibility for creating the conditions that cause us to hate each other enough to kill our own mothers, fathers, sisters, and brothers, just to get a crumb from his slice of the so-called "American Pie."

We are now our own worst enemies.

That means that the only thing we need to defeat is our own fear, ignorance, and self-hatred.

That means that the only revolution that needs to take place is the revolution within our hearts and minds.

That means that the new Black revolution can't be fought or won with guns or bombs or knives. We cannot win this war by storming the Capitol and the White House, or killing White people, or taking their land and wealth. We do not have the numerical strength, nor the military power, nor the political leadership to successfully engage the white power structure on that level.

That won't win us our freedom or the respect we're due, because the use of violence would only confirm their stereotypes of us as ruthless and dangerous savages. They will simply respond with military might and new laws to quell any physical rebellion we might launch.

The only thing white people respect is money, power, and knowledge, and those whom they perceive to be in possession of them.

Consequently, the only way to gain our freedom and our respect in this society and around the world, is by developing our intellectual abilities, striving for financial independence, and demonstrating our racial unity by protecting our families, our communities, and our interests.

You can't make White people like you, nor should you even try, but you can make them respect you. To do that, you need to first demonstrate respect for yourself and then respect for your people, because no one is ever going to respect us if we keep killing each other, and robbing each other, or peddling that chemical slavery to our own people.

Why should anybody else respect us, if we don't even respect ourselves?

How do we go about demonstrating our respect for ourselves and our people?

We demonstrate our respect by not killing each other like dogs in the street.

We demonstrate our respect by not talking down to each other like we're dirt.

We demonstrate our respect by not peddling that chemical slavery to our own people.

We demonstrate our respect by not putting the White man's poison in our bodies.

We demonstrate our respect by not reinforcing negative Black stereotypes.

We demonstrate our respect by protecting our Black Queens.

We demonstrate our respect by raising and supporting our Black children.

We demonstrate our respect by rejecting European values and embracing our African heritage.

We demonstrate our respect by doing things to uplift the Black race, instead of tearing it down.

All this talk about starting a Black revolution has been and continues to be talked about with very little to show for all the talking that has been done over the past 30 or 40 years. In my opinion, that's all it is: *all talk and no action.*

If you really want to start a revolution, then don't talk about, be about it! You can talk all that Black revolution stuff all day long, but the truth is:

The first revolution you should be fighting and winning, is the revolution within!

This is a revolution of personal freedom. That means you need to get your act together as an individual first and foremost, before taking on the cause of fixing our race, or fighting theirs.

That means you can't fix anybody else's problems until you fix your own.

That means you need to be looking at the man in the mirror to see who the real enemy is, because your worst enemy is the enemy within: *fear, false pride, material greed, mental laziness, social ignorance, self-hatred,* and *misplaced anger.*

That means there are some things you need to learn and some things you need to do to fight and win this revolution of personal freedom. If each of us expends the time, the energy, and the effort to secure our own personal freedom, then the freedom of the entire race will already be won by default.

In previous essays, I stated that in order to be free, you must think free. Now, I want to expand on that to say that "to be free, you must also act free," because thoughts of freedom without acts of freedom is the same thing as filling up your gas tank and leaving the car in the garage. You can read and study and think until you turn blue in the face, but that won't do you or anybody else any good unless you take some form of action to apply what you learn.

You have to put the Thoughts into Action! Knowledge without Action is just intellectual masturbation!

That means you need a game plan. You need to know what actions to take, and how to use the knowledge you gain to make things better for yourself, your family, and your community.

The *100 Acts of Freedom* is your game plan. It is an outline of actions that you can take, *right now*, to demonstrate to yourself and to the world that you are no longer a "free slave," but a *Black Son Rising* – a freedom fighter and a child of God, a seeker of truth and wisdom, and a soldier in the struggle for peace and justice.

Show the world that from this day forth you are a *Rising Son* – a Black man who is strong enough, courageous enough, and intelligent enough to rise up, fight back, and break free from the chains of bondage that have been placed on his mind and on his body through the systems of institutionalized racism.

This is the path to freedom! This is the blueprint for revolution!

100 Acts of Freedom

1. Invite God *back* into your life.

2. Find a faith, learn how to meditate and pray, and become a lover and seeker of truth, justice, peace, freedom, wisdom, and knowledge.

3. Read African and African American literature and poetry, and survey African and African American art to familiarize yourself with the powerful creative talents of our people.

4. Help build and/or support Afro-centered charter schools, bookstores, and libraries in your community.

5. Go into the streets, the prisons, and the schools and teach our people the truth about their history and heritage, and that of their oppressors.

6. Get off the street corners unless you are out there teaching a Brother the keys to freedom.

7. Do not allow your children to watch and idolize white superheroes until they are indoctrinated with and immunized by the knowledge and virtues of our Black heroes.

8. Do not allow your children to watch television programs or movies that do not depict Black people in positive or more realistic images, unless you are there with them to explain to them the misrepresentation of Blacks in mass media.

9. Become a school teacher or educator, or help actively recruit and promote more African American male teachers in our school systems.

10. Learn more about the true origins and teachings of the original Hebrew-Judaic Christianity, and how the altered European version of Christianity has helped to enslave the Black race.

11. Learn more about other major religions and metaphysical teachings such as Islam, Hinduism, Yoga, Zen, Judaism, and Buddhism to understand the similarities and differences in man's search for truth.

12. Study the true teachings of the world's greatest spiritual teachers, who were in fact also men of color, including Yashua (Jesus), Krishna, the Buddha, and Muhammad.

13. Reject the ways of the oppressor and choose none of his evil ways, less you become as evil as he.

14. Do not waste your divine energy harboring hatred for any man or race, but hate injustice and the evil that they do.

15. Learn the truth about the history and psychology of the European and American oppressor, and then teach that truth to both black and white students.

16. Learn more about the psychology of oppression, and the true causes and effects of Black-on-Black crime and violence.

17. Take responsibility for your own education. Don't wait or rely on others to educate you about the truth regarding your history and your heritage, or theirs.

18. Strive for self-mastery over your mind, your mouth, your body, and your behavior.

19. Find strong positive Black role models to emulate, both past and present.

20. Practice the 7 principles of African American manhood and then teach them to your sons, *and* to your daughters so that they too can understand the responsibilities of men.

21. Change your thinking and your attitude about life, and adopt an Afro-centered philosophy of peace, prosperity, and freedom.

22. Study the various forms of power and strive for principle-centered power in your life.

23. Observe the strategies and behavior of the oppressor, and note the differences in how they interact with your people and theirs.

24. Learn more about your African and African American history and heritage and take pride in it.

25. Teach your children the truth about their heritage and allow them to embrace it.

26. Learn at least two new languages – perhaps one African and one European. Language is the key to knowledge.

27. Start watching what people do and start listening to what they say, in order to become more knowledgeable about human nature, so that you can discern friends from enemies, and wise men from fools.

28. Study the social sciences like sociology, anthropology, and psychology, in order to become more knowledgeable about the theories of human behavior, and compare that to your actual life's experience with human behavior.

29. Stop giving the white law makers and law enforcement officers the excuse to take away your freedom, respect, and your manhood. Learn the laws of the land and obey them.

30. Take the time to do some deep inner reflection, identify your strengths and weaknesses, and then set goals to improve on each.

31. Identify your rational and irrational fears and set out to conquer them, one by one, until you are virtually fearless.

32. Stop sitting on your fears and take more worthwhile (purpose driven) risks in life, instead of stupid risks that only hurt you, someone you love, or some other human being.

33. Start taking personal responsibility for all of your actions and the consequences of them.

34. Set very specific, worthwhile goals for yourself and don't quit until you achieve them.

35. Kill your pride and ego that's based on ignorance and arrogance, practice humility, and admit that you don't know half as much as you should know or do half as much as you could do with your life.

36. Become the master of your destiny, instead of the slave of your environment, and stop making excuses for how and why you live like a hoodlum.

37. Set out to change the world, to make it a better and safer place to live for every man, woman, and child, but only after you have changed yourself for the better.

38. Buy your own home, and the land on which it resides, if possible, and stop helping rich White landlords get richer.

39. Don't waste time arguing with fools less you become one.

40. Control your anger and find ways to channel your anger and violent behavior into positive and constructive outlets that don't violate the law.

41. Above all else, Honor, Respect, and Protect the Black Queen from anyone or anything that would cause her harm.

42. Teach, mentor, and counsel Black boys on the responsibilities of manhood and fatherhood.

43. Provide emotional comfort, intellectual guidance, and financial support to your Black children.

44. Serve, support, rebuild, and protect the Black community, instead of tearing it down.

45. Become strong, courageous, and responsible protectors of the Black family, instead of drug-dealing, gun-toting, gang-banging, back-stabbing murderers of your own people.

46. Introduce yourself to the people living in your community and form strong, family-like, protective bonds with them.

47. Join or form your own Afro-centered organizations that promote the interests of the Black family and community.

48. Join forces with like-minded, mentally-liberated people, regardless of their race, and form think tanks to resolve the problems in the Black community.

49. Wear your skin color like a badge of honor and a source of pride, instead of a mark of shame. You descend from greatness, because yours is the first race, the "hue-man" race.

50. Become a positive mentor or role model to a juvenile offender or other at-risk youth, instead of teaching them how to hustle and peddle that chemical slavery to their own people.

51. Seek and gain knowledge that will free Black men and women from their mental, physical, and emotional bondage.

52. Remove the word "nigga" from your vocabulary and address other Black men using positive, and uplifting terms like "brother," "king," or "family."

53. Become a man of vision, find a powerful purpose or passion, and pursue it to the fullest extent possible.

54. Learn more about African, Greek, and European philosophy so that you can understand how original African metaphysical thinking has shaped and contributed to Western ideology about man, nature, and God.

55. Use your anger at racism, discrimination, oppression, and injustice to fuel your personal and professional goals. Success is the best form of revenge.

56. Become an expert on some subject that allows you to earn your money, power, and respect through legitimate endeavors the "law" can't touch.

57. Develop a rigid military style of discipline to help you accomplish your personal and professional goals.

58. Study the martial arts to improve your mental, physical, and spiritual discipline, and as another method of controlling your anger and violent tendencies.

59. Use your 2nd Amendment rights that are guaranteed in the Bill of Rights, to form a militia to protect your family and community.

60. Travel throughout the U.S. and to at least one country in Africa, Europe, and Asia, so that you can expand your worldview and gain a firsthand knowledge of other cities, countries, and cultures.

61. Find and pursue a career or occupation that is under-serviced by African Americans (i.e., computer technology, telecommunications, journalism, filmmaking, biotechnology, anthropology, education administration, and psychology), and recruit other Blacks into the field.

62. Get a college degree in the social and political sciences and then position yourself to shape and affect public policies that are advantageous to Black communities.

63. Improve your public speaking skills so that you can communicate effectively when you are called upon to speak to groups, debate issues, or give presentations.

64. Read the dictionary in order to increase your understanding of words, build your vocabulary, and improve your communication skills.

65. Read the encyclopedia to increase your general knowledge of the world so that you can carry on an intelligent, well-informed conversation on a variety of subjects.

66. Read the biographies of some of our greatest Black heroes like Malcolm X, Frederick Douglass, Marcus Garvey, W.E.B. Dubois, Hewey Newton, and Stokely Carmichael.

67. Find a subject that you are passionate about and write at least one book about it.

68. Examine the commercial and professional service needs of your community, and start your own business to provide them.

69. Become actively involved in your community, by volunteering in, or starting your own nonprofit organization that addresses the social service needs of the community.

70. Support Black businesses, and actively recruit and promote them in your community.

71. Start a savings account and an investment account, and save money by paying yourself first each time you get paid.

72. Study wealth-building strategies of successful people, Black and White.

73. Surround yourself with positive high-spirited people who live by the principles of success and self-empowerment.

74. Actively seek solutions to break this cycle of black-on-black crime and violence, and brainstorm with other intelligent, like-minded individuals trying to do the same.

75. Study the universal laws of success and apply them in achieving your personal and professional goals.

76. Change your name to one that reflects your personal beliefs and cultural heritage.

77. Familiarize yourself with the Declaration of Independence, the U.S. Constitution, and the Bill of Rights, so that you understand exactly what your rights are.

78. Learn more about the origins of the Eurocentric and pagan holidays you celebrate such as Christmas, Thanksgiving, Columbus Day, and Independence Day.

79. Stop celebrating these Eurocentric and pagan holidays that don't recognize or promote our African and African American culture and heritage.

80. Cut negative and destructive people and forces from your life, even if they are your family.

81. Change your physical environment, until you are strong enough to resist its temptations.

82. Work hard to earn your keep, do more than your fair share, and then reward yourself for your honest efforts.

83. Invite a strong, intelligent Black Queen into your life to help you rule your kingdom.

84. Learn more about computers, electronics, and telecommunications technology, all of which is being used to control our lives and monitor our activities.

85. Develop at least a conversational knowledge about popular science, history, politics, philosophy, and religion.

86. Read or watch local, national, and international news to stay up on current affairs, and discuss the issues with your children, your mate, and your friends and associates.

87. Refrain from using violence to resolve conflicts, and seek peaceful resolutions first.

88. Become a man of honor, carry yourself with the bearing of a king or prince, and conduct yourself respectfully at all times, in public and in private.

89. Respect the rights, the lives, and the property of others.

90. Be loyal to, respectful of, and compassionate toward your spouse or mate.

91. Avoid a life of crime and set personal and professional goals to uplift yourself, your family, and your community instead.

92. Make the pursuit of knowledge and education your highest priority, and avoid destructive behavior that confirms negative stereotypes about Blacks.

93. Put down the guns, pick up a book, trade your anger for knowledge, and start attacking your real enemies: fear, greed, ignorance, and self-hatred.

94. Treat everyone you meet with courtesy and respect, regardless of your opinion of them.

95. Become a great leader of men instead of a follower of fools, and take a pledge to educate, uplift, and empower other Black men.

96. Find a cause worth dying for and take a stand to defend it, even if it costs you your life.

97. Combine your material and financial resources together with like-minded people who want to uplift and empower the Black family and community.

98. Refrain from consuming drugs or alcohol and strengthen your mind and body through yoga and a diet based on African holistic health (read *African Holistic Health* by Llaila O. Afrika).

99. Live your dreams to their fullest, don't take no for an answer, and don't let any man tell you what you can and can't have because of the color of your skin.

100. Acknowledge your slave mentality, false pride, material greed, mental laziness, social ignorance, misplaced anger, and self-hatred, and then practice the 100 Acts of Freedom to remove these poisons from your mind, body, and heart.

Slaves No More

All over the world, people think that Black men in America sell drugs, commit crimes, and kill each other because they are too lazy, too weak, too greedy, and too ignorant to do anything else.

My question to you is this:

Are they right?

I know the answer to that question! Do you? If they're wrong, prove it! Not to me, not to the world, but to yourself.

How? What can you do?

It's very simple: You do *your* part, Black man.

We're not slaves anymore!

That means we are free to do anything and become anything we want. That means that there is nothing stopping you from achieving anything you set your mind to, as long as you have the strength, courage, and discipline to follow through.

Does that mean racism and discrimination won't have any effect on our lives? Does that mean we'll wake up one day and find that White people have stopped oppressing Blacks?

Hell no! We're not stupid. Racism and oppression are an unfortunate fact of life.

Get over it! Or through it! Or around it!

Or whatever you have to do to overcome it, because sitting back and throwing your hands up, or crying about it, or taking the easy, lazy, dishonest way around the problem, or taking your anger and frustration out on your own people, doesn't do you or our people any good.

That means you have to stop giving the "system" the power and the excuse to put us where they want us anyway: *in graves* or *in prison*.

That means you have to stop making excuses for failing and start finding ways and reasons to succeed.

That means that you have to stop doing all of the stupid things you see everybody else doing, like selling drugs and killing your own people, just so you can put money in your pockets or earn some false idea of "respect."

You know, there was a brief period in history, during the civil rights movement, when White people were afraid of us, because they saw us accomplishing the one thing that scares the hell out of them: *Black Racial Unity*.

Now when they look at us, all they see is a people too weak from drugs, crime, violence, and incarceration to enjoy the freedom that was paid for by the blood of our forefathers.

However, we are not weak! In fact, we're stronger than they are. And we are stronger than they think we are.

Just look around you. Look at all that Black people have accomplished, and continue to accomplish, despite the numerous forms of oppression to which we have been subjected. Yet, despite that oppression, Black people are successful in every field of endeavor.

It might not seem like it because the media won't depict our success unless it's on the basketball courts, the football fields, the boxing rings, or the music studios.

They won't show you all of the successful Black CEOs of Fortune 500 companies, or the brilliant Black Ph.D.s teaching in the nation's top universities, because if they do, that will prove that we're not the lazy, ignorant, inferior, and trifling race they try to portray us as.

I'm telling you we're stronger than they are, because they have never been subjected to the kind of oppression that we have been living with, and thriving under, for the past 400 years.

We are stronger than they are, for people who suffer the most are the strongest. Our very existence is proof of this fact. If we were not so mentally and physically strong, we would have perished a long time ago under the yoke of physical and psychological slavery and oppression.

Yet, we are still here!

What does that tell you?

That tells me that you can do anything, survive anything, and become anything!

No one is stronger than you, Black man!

No one!

Nothing is stronger than you, Black man!

Nothing!

Not drugs.
Not poverty.
Not crime.

Not racism.
Not oppression!
Not even slavery!
Nothing!

Do not be afraid of, intimidated by, or impressed with the accomplishments of the White race, and do not allow them to manipulate you into destroying the Black family and the Black community.

There is nothing they can do that you can't. You alone hold the keys of responsibility for your personal destiny, and the collective destiny of the Black race.

We're not slaves anymore! And it's time we stop acting like we are!

21

THE RETURN OF THE KING

Returning to the Principles of African American Manhood

I believe in pride of race and lineage and self; in pride of self so deep as to scorn injustice to other selves. Especially do I believe in the Negro Race; in the beauty of its genius, the sweetness of its soul, and in its strength in that meekness which shall inherit the turbulent earth.
- **W.E.B. Du Bois, Intellectual and Activist**

The Black man is the first father and first King of the entire "hue-man" race. That means you *are* the original Father-Kings of the earth, and it's time for you to resume your rightful place as its ruler. You alone can restore balance, peace, freedom, and justice to a world that is drunk with hatred, greed, violence, and an insatiable lust for power.

Wake up, Black man! You are the Father-King of the Black family, and it's time for you to start acting like one!

Wake up, Black King! You are not living in your natural state of mind, the mind of a Father-King, and it's time for you to return to that natural of state of mind, and become a man of peace and justice, a seeker of truth and wisdom, and the leader and protector of the Black family.

Right now, you are living in a dangerous European state of mind (a slave mind) that runs contrary to everything you know to be good, honest, natural, and in alignment with the attributes of a King, or God.

You can no longer pretend that your devious ways and your irresponsible behavior are acceptable to anyone, except the white supremacists who have conditioned you into this unnatural, unhealthy state of mind, which serves their evil purposes.

I wrote this book for you Black man, because I love you, and I hate to see you suffering in the grips of a disease called slavery, that's based on fear, false pride, material greed, mental laziness, social ignorance, self-hatred, and misplaced anger, which controls every aspect of your life, and runs contrary to the natural state of mind of a healthy Black King.

What is a King and what are his attributes? A King is a male sovereign, a hereditary ruler of people and kingdoms and lands, a person who is the symbol of the strength and greatness that lies within the people that he has been chosen to govern. Not surprisingly, his attributes coincide with the attributes of God: power, strength, courage, mercy, compassion, truth, justice, peace, wisdom, and love.

Great African Kings

(source: The AfroCentric Experience http://www.swagga.com/king.htm)
Come experience the power, the glory, the splendor, the greatness, and the intelligence of Great African Kings, the makers and creators of the world's first known high civilizations.

BLACK SON RISING

AFFONSO I – King of the Kongo (1506-1540)

Affonso I was a visionary, a man who saw his country not as a group of separate cultures, but as a unified nation fully equipped with advance knowledge and technology. He was also known as the first ruler to resist the most despicable act ever known to man, the European slave trade.

AKHENATON - The Creator of Monotheism (1375-1358 B.C.)

Akhenaton was the first ruler in recorded history to believe in the concept of One God. He also taught this concept to all his citizens. He built a new city in the desert that was dedicated to religion, art, and music. This new city, Akhenaton (now Tell el Amara), with its lush gardens and magnificent buildings is where Akhenaton and his wife Queen Nefertiti changed Kemet's culture so radically that their influence has been felt for centuries right up until today. Akhenaton was also the first Pharaoh of whom a true likeness is recorded as shown in the picture to the left.

ASKIA TOURE – King of Songhay (1493-1529)

Askia Toure united the entire central region of the western Sudan, and established a governmental machine that is still revered today for its detail and efficiency. He divided his country into provinces, each with a professional administrator as governor, and ruled each fairly and uniformly through a staff of distinguished legal experts and judges.

BEHANZIN HOSSU BOWELLE – The King Shark (1841-1906)

Behanzin was the most powerful ruler in West Africa during the end of the nineteenth century. He strongly resisted European intervention into his country. This was done with a physically fit army which included a division of five thousand female warriors. He is often referred to as the King Shark, a Dahomeyan surname which symbolized strength and wisdom. He was also fond of humanities and is credited with the creation of some of the finest songs and poetry ever produced in Dahomey.

HANNIBAL – Ruler of Carthage (247-183 B.C.)

Hannibal is well known as the greatest general and military strategist who ever lived. He used his overpowering African armies to conquer major portions of Spain and Italy and came very close to defeating the Roman Empire. His audacious moves-such as marching his army with African war elephants through the treacherous Alps to surprise and conquer northern Italy and his tactical genius, as illustrated by the battle of Cannae where his seemingly trapped army cleverly surrounded and destroyed a much larger Roman force, won him recognition which has spanned more than 2000 years. His tactics are still being studied in many military schools today.

IDRIS ALOOMA – Ruler of Bornu (1580-1617)

He is credited with reuniting two of Africa's kingdoms: Kanem and Bornu. This union lasted many generations with sustained peace becoming a part of the Bornu.

IMHOTEP – The World's First Known Genius (2800 B.C.)

Imhotep was the royal advisor to King Zoser during the Third Dynasty of Kemet. Regarded as the world's first recorded multi-genius, Imhotep was an architect, astronomer, philosopher, poet, and physician. As an architect he was responsible for designing the Step Pyramid and the Saqqara Complex. During his lifetime he was given a host of titles, among them: Chancellor of the King of Lower Kemet, the First after the King of Upper Kemet, High Priest of Heliopolis and Administrator of the Great Palace. As a physician, Imhotep is believed to have been the author of the Edwin Smith Papyrus in which more than 90 anatomical terms and 48 injuries are described. This is well over 2200 years before the Western Father of Medicine Hippocrates was born. Some 2000 years after his death, Imhotep was deified by the inhabitants of Kemet and was known later as Asclepius, God of Medicine, to the Greeks. His very name, Im-Hotep, translates as the Prince of Peace. His tomb near Memphis became a sacred place and the site of pilgrimages for those seeking a cure. As a philosopher and poet, Imhotep's most remembered phrase is: "Eat, drink, and be merry for tomorrow we shall die." There still remain many bronze statuettes, temples, and sanatoria bearing his name, as is depicted in the picture of the statue above.

JA JA – King of the Opobo (1821-1891)

He was the founder and leader of the territory of Opobo, an area near the eastern Niger River. This area was very favorable to trading. This trading route soon attracted the greedy Europeans sought to control it. Ja Ja put up fierce resistance to this outside intervention. This resistance lasted for many years until at the age of 70 he was finally captured by the British and sent into exile to the West Indies. The greatest Ibo leader of the nineteenth century never saw his kingdom again.

KHAMA – The Good King of Bechuanaland (1819-1923)

Khama distinguished his reign by being highly regarded as a peace-loving ruler with the desire of advancing his country in terms of technological innovations. He instituted scientific cattle feeding techniques which greatly improved his country's wealth and prestige. During his reign crimes were known to be as low as zero within his country.

KHUFU – The Father of Pyramid Building (2551-2528 B.C.)

King Khufu, who is also known by the Greek name "Cheops," was the father of pyramid building at Giza. He ruled from 2551 - 2528 B.C. and was the son of King Sneferu and Queen Hetpeheres. Dates built: c. 2589-2566 B.C. Total blocks of stone: over 2,300,000.

Base: 13 square acres, 568,500 square feet, or 7 city blocks. The length of each side of the base was originally 754 feet (230 m), but is now 745 feet (227 m) due to the loss of the outer casing stones.
Total Weight: 6.5 million tons. Average Weight of Individual Blocks of Stone: 2.5 tons. The large blocks used for the ceiling of the King's Chamber weigh as much as 9 tons.

BLACK SON RISING

Height: Originally 481 feet (146.5 m) tall, Khufu is now, 449 feet tall as the top stones have since fallen off or been removed. Until early in the 20th century, this pyramid was the tallest building on earth.
Angle of incline: 51 degrees 50' 35"
Construction material: limestone, granite

MANSA KANKAN MUSSA – King of Mali (1306-1332)

A scholar, a great economist and a true man of the arts, Mansa Mussa is well known for the impact he created with his flamboyant style. In 1324 he led his people on the Hadj, a holy pilgrimage from Timbuktu to Mecca. His caravan consisted of 72,000 people whom he led safely across the Sahara Desert and back, a total distance of 6,496 miles. So spectacular was this event that Mansa Mussa gained the respect of scholars and traders throughout the world. Also during his reign, Mali was one of the most prestigious and wealthiest empires in the world. This empire also contained one of the world's most prestigious universities in Timbuktu.

MENELEK II – King of Kings of Abyssinia (1844-1913)

Menelek II united many independent kingdoms into the United States of Abyssinia (Ethiopia). The feat of pulling together several kingdoms which often fiercely opposed each other earned him a place as one of the great statesmen of African history. His further accomplishments in dealing on the international scene with the world powers, coupled with his stunning victory over Italy in the 1896 Battle of Adwa, which was an attempt to invade his country, place him among the great leaders of world history.

MOSHOESHOE – King of Basutoland (1815-1868)

Moshoeshoe was a wise and just king who was as brilliant in diplomacy as he was in battle. He united many diverse groups into a stable society where law and order prevailed. He knew that peace made prosperity possible, so he often avoided conflict through skillful negotiations. Moshoeshoe solidified Basotho defenses at Thaba Bosiu, their impregnable mountain capital.

MUTATO – The Great Mutota (1440 - ?)

The year was 1440. The King was Mutota. In any European country he would have been known as Mutota the Great. He and his council were quick to see that even the most advanced states each standing independently and alone, were doomed to European criminal exploits unless unified into a single nation with a strong central government. This also should be achieved through voluntary association if possible. Mutota and the new leaders understood this very well. Therefore, Mutota, in 1440, began the campaign to carry out his grand design. This was a great plan aimed at nothing less than uniting Africans into a vast empire that cut across South Africa below the Limpopo River, and covered Zimbabwe with an indefinite boundary beyond the Zambezi River in Zambia, and on over Mozambique to the Indian Ocean, sweeping southward again to include the entire coastline fronting the New Empire. This area contained the majority of the world's precious metals such as gold, copper, tin, and iron held in over 4000 mines. After 30 years of struggle, unity was finally achieved, consolidating in 1480 into the Empire of Monomotapa.

The Return of the King

NARMER – The Founder of the Dynastic Kemet (3200 B.C.)

Narmer, or Aha, was called Menes by the Greeks. Regarded as the founder of Dynastic Kemet, he led an army from Upper Kemet in the south to conquer Lower Kemet in the north around 3200 B.C. Upon victory, Narmer united Upper and Lower Kemet into one nation, after which thirty dynasties would follow. It was at this time that hieroglyphic writing made its first appearance, in the tombs and treasures of the pharaohs. One of Narmer's first tasks was to build a city on his newly conquered lands. Here he was met with a difficult task as the Nile Delta region was covered by an immense swamp. To remedy this situation, Narmer drained the swamp by actually diverting the course of the Nile River. Upon this new land he built a city which he named Men-Nefer: The Good Place. This city served as the capital of Kemet for several centuries. An Arab traveler writing as late as the Middle Ages reported the city as "stretching a day's journey in every direction." The Greeks would rename Men-Nefer "Memphis," a name that even today honors an African king who lived 5000 years ago.

OSEI TUTU – King of Asante (1680-1717)

Osei Tutu was the founder and first king of the Asante nation, a great West African kingdom in what is now Ghana. He was able to unite over six different nations under his leadership. The Golden Stole became a sacred symbol of the nation's soul, which was especially appropriate since gold was the prime source of Asante wealth. During Osei Tutu's reign, the geographic area of Asante tripled in size. The kingdom became a significant power, that with military and political prowess would endure for two centuries.

RAMSES II – The Great (1292-1225 B.C.)

Ramses II (The Great) was one of the most prolific builders of ancient Egypt. Hardly a site exists that he did not initiate, add to, complete, or build entirely himself. Some of the greatest monuments on any tour of Egypt bear his stamp: Abu Simbel, Karnak and Luxor Temples, the Ramseseum, and many others. He also commissioned the largest monolithic statue ever, a seated statue of himself at the Ramseseum. Now lying in pieces, the giant red-granite statue inspired many.

SAMORY TOURE – King of the Sudan (1830-1900)

The ascendance of Samory Toure began when his native Bissandugu was attacked and his mother taken captive. After a persuasive appeal, Samory was allowed to take her place, but later escaped and joined the army of King Bitike Souane of Torona. Following a quick rise through the ranks of Bitike's army, Samory returned to Bissandugu where he was soon installed as king and defied French wicked exploits in Africa by launching a conquest to unify West Africa into a single state. During the eighteen-year conflict with France, Samory continually frustrated the Europeans with his military strategy and tactics. This astute military prowess brought him respect worldwide.

SENWOSRET I – Pharaoh of the 12TH Dynasty (1962-1926 B.C.)

Senworsert I was a Twelfth Dynasty King of Kemet (1897 B.C.). Also known as Kepre Kare Senworsert I, he was known to the Greeks as Kekrops and Sesostris. Interestingly enough, Herodotus, Greece's Father of History, reported that Greece had once been conquered by a king named Sesostris. Greek mythology also indicated that the legendary founder of Athens was an Egyptian named Kekrops.

SHAKA – King of the Zulus (1818-1828)

A strong leader and military innovator, Shaka is noted for revolutionizing 19th-century Bantu warfare by first grouping regiments by age, and training his men to use standardized weapons and special tactics. He developed the "assegai," a short stabbing spear, and marched his regiments in tight formation, using large shields to fend off the enemies throwing spears. Over time, Shaka's troops earned such a reputation that many enemies would flee at the sight of them. He built the Zulus into a nation of over a million strong. He was also successful in uniting all the ethnic groups in southern Africa against the despicable vestiges of colonialism.

TAHARKA – King of Nubia (710-664 B. C.)

Taharka is probably one of the most famous rulers of Napatan Kush. He was 32 when he became king and was heir to a kingdom that included not only Kush but KMT(Kemet) as well. He is said to have commanded military campaigns in western Asia as far away as Palestine and led expeditions all the way to Spain. Mention of his great campaigns can be found in the Bible (Isaiah 37:9, 2 Kings 19:9). During his reign, Taharka controlled the largest empire in ancient Africa. He was able to initiate a building program throughout his empire which was overwhelming in scope. The numbers and majesty of his building projects were legendary, with the greatest being the temple at Gebel Barkal in the Sudan. The temple was carved from the living rock and decorated with images of Taharka over 100 feet high.

TENKAMENIN – King of Ghana (1037-1075)

The country of Ghana reached the height of its greatness during the reign of Tenkamenin. Through his careful management of the gold trade across the Sahara desert into Western Africa, Tenkamenin's empire flourished economically. But his greatest strength was in government. Each day he would ride out on horseback and listen to the problems and concerns of his people. He insisted that no one be denied an audience and that they be allowed to remain in his presence until satisfied that justice had been done. His principles of democratic monarchy and religious tolerance make Tenkamenin's reign one of the great models of African rule.

THUTMOSE III – Pharaoh of Kemet (1504-1450 B.C.)

Thutmose III was a member of one of the greatest families in the history of royalty anywhere in the world, the 18th Dynasty of Kemet (ancient Egypt). He is credited with strengthening the sovereignty of Kemet and extending its influence into western Asia.

TUTANKAMUN – Boy Pharaoh of Kemet (1341-1323 B.C.)

Tutankhamen became pharaoh after the death of Smenkhkare, and became one of history's most famous royals. Tutankhamen's story has since come out, and we know more about this boy-king than we do about any other person in the Kemetic period. Tutankhamen became pharaoh at the age of nine. He married Ankhesenpaaten and ruled from Akhetaten. Four years after he became king, Tutankhamen moved his capital back to Memphis, and changed his name to Tutankamun, in honor of the god Amun. Tutankamun ruled for nine years, until he was 18. The mummy discovered in the Valley of the Kings has an injury to the skull, and it is believed that Tutankamun was either the victim of an accident or was assassinated. His tomb is one of very few that have been discovered almost untouched by thieves.

As you can see from the above biographies, we have a long and illustrious history of great Black African Kings. Did you ever hear anything about any of these great leaders in public school? No!

Why?

Because they were too busy teaching you about white European and American leaders and heroes like Winston Churchill, and George Washington, and Thomas Jefferson, and Abraham Lincoln, and all the rest of the "good-ole-boys."

These white boys couldn't hold a candle to our great Black Kings and heroes.

We know how to be great men. We know how to lead our people. We know how to be strong, courageous, intelligent, wise, just, and compassionate. We had been doing just that thousands of years before the Caucasians arrived on the scene.

The problem is this:

When we assimilated into this Euro-American culture, we lost our Afro-centric concept of manhood and Kingship. As a result, instead of being strong, courageous, and responsible protectors and leaders of the Black family and Black community, Black men have become selfish, arrogant, petty, childish, materialistic house and field niggas, who have adopted and adapted to a Darwinist view of survival of the fittest.

In other words, because of our socialized Euro-American mindset, we don't give a damn about nobody but ourselves. And that is what's killing the Black community!

This self-centered, paranoid, and ruthless code of conduct, which is the character and history of the entire European race of men, is what now drives the mentality of the Black male in the streets and ghettos and prisons all over this country.

However, all is not lost. We come from greatness and with the proper knowledge and guidance we can return to greatness. To resume our rightful places as strong, courageous, intelligent, and responsible protectors of the Black family and Black community, and restore balance, peace, justice, and harmony within our homes and our lives, there are twelve (12) stages of development that Black males need to journey through. I call these twelve stages of development, *The 12 Keys to the Kingdom.*

The 12 Keys to the Kingdom

1. Apply the Principles of African American Manhood
2. Change Your Attitude and Your Way of Thinking
3. Take Control of Your "Self-Education"
4. Take Responsibility for Your Actions
5. Strive for Self-Mastery
6. Study and Apply the Laws of Success
7. Find Positive Black Role Models to Emulate
8. Become a Man of Honor
9. Fight for Your Human and Civil Rights
10. Walk the Path of the Spiritual Warrior
11. Honor, Respect, and Protect the Black Woman
12. Pay Your Love and Respect to God Before All Others

In the next twelve (12) chapters, I describe in detail each of these twelve stages of development for Great Black Men and Kings.

22

FROM NIGGAS TO GODS

Apply the Principles of African American Manhood

If the Negro is to be a man, full and complete, he must take part in everything that belongs to manhood. If he omits a single duty, responsibility, or privilege, to that extent he is limited and incomplete.
- **Henry McNeal Turner, Minister and Militant Activist**

As Black men, we can no longer afford to live by a Euro-American code of conduct that justifies the use of ruthless and violent aggression against our own people just to survive in the ghettoes that were created by this racially hostile and oppressive nation.

What we need is a definition of manhood that is Afro-centered, and a set of principles that are consistent with the attributes of God: truth, love, wisdom, mercy, justice, peace, and freedom.

What we need is a standard of conduct, based on honor, respect, responsibility, and loyalty, that we can live by with our African American manhood and dignity intact, and our responsibilities as Father-Kings fulfilled.

What we need is a moral code of conduct that teaches Black men and Black boys to carry themselves with the bearing of Kings and Princes.

We need a set of moral principles that teaches all Black males:

- To Refrain from using violence to resolve conflicts, and seek peaceful resolutions first.

- To Be strong, yet gentle and compassionate, and to refuse to do anything that causes other people to suffer.

- To Respect the rights, the lives, and the property of other men, and to refuse to infringe upon these things without lawful justification.

- To Be loyal to and respectful of their mates, and when they are ready for fatherhood, to become responsible and supportive fathers to their children.

- To Avoid a life of crime, and to set personal and professional goals for their lives.

- To Make the pursuit and application of knowledge and education their highest priority in realizing those goals.

- To Refrain from abusing their bodies with drugs and alcohol, and to conscientiously object to the sale, marketing, and distribution of drugs in Black communities.

145

I've searched far and wide for a standard of conduct that meets these criteria, and asked hundreds of Black men what this standard of conduct should consist of.

As you know, it's hard enough to get two or more people to agree upon anything, let alone something as important as this.

However, based upon hundreds of interviews and discussions with my students at the prison where I teach, and with dozens of other Black men in the community, about what Black men are obligated to do for their families and communities, we finally developed what has become known and accepted in our circles as *The 7 Principles of African American Manhood.*

The 7 Principles of African American Manhood

Lest we forget our divine nature and our attributes as men and kings, we hereby affirm, embrace, and live by the following principles as the duties and responsibilities of all African American men:

1. To seek and gain knowledge that will free Black men and women from their mental, physical, and emotional bondage.

2. To educate, uplift, and empower Black men, who are the "Father-Kings" of the Black family.

3. To honor, respect, and protect the Black woman, who is the "Queen-Mother" of the Black family.

4. To teach, mentor, and counsel Black boys on the responsibilities of manhood, fatherhood, and leadership.

5. To provide emotional comfort, intellectual guidance, and financial support to our Black children.

6. To serve, support, and protect the Black family and the Black community.

7. To build and maintain a strong, spiritual relationship with God.

23

AS A BLACK MAN THINKETH

Change Your Attitude and Your Way of Thinking

As a man thinketh in is heart, so is he.
- **James Allen, Inspirational Philosopher**

As a Black man thinketh in his heart, so is he. And what a Black man thinks about, and believes, becomes true in his life. This truth becomes his *philosophy.*

To become a Man, you must first think like a Man!
To become a King, you must first think like a King!

That means we must first learn and embrace a new Afro-centered philosophy that exemplifies the qualities and attributes of a Man and a King.

What is Philosophy? The word itself means to think and reason about the truth of one's existence. In laymen terms it means to think about *who you are,* and *what you are,* and *why are you here.*

It means to think about the environment around you, your relationships with other people, and the social, economic, political, and spiritual influences of everyday life.

Your personal philosophy is simply how you see the world around you, and how you fit into the world. It's your attitude toward life in general, and your life in particular.

Your philosophy is your view of the way things are, or the way you think they should be in life.

However, like anything else, there is a positive and a negative aspect to just about everything that has to do with the way men think and act. As Black men we have adopted some very negative attitudes and views about how life is or should be for ourselves as individuals.

These negative attitudes and views have become our philosophy, and this philosophy has become our way of life. Unfortunately, our philosophy and our way of life are what perpetuate the cycle of black-on-black crime and violence in our communities.

Have you ever heard the expression, "Attitude is everything"?
It's just another way of saying, "You are what you think, and what you think is what you become." It's absolutely true.

Your attitude about life, in other words, your philosophy, determines to a large degree how you think and how you act.

The good news is that when you change your attitude, you can change your life.

One of the most powerful ways of changing your attitude is through the use of positive affirmations. Affirmations are a series of written and spoken thoughts that when repeated often enough, with sincerity, can replace old negative attitudes with new positive ones.

BLACK SON RISING

Below are seven affirmations I use to remind myself of how I should be thinking and acting as a Black man, and as a Father-King. I call these seven affirmations, *The 7 Attributes of a Black King.*

The 7 Attributes of a Black King

From this day forth, I will change my way of thinking and change my attitude about myself, my life, my family, my community, and my God, and adopt the following attributes as the inherent qualities of a Man and a Black King:

1.   I Am a Responsible Black King

A good, capable, and dependable Black King – one who is a good provider to his children, and a loyal friend and lover to his mate; one who holds himself personally accountable for all his actions, good and bad, and doesn't blame others for his mistakes; one who doesn't make excuses for his faults and failures; one whom others can trust to do what he's supposed to do, when and how he's supposed to do it.

2.   I Am an Intelligent Black King

A smart, resourceful, and educated Black King – one who recognizes that his mind is his most powerful weapon, and that knowledge is the best source of ammunition; one who refrains from violence, and channels his anger and energy into positive directions; one who uses his mind to bring positive changes to his life, and the lives of others.

3.   I Am an Honorable Black King

A dignified, respectable, and honest Black King – one who earns his living through legitimate pursuits, without doing harm to others; one who speaks the truth, because his integrity is more valuable than any material possession he has; one who doesn't lie to impress others, or to cover his mistakes, or to avoid the consequences of his actions.

4.   I Am a Powerful Black King

A strong, confident, and disciplined Black King – one who understands that real power is the ability to have a positive influence on other people's lives; one who knows that true power can only be developed through the Power of Self-mastery and the 5 Aspects of Spiritual Practice.

5.   I Am a Courageous Black King

A brave, assertive, and undaunted Black King – one who faces his fears instead of hiding behind them; a man who admits that he has fears and knows how they can negatively effect his behavior; one who knows the difference between right and wrong, and does the right thing without regard to the consequences of his actions.

6.   I Am a Compassionate Black King

A gentle, sympathetic, and generous Black King; one who tolerates the differences in others, and accepts people as they are; one who recognizes each person's right to live and be free from persecution because of his race, ethnicity, religion, or socioeconomic status; one who knows that the true value of a person is not measured by what a person has, but by what they do for others.

7.   I Am a Spiritual Black King

A thinking, philosophical, and God-loving Black King; a seeker of truth, knowledge, peace, justice, freedom, wisdom, and love – being all the attributes of God; one who knows that the first and most important relationship is the one he builds between himself and God.

As a Black man, and as a Black King, let the above affirmations be your philosophy, your attitude, and ultimately, your new way of life. Write down and then recite these affirmations in a quiet place, as often as you can, and believe them in your heart as you say them, and in a short while, you will begin to see a significant change in the way you think about yourself, your family, and your world.

24

FREE YOUR MIND

Take Control of Your "Self-Education"

If Southern whites found the prospect of an educated slave so threatening, education must hold the promise of liberation.
- **Audrey Edwards, Publisher**

For hundreds of years the White race has purposefully and willfully lied about the history of the world and history of the Black race, in an effort to make the Black race feel inferior, thereby keeping them subservient to the White race.

The public school system in this country is one of the white power structure's greatest tools in keeping the Black race ignorant about the truth of their history and heritage.

Consequently, if you rely solely on a public school education, you will never hear the full truth about the significant contributions the Black race has made to the world. Nor will you ever hear the truth about the White race's horrific acts of brutality and treachery throughout history.

It is your responsibility to seek out the truth for yourself and research your history and heritage, as well as the history and psychology of the White race.

To liberate your mind from your ignorance about who you are, you must educate yourself beyond the institutions of white racism.

Therefore, Black man, if we want to live and stay free, mentally and physically, you must educate yourself. To educate yourself, you must read!

You would never know anything about the significant contributions of the Black race, if you relied solely on what the White race tells you via their systems of "mis-education."

Therefore, one of the keys to breaking the cycle of black-on-black crime and violence is to encourage Black people to learn about their history and heritage, and world history through self-directed education. By learning the truth about the extensive history and significant contributions of their own race, and how the white race has willfully deceived the world about its own history and heritage, Black people can begin to free themselves from their mental, physical, and emotional bondage.

Your freedom from these various forms of bondage begins with the way you *think*.

That means to become free, you must think free.

To think free, you must free your mind.

To free your mind, you must educate yourself.

To educate yourself, you must read!

The knowledge you can gain through self-education is the White man's greatest fear, because he realizes that with this knowledge, a self-educated and free-thinking Black man cannot be tricked or manipulated into destroying his own race.

25

KEEPING IT REAL

Take Responsibility for Your Actions

None of us is responsible for our birth. Our responsibility is the use we make of life.
- **Joshua Henry Jones, Novelist**

One of the things that separates a man from a boy, and a King from a Prince, is his willingness to accept responsibility for his actions, and the consequences of those actions.

As a former law enforcement officer, I've locked up hundreds of young Black men for every kind of crime you can think of. The one thing they all had in common was their failure to accept responsibility for their actions and their behavior.

Black men have to stop blaming everybody else for their failures and faults, and start accepting responsibility for all of their actions, and the consequences that follow.

Every time I talk to Black men, I hear the same tired excuses over and over again:

It's somebody else's fault that you dropped out of school and can't get a job making minimum wage.

It's somebody else's fault that you're on lock-down for the 5th time this year.

It's somebody else's fault that you have 2 or 3 babies you can't or won't take care of.

It's somebody else's fault that you're standing on the corner slinging rock, and carrying illegal, unregistered handguns.

It's somebody else's fault that you robbed the liquor store down the street, and shot the owner for no good reason.

Being a man and being a King means being responsible for your actions. That means that you hold yourself personally accountable for everything that happens in your life, where you have some control.

This means you make no excuse for your weaknesses, failures, or mistakes. This means that you don't waste time blaming others, or trying to find the easy, lazy, or dishonest way out of bad, or unpleasant situations.

The ability to accept and face the consequences of your actions automatically sets you apart, and above the average man around you, because the average man is afraid to accept responsibility for his actions.

The fear of responsibility makes a man weak, ineffective, and powerless. However, the acceptance of responsibility makes a man strong, effective, and powerful, and the willingness to accept responsibility is one of the most important qualities of a King.

26

SMARTER CHOICES

Strive for Self-Mastery

You can master yourself, or you can be "mastered." The choice is yours.
- **Michael Samir Mohamed**

The other thing that separates a man from a boy and a King from a Prince, is his ability to control his behavior. This ability is called *Self-Mastery*, and it goes hand-in-hand with responsibility.

You can master yourself, or you can be "mastered." The choice is yours. That means that if you don't take control over your life, somebody else will. Usually that means a person or an institution like the criminal justice system, that has the authority to rob you of your freedom, your respect, and your manhood.

Jail and prisons are full of Black men who failed to exercise any degree of self-control. Ask any man in prison who's honest enough to admit it, why he is where he is.

If he has accepted responsibility for his actions, he will tell you quite simply, "I was out of control, and I'm paying for it, every day."

Self-mastery means that you must take control over your anger, instead of letting your anger take control of you. Anger unchecked leads to aggression. Aggression often leads to violence. And violence can only lead to pain, prison, or death.

Self-mastery means that you must take control over your fate, instead of letting your friends and peers decide your fate for you. Everybody wants to fit in, but if your so-called friends are committing crimes or engaged in other negative behavior, then you need to walk away from your friends and do what's right for your life.

Self-mastery means that you must take control of the substances you put into your body, instead of letting the substances you put in your body take control of you. Besides the negative effects on your body, drugs and alcohol severely impair your ability to control your behavior. If you can't control your behavior, you can't control your life.

As Black men and Kings, the first power we must exert is power over ourselves. This form of power is called *Self-Mastery*, and no man is free, nor can he prosper, until he has it.

27

MAKE IT HAPPEN

Study and Apply The Laws of Success

The guy who takes a chance, who walks the line between the known and the unknown, who is unafraid of failure, will succeed.
- **Gordon Parks, World Famous Photographer**

In 1928, Napoleon Hill, one of the world's leading experts on success psychology and personal achievement, published the landmark book, *The Law of Success in Sixteen Lessons*. This book continues to be the world's most comprehensive text on the philosophy of personal achievement.

To research the psychology of success, Napoleon Hill personally interviewed hundreds of the most successful men on the planet at that time, including Andrew Carnegie, Henry Ford, Thomas Edison, John D. Rockefeller, and Alexander Graham Bell.

What he discovered was that no matter what industry successful people worked in, they all possessed the same success characteristics, to some degree or another. He identified 16 consistent personality traits in hundreds of successful men and women, over a period of 25 years of research.

To this day, *The Law of Success* is used by countless business and industry leaders, and is considered one of the most powerful tools for personal achievement, 78 years after it was first published. It stands as the classic text on success psychology.

Why is this important to you?

Because most people have no idea what it takes to succeed, and I know for a fact that most people don't get a success curriculum taught to them in the public school system. So then when and where are you supposed to learn the laws of success?

Answer: Normally you never learn them. And that's the problem. Too many Brothers out here have no idea what the principles of success are, or that there are principles of success to begin with.

So then how does one learn how to succeed if one doesn't know what the principles of success are?

Answer: Normally you don't. That's why most people fail to achieve anything of significance in their life. The average person spends his entire adult life working a 9 to 5 that they absolutely hate, because they don't know how to break away and do something with their lives that gives it meaning.

Learning the principles of success is no different from learning the principles of reading or writing. There are rules and regulations to each, but somebody has to teach you what the rules are. Some of us are smart enough to teach ourselves how to read, write, and succeed, but most of us can't and don't.

The bottom line is this: If we never learn the principles, then we can't apply them in our life to our advantage. The good news is that as long as you are breathing, it's never too late to learn.

So let's start changing our lives and learning how to succeed by studying *The 16 Laws of Success!*

The 16 Laws of Success

1.   Develop a Definite Major Purpose

Success and progress toward achieving your goals in life begin with knowing where you are going. Any dominating idea, plan, or purpose held in your conscious mind through repeated effort and emotionalized by a burning desire for its realization is taken over by the subconscious and acted upon through whatever natural and logical means may be available.

Your mental attitude gives power to everything you do. If your attitude is positive, your actions and thoughts further your ends. If your attitude is negative, you are constantly undermining your own efforts. The starting point of all human achievement is the development of a Definite Major Purpose. Without a definite major purpose, you are as helpless as a ship without a compass.

2.   Establish a Mastermind Alliance

A mastermind alliance consists of two or more minds working actively together in perfect harmony toward a common definite objective. Through a mastermind alliance you can appropriate and use the full strength of the experience, training, and knowledge of others just as if they were your own. No individual has ever achieved success without the help and cooperation of others. The value of "gathering together those of a like mind" is self-evident. A group of brains coordinated in a spirit of harmony will provide more thought energy than a single brain, just as a group of electric batteries will provide more energy than a single battery.

3.   Use Applied Faith

Faith is awareness of, belief in, and harmonizing with the universal powers. Faith is a state of mind which must be active not passive, to be useful in achieving lasting success. Close the door to fear behind you and you will quickly see the door of faith open before you. Fear is nothing more than a state of mind, which is subject to your own direction and control. Faith will not bring you what you desire, but it will show you the way to go after it for yourself.

4.   Go the Extra Mile

Strength and struggle go hand in hand. Render more and better service than you are paid for, and sooner or later you will receive compound interest from your investment. The end of the rainbow is at the end of the second mile. The quality of the service rendered, plus the quantity of service rendered, plus the mental attitude in which it is rendered, equals your compensation. The more you give, the more you get.

5.   Develop a Pleasing Personality and a Positive Mental Attitude

A Positive Mental Attitude is the single most important principle of the science of success, without which you cannot get the maximum benefit from the sixteen principles. Success attracts success and failure attracts more failure. Your mental attitude is the only thing over which you, and only you, have complete control. A Positive Mental Attitude attracts opportunities for success, while a Negative Mental Attitude repels opportunities and doesn't even take advantage of them when they do come along. A positive mind finds a way it can be done... a negative mind looks for all the ways it can't be done.

A Positive Mental Attitude is the right mental attitude in any given situation. Courtesy is your most profitable asset... and it is absolutely free! Emotions are nothing but reflections of your mental attitude, which you can organize, guide, and completely control. Your personality is your greatest asset or your greatest liability because it embraces everything you control ...your mind, body, and soul. To be happy, make someone else happy!

6. Take Personal Initiative

It is better to act on a plan that is still weak than to delay acting at all. Procrastination is the archenemy of personal initiative. Personal initiative is contagious. It succeeds where others fail. It creates work, opportunity, and future advancement. Procrastinators are experts in making excuses. Personal initiative is the inner power that starts all action.

7. Show Your Enthusiasm

To be enthusiastic act enthusiastically! Enthusiasm is to progress toward success as gasoline is to a car's engine. It is the fuel that drives things forward. Enthusiasm stimulates your subconscious mind. By feeding your conscious mind with enthusiasm, you impress upon your subconscious that your burning desire and your plan for attaining it are certain. Enthusiasm is a state of mind. It inspires action and is the most contagious of all emotions. Enthusiasm is more powerful than logic, reason, or rhetoric in getting your ideas across and in winning over others to your viewpoint.

8. Develop Self-Discipline

Self-discipline is the process that ties together all your efforts of controlling your mind, your personal initiative, positive mental attitude, and controlling your enthusiasm. Self-discipline makes you think before you act. The subconscious has access to all departments of the mind, but is not under the control of any. If you don't discipline yourself, you are sure to be disciplined by others. Without self-discipline, you are as dangerous as a car running downhill without brakes or steering wheel.

9. Think Accurately

Thoughts have power, are under your control, and can be used wisely or unwisely. Accurate thinkers accept no political, religious, or other type of thought, regardless of its source, until it is carefully analyzed. Accurate thinkers are the masters of their emotions. Accurate thought involves two fundamentals. First you must separate facts from information. Second you must separate facts into two classes: the important and unimportant. Accurate thinkers allow no one to do their thinking for them.

10. Stay Focused

Keep your mind ON the things you want and OFF the things you don't want! It is much easier to focus your attention on something you believe will happen than on something you believe is unlikely. Controlled attention is the act of coordinating all the faculties of your mind and directing their combined power to a specific end. Positive and negative emotions cannot occupy your mind at the same time. You can not hold a good thought and a bad thought in your mind simultaneously. It has to be one or the other. Stay focused on the good thought and activity, instead of the bad one.

11. Inspire Teamwork and Cooperation

There is no record of any great contribution to civilization without the cooperation of others. Enthusiasm is contagious and teamwork is the inevitable result. A good football team relies more on harmonious coordination of effort than individual skill. Most people will respond more freely to a request than they will to an order. Helping others solve their problems will help you solve your own.

12. Learn from Adversity and Defeat

Everyone faces defeat. It may be a stepping-stone or a stumbling block, depending on the mental attitude with which it is faced. Failure and pain are one language through which nature speaks to every living creature. You are never a failure until you accept defeat as permanent and quit trying. Thomas Edison failed 10,000 times before perfecting the electric light bulb. Don't worry if you fail once. Every adversity, every failure, and every unpleasant experience carries with it the seed of success, the silver lining in the dark cloud.

13. Cultivate Your Creative Vision (Imagination)

Creative imagination has its base in the subconscious and is the medium through which you recognize new ideas and newly learned facts. Synthetic imagination springs from experience and reason; creative imagination springs from your commitment to your definite purpose. Imagination recognizes limitations. Creative vision sees no limitations. Your imaginative faculty will become weak through inaction. It can be revived through use. In other words, the more you use your creative vision the stronger it will become. Creative vision allows you to "think outside the box" and "take the road less traveled."

14. Maintain Sound Health

To maintain a Positive Mental Attitude and develop a healthy mind and body, you must conquer fear and anxiety. Anything that affects your physical health also affects your mental health. A Positive Mental Attitude is the most important quality for sound mental and physical health. Exercise produces both physical and mental stability. It clears sluggishness and dullness from your body and mind. If you don't have the willpower to keep your physical body healthy, you also lack the power of will to maintain a Positive Mental Attitude in other important circumstances that control your life.

15. Budget Your Time and Money

Tell me how you use your time and how you spend your money, and I will tell you where and what you'll be ten years from now. Take regular inventory of yourself to learn how and where you are spending your time and money. The secret of getting things done is: DO IT NOW! Time is too precious to be wasted on arguments and discontent. Some mistakes can be corrected, but not the mistake of wasting time. When time is gone, it's gone forever.

Use your income to pay yourself first, and distribute your income systematically so that a certain percentage of it will steadily accumulate (savings). Like time, don't waste money on objects that don't move you closer to your Definite Major Purpose. Having luxury items is nice, but if having them prevents you from achieving your Definite Major Purpose, then put them on hold until you accomplish your objectives.

16. Live By the Golden Rule

The Golden Rule is very simple: Treat people the way you would wish to be treated. That means don't do things to people you don't want done to yourself. It also means deal with people with the same level of respect and courtesy with which you want to be treated. In fact, treat them even better than what you are used to, and you will become known as a good, decent, and respectful person, in business and social affairs.

The 16 Laws of Success are about developing new success habits. It takes a habit to replace a habit. All of your successes and failures are results of habits you have formed over the years. Some of your habits are good, others are bad. If you are failing more than you are succeeding, then you need to change some of your bad habits into good ones.

That means you have to identify what your bad habits are, then identify a good habit you would like to replace it with. Use the 16 Laws of Success as your guide. If you don't have any of these success habits, then it's time for you to start developing them. Now!

Don't wait until you are 60 or 70 years old to start trying to figure out why you have been a failure most of your life. Take action now! Get off your butt and start taking charge of your life and your success. That means start learning about something other than hustling, and rap, and basketball. Everybody can't be a basketball star or a rap artist. And hustling will eventually land you in one of two places: in the prison or in the graveyard.

Find some truly unique purpose in life and do everything in your power to be successful at that. Think outside the box. Do something that's never been done before, or do some old thing in a new way that's never been done before. Get creative with it, and don't let anything stand in your way.

But first you must learn the laws of success!

157

28

UP FROM SLAVERY

Find Positive Black Role Models to Emulate

Youth are looking for something; it's up to adults to show them what is worth emulating.
- **Jesse Jackson Sr. Minister and Civil Rights Activist**

If you want to be remembered as a fool, continue doing the things that fools do. However, if you want to be remembered as a great man, start doing the things that great men do.

It's very unfortunate that so many of our young Brothers today look up to drug dealers, gang-bangers, and ruthless Black street hustlers as their role models. They see the fast cash, the spinning rims, the fly gear, the "bling," and the loose easy young women who flock to the gangsta lifestyle.

Our young Black men are easily drawn to that lifestyle because it appears to be fun, carefree, a *little* dangerous, and *very* exciting, and the women are a dime a dozen.

Who wouldn't want that kind of lifestyle?

I have to admit whenever I watch BET Rap City videos and see all that "cash and women" on display, it seems like a very exciting and plush lifestyle, with fast cars, fast cash, and even faster women.

Yeah, at first it might appear that these gangstas and hustlers have it going on with their flashy lifestyle, but then I remember why I am writing this book and why black-on-black crime and violence is escalating out of control. Because once you get past all the glamour and glitz you think about the truth going on behind the scenes. Your first inclination is to admire these brothers for their cool and hip and enviable lifestyle, but instead of admiring them, you might want to consider this:

That drug-dealing, gun-toting, and ruthless Black street hustler you want to be like, is that same dangerous brother hanging on the corner at 3a.m. slinging rock to your mother and father, or your son and daughter.

That's the same trifling brother who would rather steal your possessions, than work for his own.

That's the same ignorant brother who knows all the lyrics to the latest "gangsta" rap, but can't put 2 correct sentences together.

That's the same lazy brother who's got enough energy to play b-ball all day, but not enough energy to pick up a book or look for a job.

That's the same irresponsible brother who's not only 1 baby's daddy, but 3 other babies' that he can't or won't take care of.

That's the same ruthless brother who will put a bullet in the head of another young brother over a dime bag of crack.

That's the same cowardly brother standing in front of a judge begging and pleading for mercy, even though he didn't show any mercy to that brother he just smoked.

That's the same sorry brother on lock-down in the modern day slave plantation called prison, doing 25 to life, for killing his brother over the white man's poison.

That's the same pathetic brother with no goals, no dreams, and no future, who doesn't give a damn about anything or anyone but himself.

So if this is the kind of man you want for a role model and if that's the kind of man you want to be, then that lifestyle is definitely there waiting for you in the streets, in the prisons, and in the graveyards. All you have to do is start doing the same stupid things you see all the other ignorant and uneducated Brothers doing: *getting high, dropping out of school, hanging on the corners like bums until they get locked up, peddling that chemical slavery to their own people, and making a bunch of fatherless children who have to suffer because their "daddy" is in prison.*

I know how quick we are to put celebrities up on peddle-stools and make icons out of people who make more money than we do, but let me ask you this:

What has 50 Cent, Ludakris, Little Scrappy, Lil Wayne, Mobb Deep, Lil Jon, Snoop Dogg, Boyz n Da Hood, The Dogg Pound, Above the Law, the Gheto Boys, Hot Boys, or the Eastside Boyz, or any other "boys" ever done to educate, uplift, and empower the Black race?

Absolutely nothing! They spend most of their time and talent talking about how much dough they bank, how many hos they pimp, and how many "niggas" they pop.

The truth is they are the ones getting pimped, because they are the ones prostituting themselves for rich white record company executives who want them to pump that negative destructive message into their own Black communities, just so they can make a profit and keep Black people in ghettos and prisons and graveyards.

These Brothers ain't heroes, they are whores. They will sell their honor and their people for a piece of chicken and a biscuit if they thought it would get them some airtime on the radio or television.

So stop putting these ignorant, music industry prostitutes up on peddle stools, and find some real Black man of honor and respect to look up to and emulate.

I understand that psychologically, most people need someone they can look up to as a role model, but if you want to emulate somebody, why not emulate Malcolm X (born Malcolm Little)? Malcolm X was arguably the most brilliant Black man in history, and the perfect living example of what one man can do for his race once he removes the shackles of fear, ignorance, and self-hatred from his own mind.

A lot of today's young hoodlums think they are so hard and tough and gangsta, but nobody was more gangsta than Malcolm Little. He stole, robbed, pimped, whored around, vandalized, victimized, and peddled that chemical slavery with the worst of them, until he woke up from his ignorance and slave mentality, and became a man of honor.

Not surprisingly, it was during his incarceration that he first got the opportunity to change his way of thinking. It's unfortunate, but Black men seem to do their best self-analysis and deepest thinking on the slave plantations called prisons.

Nonetheless, Malcolm made real good use of his time in the joint, and began studying world history, philosophy, and religion, including Islam. As a result of his Islamic studies, and his desire to educate himself, he realized how successfully and thoroughly the white race had mentally enslaved not only him, but most of the Black race in America as well. Once he realized the depth of his own slave mentality, he made it his life mission to overcome that condition for himself, and the entire Black race.

Before his assassination at the hands of Black sell-out field niggas, Malcolm had touched and positively impacted the lives of millions of men, women, and children, Black and White.

That's a role model!

My point is that the Black race is not short of positive role models, past or present. We have throughout our entire history thousands of courageous Black men and women who have successfully overcome poverty, crime, racial hatred, discrimination, institutionalized racism, violence, drug abuse, physical handicaps, poor education systems, physical abuse, and other social injustices.

They are there if you bother to look for them and seek them out.

The question is: If these true heroes and heroines found the strength, the courage, and the discipline to achieve their goals, why can't you?

What qualities of character do they have that you don't, yet?

29

RISE AND SHINE

Become a Man of Honor

Black men, you were once great; you shall be great again.
- **Marcus Garvey, Nationalist Leader**

Why is it that young Black men would rather follow the example of some drug-dealing, gun-toting, gang-banging, ruthless Black gangsta, but don't want to follow the example of honorable and respectable men like Fredrick Douglass, Paul Robeson, W.E.B. Dubois, Marcus Garvey, Malcolm X, Huey Newton, Stokely Carmichael, Medgar Evers, Steve Biko, and Dr. Martin Luther King, Jr.?

The answer is simple:

It is much easier to be a hoodlum than it is to be a man of honor and respect!

There are no special qualifications to become a hoodlum. All you have to do is be lazy, irresponsible, cowardly, disrespectful, deceitful, trifling, ignorant, and ruthless.

However, being a man of honor and respect is much more difficult, because it requires you to be kind, considerate, humble, generous, honest, courageous, compassionate, responsible, respectful, respectable, merciful, and knowledgeable about yourself and your heritage.

That's a very difficult way to live, especially if you don't know how, and no one is teaching you or showing you the way.

Even if someone were to show you, the truth is, a lot of you brothers "ain't" ready to be that kind of man, because it requires too much strength and courage and discipline to follow that way of life.

Let's be honest, Black men, we have a bad habit of taking the path of least resistance and taking the easy, lazy, and dishonest way out of difficult situations, which then turn around and bite us later on down the road.

You and I both know that if you had exercised a little strength and discipline up front, you wouldn't have half the problems you now face in terms of poverty, unemployment, and prison.

Strength and discipline would have kept you from dropping out of school.

Strength and discipline would have kept you from hanging on the corner.

Strength and discipline would have kept you from slinging rock and packing heat.

Strength and discipline would have kept you from doing that 5-year stint at the pen.

Strength and discipline would have kept you from becoming just another "boy in the hood," instead of a "man of honor."

Why am I making such a big deal about being a man of honor and respect?

Why can't Black men just do whatever they want to do, or live however they want to live?

What's wrong with being a thug or gangsta or hustler?
What difference does it make?
Why do we need men of honor, anyway?
Let me ask you this:
Where would we be if Frederick Douglass had been a gangsta?
Where would we be if Marcus Garvey had been a hustler?
Where would we be if Martin Luther King, Jr., had been a gang-banger?
Where would we be if Malcolm X had continued to live like a thug, instead of becoming the great man he came to be?
Where would we be if every great Black leader we ever had had decided to be a ruthless, ignorant, dishonest black gangsta and street hustler?

Being a man of honor requires great commitment and great sacrifice.
Be honest with yourself: *Are you half the man Malcolm X was?*
If not, could you be if you really tried?
What is it going to take for you to become a man of honor and respect?
What is it going to take to turn you into a strong and courageous protector of the Black race instead of a drug-dealing, gun-toting, gang-banging, back-stabbing murderer of your own people?
To become a Black man of honor, you need to know what a Black man of honor will and won't do. That means you need to familiarize yourself with some form of moral and spiritual instruction.
One of the oldest sources of African moral and spiritual instruction is the Principles of MA'AT developed in ancient Egypt. The Principles of MA'AT existed at least 2000 years before Moses and the Hebrew Bible. Ma'at, the dynamic Principle of Right, Truth, and Justice, was the source of harmony with the self, the universe, and God.
The Egyptians believed that when they died, their souls would be judged by these principles. After revising and shortening the list, Moses taught these principles to the Israelites as the 10 Commandments. Moses added three new commandments; the ones about not honoring other gods, the honoring of parents, and not coveting one's neighbors' wives and slaves.
There are 42 Principle of MA'AT. However, I have provided only 24 of the principles of MA'AT that are more relevant to our times. Learn these principles and apply them in your life to become a man of honor and respect.

The 24 Principles of MA'AT

1. I will do no evil to any man, woman, or child.
2. I will not use violence unless it is necessary to protect life and limb.
3. I will not rob or steal from others.
4. I will not cause the suffering of others.
5. I will not defraud my friends, my family, or my associates.
6. I will not murder or cause anyone to be murdered on my behalf.
7. I will not lie to save myself from the consequences of my actions.
8. I will not dishonor God by bringing harm to his creations.
9. I will not transgress against God or anger Him.
10. I will not cause the shedding of blood or tears.
11. I will not deal deceitfully with any man or woman.
12. I will not speak hurtful words toward or against anyone.
13. I will not act angrily or wrathfully without just cause.
14. I will not lust after or defile another man's wife or mate.

15. I will not pollute my body with drugs or alcohol or cigarettes.
16. I will not terrorize my family or my community.
17. I will not commit any abominable acts such as murder, torture, or rape.
18. I will not speak angrily toward any man, woman, or child.
19. I will not judge others without first trying to understand their situations.
20. I will not act uncontrollably out of rage.
21. I will not act out of arrogance.
22. I will not act out of vengeance or retribution.
23. I will not create trouble or strife in other people's lives.
24. I will not abandon my children or cause them harm.

30

FIGHT THE POWER

Fight for Your Human and Civil Rights

We have the longest revolutionary heritage of any people on the face of the earth.
- **John Henrik Clarke, Historian**

Black people have the longest history of revolutionary heritage of any people on the planet. We have been fighting racism, discrimination, and racial oppression for thousands of years. I don't know who originated the saying, but whoever said it first, truly understood the importance of fighting for your beliefs. In two sentences, he perfectly summed up the strength, courage, philosophy, and mentality of the world's greatest Black freedom fighters and revolutionaries.

The saying I'm referring to is the one that goes:

You can die on the field, or you can die on the bleachers. Either way you're going to die, so why not go out swinging?

The problem is a lot of us are sitting on the bleachers, waiting for someone else to fight our battles for us, instead of getting our there and punching and swinging to demand freedom, respect, and manhood.

Who are you Brothers waiting for? Another Malcolm X or Marcus Garvey?

Why should someone else have to fight your battles, that you can't or won't fight for yourselves.

When are you going to get off your butt and demand the freedom and respect that all men are due?

Of what, or should I say of *whom*, are you afraid?

I think Black men forget, or they never knew, that the Black race has had a long, proud history of fighting back against slavery, racism, inequality, oppression, and other forms of social injustices.

For hundreds of years, European and American white supremacists have tried to rob our people of our glorious African history, and rewrite world history based on racist lies, deceptions, and the deliberate mis-education of both races, *ours* and *theirs*.

We have been denied our honor as the world's first great civilization.

We have been used and exploited as cheap slave labor for capitalist greed.

We have been lynched, castrated, mutilated, humiliated, and mis-educated, as European and American white supremacists attempted to turn our people into deaf, dumb, and blind slaves who hate themselves and love their oppressors.

But all along the way, there have been thousands of courageous Black men and women who dared to fight these white supremacists tooth and nail, refusing to bow their heads or hold their tongues, without regard for the consequences of rising up, fighting back, and breaking free from the chains of oppression.

164

Fight the Power

They fought on their terms, not the "masta's," for freedom, justice, and equality in every aspect of Black social life including education, politics, business, economics, and religion.

This struggle, fought on numerous battlefronts, has cost us the lives of some of our most intelligent and courageous heroes.

Cornel West once said:

Anytime there is a self-loving, self-respecting, and self-determining Black man or woman, he or she is one of the most dangerous folks in America. Because it means you are free enough to speak your mind, you're free enough to speak the truth.

And it's true. Anyone who dares to stand up and speak out against the racist policies and practices of this country automatically places his or her freedom and life at risk, because if you're brave enough to speak your mind and speak the truth, you immediately become a danger to the white racist power structure in this country.

Many of these Brothers and Sisters who were brave enough to stand up and speak out, have sacrificed everything, including their lives, to bring the truth to Black people who are in mental and physical bondage.

As proof of their danger to the white power structure, consider this:

With few exceptions, every last one of our greatest Black freedom fighters, famous and unknown, have been killed, discredited, or forced into exile, simply for speaking the truth and openly defying the creators and supporters of the systems of institutionalized racism.

To quote the Talking Drum regarding Black freedom fighters:

Nameless thousands have resisted even unto death for the liberation of African people, beginning on the shores of the Mother continent itself and continuing through the Middle Passage, Slavery, Jim Crow, the Civil Rights Struggle, the Black Liberation Struggle, and the struggles of today. The fact that the names of many of those individuals are not known does not reduce the significance of their contribution to the struggle for Black Liberation. This compilation is an attempt to recognize and pay homage to those individuals who made the ultimate sacrifice for the liberation of Black/African people and should not be looked upon as discrediting the thousands, perhaps even millions of others that have also struggled for true freedom, justice, and equality. Our generation must now accept the torch that has been passed to us to guarantee our existence and our children's future. The Struggle Continues!

A lot of Brothers have lost their lives just for having the courage, self-respect, and racial pride to participate in social movements that were attempting to develop political and economic power in Black communities.

Make no mistake!

If you stand up for yourself and fight back against the systems of institutionalized racism in this country, there will be consequences for your actions.

The question is: Are you prepared to deal with the consequences?

BLACK SON RISING

When I first received my awakening I had to ask myself that same question, and what I decided was that I would rather die a free man than live like a slave.

The choice is yours, and you are the only one who can make it.

The real question is how do you want to be remembered:

As someone who fought and died for your principles? Or as someone who continued to live in bondage because you were too afraid to fight back against the systems of institutionalized racism?

31

A MAN ON FIRE

Walk the Path of the Spiritual Warrior

Our emphasis [as an African people] was not on religion, but rather on spirituality; and spirituality is higher than religion.
- **John Henrik Clarke, Historian**

You can fight for yourself, you can fight for your people, or you can fight for God; either way, you are going to have to fight if you want to be free.

If you decide to fight, you are going to need the mental, physical, and spiritual strength and power to do battle with your enemies, including the internal ones like fear, greed, and ignorance, as well as the external ones like the white racist power structure and their agents.

That means equipping your mind, body, and spirit to do battle with those who seek to destroy your efforts and stand in the way of your individual freedom, and the collective freedom of your people.

To prepare for battle, you should set your foot on the path of the *Spiritual Warrior.*

When you hear the word "warrior," it brings up images of fighting, conflict, war, and killing. When we think of warriors, we tend to think of angry, vengeful men blazing a path of havoc, death, and destruction with their weapons of swords, guns, and bombs.

The dictionary defines "warrior" as "a person engaged in some struggle or conflict," as all Black men are whether they actively struggle or not. You are involuntarily enrolled into conflict from the day you are born. Some of our Brothers tend to forget this, after they have accumulated some material wealth or realized some measure of success.

Make no mistake, Black man, you are part of the struggle whether you like it or not.

When "spiritual" is attached to the word "warrior," it takes on a whole new meaning, and becomes a larger, much more holistic concept than anger, vengeance, death, and destruction.

A Spiritual Warrior is an individual whose goals and purpose are in alignment with the natural order of the universe, and whose attributes are consistent with the attributes of God.

Malcolm X, Marcus Garvey, and Martin Luther King, Jr., were all spiritual warriors. They fought for themselves, their people, and their God; their purpose was in alignment with the natural order of things, and they possessed the attributes of God, including strength, courage, compassion, kindness, generosity, patience, wisdom, knowledge, and love.

To become a Spiritual Warrior like Malcolm, Marcus, and Martin, you must learn, embrace, and practice *The 5 Aspects of Spiritual Practice.*

The 5 Aspects of Spiritual Practice

1. **The first aspect of spiritual practice is Meditation.**

    Meditation is a quiet mental state that allows the individual to reflect on his world, his strength and weaknesses, and his relationship with God. Meditation means literally to *sit in silence*.
    Meditation brings about order and focus. It is not a place for you to obsess about life's problems. It provides a comfort zone in the silence or emptiness, and a closeness with God.

    In order to bring about the best results, it is important to set the stage for your meditation. Before you meditate, take fifteen or twenty minutes to sit down and quietly read some teaching from whatever faith you observe.

    Turn off the television, CD players, and radios, and unplug the phone. Background music, even though you think it relaxes you, is a disturbance. I say this because, while such music can sound pleasant, the melody will have a way of carrying you off in thought. It is better to have your meditation space completely quiet.

    Eat light before you study and meditate, because if you eat heavy food it will make you sleepy, so I suggest that you do your meditation an hour or two after you eat.

    After you have quietly studied some spiritual or philosophical Teaching, sit comfortably, and let your mind go naturally to that Teaching. Don't force the thought, just let it soak in.

2. **The second aspect of spiritual practice is Service.**

    Service can take on many different forms, but it should play to your strengths, and give you a sense of personal satisfaction while you are engaged in it. Whether you are feeding the homeless, or teaching adults to read, or mentoring an at-risk youth, giving service to someone other than yourself can increase your sense of compassion for your fellow man. And compassion is one of God's greatest attributes.

    However, the most important aspect of service is that it should be given without any expectation of reward. Service should be given or performed from your heart.

    Therefore, you do something for someone else, just because it is there to do. If you have expectations attached to the service you give, then what you do is not service. It is instead an exchange of energy, or a bargain. When you do something for someone with a reward in mind, you have already limited your return.

3. **The third aspect of spiritual practice is Concentration, or Focus.**

    Find a divine mission or service and concentrate on accomplishing that. This means to be totally present with it. When you give service, focus on the gift of that service, whether it be handing a beggar some money on the street, or working in a soup kitchen, or teaching classes to prison inmates.

When you set your mind to resolve an issue like poverty or violence, or to create something like a shelter for the homeless, give it your full attention. Be totally present as you do it. If you are writing a book on helping people to achieve self-empowerment, do not think about how the book will end, stay focused on the thought that you are writing about at that moment, and the book will finish itself.

Concentrating, or focusing, means not letting yourself become easily distracted by trivial thoughts or desires, like sex, drugs, alcohol, TV, or video games that don't move you closer to your purpose and goals. There will be plenty of time to play, but you have played long enough; it's time to get serious and focus on some mission or goal of spiritual importance.

4.   The fourth aspect of spiritual practice is Study.

To be free, you must think free. To think free, you must educate yourself. To educate yourself, you must read.

This applies to spiritual studies as well. You must spend as much time studying the philosophy and meaning of life, religion, and God, as you do with your rap music, video games, TV, or basketball. In fact, you should be spending more time on spiritual studies than these other distractions, because none of these distractions will move you any closer to the completion of your mission and purpose; but your spiritual studies can.

Study some spiritual teachings or philosophy some part of every day, for at least fifteen or twenty minutes, preferably more. And open up your spiritual horizons. In other words, if you are a Christian, learn something about Islam or Judaism or Buddhism. You will be surprised at how many similarities there are between your faith and others, and you might just learn something from one of them that will help bring you closer to God, and closer to your divine purpose.

5.   The fifth aspect of spiritual practice is Living Impeccably.

Living impeccably means carrying and conducting yourself with the bearing and dignity of a King or Prince. Living impeccably means knowing the difference between right and wrong and choosing to do the right thing, simply because it's the right thing to do, and for no other reason.

This doesn't mean living like a monk or a saint. I don't expect anyone to give up all of their vices, whatever they may be, or to live a completely sinless life. That's impossible. There's sin in every living human being, and it comes in many different shapes, sizes, and colors. However, I do expect and hope that you strive to control your vices rather than letting your vices control you.

BLACK SON RISING

Living impeccably means living in a way that doesn't bring shame to yourself or your family. That means that if you can't do it in the light, then don't do it in the dark, because everything done in the dark eventually comes to the light of truth, and it could embarrass you, your family, and the community you are trying to serve.

To live impeccably means living in emotional cleanliness. That means there can be no hidden agenda in your thoughts, words, or actions. That means you shoot straight from the heart with no personal or selfish ulterior motives.

Nor can you have any destructive emotions like anger, hatred, pride, lust, greed, vanity, envy, revenge, or jealousy attached to any part of your efforts, service, or goals. If you harbor these destructive emotions in pursuit of your mission and purpose, they are already doomed to fail, because none of these emotions are consistent with the highest attributes of God.

To live impeccably learn and apply The 24 Principles of Ma'at.

The 5 Aspects of Spiritual Practice are not meant to be easy or fun, but they can become both eventually, with sincere and consistent practice. They are only for the serious individual who has made the firm decision in his mind, body, and spirit to become a Spiritual Warrior.

Think of it this way: any man can be a reckless, ruthless, and irresponsible fool. It takes no effort whatsoever to do that. But if you want to set yourself apart from the average man, and live in a way that you and your family and community will be proud of, then the path of the Spiritual Warrior can certainly help you do that.

If you can combine these 5 spiritual practices into your daily life consistently, and use them to prepare for your upcoming struggle for freedom for yourself and your people, then you will be well on your way to becoming a true Spiritual Warrior.

32

PROTECTING THE BLACK QUEEN

Honor, Respect, and Protect the Black Woman

Obviously, the most oppressed of any oppressed group will be its women.
- **Lorraine Hansbury, Dramatist**

The biggest mistake the Black man ever made, and continues to make to this day, is allowing anyone and everyone, including himself, to disrespect, abuse, and misuse our Black women, the Queen-Mothers of the Black race.

There is no denying that Black men have a legitimate complaint about being oppressed by the white power structure in this country. No intelligent person could argue otherwise. Every reasonably educated person on the planet knows that Black men have been brutalized and marginalized, in this society, from the days of slavery up to this present day.

However, Black men tend to forget or ignore the fact that Black women have been just as oppressed and exploited as Black men, if not more so.

In fact, in many ways, Black women have had it worse, because they've been born with two strikes against them instead of one: being Black *and* being a woman, for their race *and* gender have been used as both a social *and* sexual weapon against them.

A lot of Black men resent the current level of success that Black women are experiencing. These men overlook the fact that long before experiencing any significant degree of success in the work place, Black women suffered the worst acts of mental, physical, and economic oppression in the bedroom, in the boardroom, and in the home.

She has been used as a sexual toy by lustful white slave masters, and as a punching bag by cowardly, insecure Black men.

She has been forced to serve as a white woman's servant and nanny for white babies, while her own children were starved and neglected.

She has been sexually molested and physically abused by her own fathers and brothers, the same men who were supposed to protect her.

She has been stepped on, used up, abandoned, and left unprotected by Black men, after giving these ungrateful men her heart, her body, her mind, and her soul.

She has been socially manipulated and psychologically conditioned to undermine the strength of the Black man and the structure of the Black family, in order to keep the Black race in check.

She has had to watch her fathers, husbands, and children beaten, lynched, killed, and thrown in prison by white supremacists, for no other reason than the color of their skin.

She has been forced to assume the unenviable role as the "head of the house" and surrogate father in the Black family, because Black men are dying in streets or rotting in prisons.

She has been told, even by our own men, that she is good for nothing except cleaning up someone else's dirt, satisfying our physical desires, and making babies that Black men sire and then abandon.

BLACK SON RISING

She has had to standby and watch as her co-workers, usually some incompetent but pretty young White women, get promoted over her even though she trained them for their positions and had significantly more time on the job.

She has been told that her skin color is too black, her hair is too nappy, her lips are too thick, her butt is too big, and her hips are too wide, and that she doesn't fit the European standard of beauty found in flat-chested, bone-thin, and blue-eyed so-called "supermodels."

She has been cast as either a lazy, trifling, and irresponsible welfare queen who would rather watch soap operas than look for a job, or as a gold-digging, money-hungry hoochy who will suck men dry of every penny they own.

She has been labeled and mislabeled every negative thing in the book: ho, tramp, heifer, and slut – usually by some trifling, insecure Black man – all the while making sure her Black children were loved, fed, clothed, and nurtured above all else.

She has had to endure all of this. And still she rises.

What is the source of her incredible strength and resilience?
How is it that she is able to stand, with so many forces working to bring her to her knees?
What is this power that allows her to persist, when all reasonable logic dictates that she should just lie down and die?
Who is this Black woman?

She is the Black Queen, the mother of the human race, the backbone of the Black family, and God's greatest, most precious gift to mankind.

There is an old saying, "People who suffer the most are the strongest. Their very existence is proof of this fact."

If that statement is true, and I believe that it is, then by definition Black women are the strongest people on the planet, for who have suffered more than they?

Black men need to stop whining and crying about their condition, and take a lesson from Black women on how to suffer, bleed, and cry, and keep on stepping. Black men think that Black women are purposely trying to replace them as the "breadwinner" and "head of the household."

Contrary to popular belief, Black women don't resent the power and success that Black men have achieved. In fact they welcome it.

Black women are still waiting for Black men to step up to the plate and resume their rightful places as the head of the Black family. However, Black men are too busy trying to be thugs, gangstas, playas, pimps, and hustlas, to assume their traditional roles as the "men" of the house, instead of the "boyz" in the hood.

Black women have no desire to take Black men's place as the breadwinner and the head of the house.

It is only the insecurity of the Black male ego, resulting from fear, ignorance, and emotional immaturity, that causes Black men to feel inferior in the face of the Black woman's success, and keeps the Black man from standing alongside the Black woman, instead of falling behind her as she climbs higher and higher.

Protecting the Black Queen

Black women are not a threat to Black men. They are not our enemies. In fact, they have always been our greatest supporters, and our greatest source of inspiration.

Have you forgotten that it was a Black woman who raised you?

Or that it was a Black woman who loved and nurtured you?

Or that it was a Black woman who fed you and changed your nasty diapers?

Or that it was a Black woman working two jobs, while going to school at night, but still made time to cook for you and wash your dirty clothes and help you with your homework?

Or that it was a Black woman who supported you when you couldn't or wouldn't support yourself?

So then why don't we honor her and respect her and protect her like any good king would do for his queen?

Instead of honoring the Black Queen, we humiliate her.

Instead of respecting the Black Queen, we despise her.

Instead of inspiring the Black Queen, we control her.

Instead of protecting the Black Queen, we violate her mind, body, and spirit.

Why?

Because in the eyes of Black men, the Black Queen has become the tool of the "white devil," the pawn of the white power structure, and a threat to Black manhood, all rolled into one.

The greatest tool of the "white devil" is the evil that Black *men* do.

The biggest pawns in this "game" are the thugs, gangstas, playas, pimps, and hustlers out here selling the "white devil's" product.

The only threat to "Black manhood" is ignorance, arrogance, and stupidity.

Truth be told, Black man, the Black Queen is the one person in the world that has always been there to cheer you on, lift you up, carry your load, and love you, unconditionally, while you learned the ways of the world.

So instead of hiding behind your ignorance, arrogance, and excuses, Black man, it's your turn to give something back to these brave, beautiful, and incredibly strong Black Queens.

It is your turn to lend her your strength, and courage, and intelligence so that she no longer has to bear the weight of the survival of the Black family on her lone, broad shoulders.

It is your turn, Black man, to assume the responsibilities of manhood that God Himself has ordained as your natural birthright and your social obligation.

It is your turn, Black man, to loudly protest against anyone who would dare disrespect the Black Queen, or otherwise cause her harm.

Instead of hiding from your so-called "Black manhood" and making excuses for letting anyone and everyone heap atrocities and insults upon her, day after day, it is your turn, Black man, to protect the Black Queen, the sparkle in God's eye, the mother of our children, the woman of our dreams, and the hope for the future of the Black race.

BLACK SON RISING

See That Black Queen?

See that Black Queen?
Love that Black Queen.
Never put another above that Black Queen.
Hold that Black Queen.
Don't try to mold or scold that Black Queen.
Respect that Black Queen.
Always protect that Black Queen.
Don't neglect that Black Queen,
Or disrespect that Black Queen.

See that Black Queen?
Admire that Black Queen.
Desire that Black Queen.
Be inspired by that Black Queen .
Use your mind to set fire to that Black Queen.
Bow your head and pray with that Black Queen.
Remember to stay with that Black Queen.
Stop trying to just lay with that Black Queen.
Never mind what they say about that Black Queen,
No other will ever make your day like that Black Queen.

33

HONORING THY FATHER (GOD)

Pay Your Love and Respect to God Before All Others

The one thing more than anything else that I wish for you is to discover that you are not alone, and that the stranger in the fire with you is God. That discovery is the discovery of God in your life and work, and I could wish no greater discovery for you – here and now – than that, and when you have discovered that, you have discovered everything.
- **Peter J. Gomes, Minister**

Black men honor the pimped-out cars they drive with their ridiculous spinning rims; they honor the gear they wear with the rich White man's name on the label; they honor their sports icons and their music gods and goddesses; they even honor the big screen TVs and the video games that they are mindlessly plugged into for hours at a time; Black men honor every thing you can think of, except the one thing they should be honoring: God, their Father.

Go into any Black church, on any given Sunday, and what do you see: pews full of grandmothers, mothers, and daughters, representing 3 or 4 generations of strong Black women. Nearly 75% of the congregation in "Black Churches" are Black women.

Where are the Black men?

If they are not in the church, the temple, the mosque, or the synagogue, where are they?

Why have Black men abandoned God?

Have we lost faith in God, or have we lost faith in the institutions (i.e., the churches) that are supposed to represent God?

If we have lost faith in the institutions like the Black Church, I can understand that because "the Black Church is itself in a struggle for its collective soul - to find itself in an age when it is consumed by the God of materialism." Few, if any of these churches seem willing or inclined to reach out to Black men in the places that Black men need them the most: *in the streets of poor, drug-filled and gang-infested neighborhoods.*

However, if they have lost faith in God, that's a much more serious dilemma, because you can still Honor God without necessarily going to a church or temple.

Should you support the churches and the temples in your community?

Absolutely, as long as they are fulfilling the spiritual needs of their congregations.

But do you need to be in a church or temple to Honor God?

Absolutely not!

You Honor God, the Father, not by showing up to church service one day out of the week, because you were to busy for Him the other six days.

You Honor God, the Father, not by giving lip service to the prayers the pastor has you recite, that you don't really understand or feel.

You Honor God, the Father, not by dropping a few coins in the collection plates that seem to get passed around more than the "Word of God" itself.

No, you Honor God, the Father, simply by raising the children you sire, instead of abandoning them to the streets, just because you weren't ready to be a father, but you were ready to be a "man" when you laid down with that sister.

You Honor God, the Father, simply by protecting our Black mothers, sisters, and daughters, instead of letting anybody and everybody disrespect them, or otherwise do them harm.

You Honor God, the Father, simply by spending as much time giving thought to His Divine Purpose for you, as you do the video games or the sports channels you just can't seem to get away from.

You Honor God, the Father, simply by putting as much effort into trying to understand His Word, as you do the word of some thugged-out, highed-up gangsta rapper who isn't even half a man, let alone half a dollar.

You Honor God, the Father, simply by taking advantage of the numerous opportunities for you to succeed, that have been laid out before you and bought with the blood, sweat, tears, and lives of Black freedom fighters, like Malcolm and Martin.

You Honor God, the Father, simply by preserving and respecting and living life, instead of doing everything you can to destroy life, including yours and everybody else's, just because you *think* you got a raw deal in life.

You Honor God, the Father, simply by growing in knowledge and wisdom, and applying that knowledge and wisdom to change the world for the better, instead of growing in ignorance and stupidity and adding to the problems of the world.

You Honor God, the Father, simply by honoring your commitments and your responsibilities to your children, your family, and your community.

You Honor God, the Father, simply by living and walking in His example of Mercy, Kindness, Compassion, Truth, Peace, Justice, Wisdom, and Love. That's how you Honor the Father. That's how you Honor God.

Losing Faith

But how do you Honor God, if you don't even believe He exists?

That's a much tougher question to answer.

I don't pretend to be a theologian or religious philosopher, so I'm not sure I'm really qualified to answer that question in any meaningful way that might be useful to anyone struggling with this matter of faith.

Let me just say this: I think that deep down inside, every man *knows* that there is a power in the universe greater than he is, and that Someone or Something created the world in which we live.

Yet, it's hard to come to grips with the concept of an All-Powerful, All-Merciful, and All-Loving God, when everything around is going to hell, and dramatically contradicts God's presence in the world.

It's no secret that a lot of people are living some pretty horrible existences. There are so many people suffering in this world that it's easy to see why anyone would question God's existence:

- People are being burned and raped and tortured because of their race or religion.
- People's children are being kidnapped, molested, and murdered.
- Thousands of people are dying every day because nations are at war over financial greed and bad politics.
- Children are suffering from poverty, famine, and disease.
- Plagues like AIDS have destroyed the lives of millions of innocent people.

Honoring Thy Father (God)

Let's be real: the world we live in is a very scary place to be in right now. In fact, it always has been, but things seem to be getting worse every day.

And in the midst of all of that death, disease, and destruction, we're supposed to believe that there is a God somewhere who loves us unconditionally? A lot of Black men "ain't" buying it. Truthfully, I don't blame them.

It's easy for people to talk about how much they love God, and how much God loves them, when their lives are full of wealth and peace and prosperity.

You don't have to look any further than the Book of Job in the Bible, to see a perfect example of the this kind of "I love God and God loves me as long as everything is perfect in my life" mentality.

But try telling that young Brother whose father is doing 25 to life for killing his crack-addict mother, that there is a God.

Try telling that young Brother who's getting gang-raped in prison every day, by 3 or 4 of his so-called "boyz from the hood" that there is a God.

Try telling that young Brother that witnessed his best friend get his brains blown out the back of his head over some stupid, petty crap game, that there is a God.

Try telling that young Brother that has to watch rich White men get richer despite the evil that they do, while his poor but honest and hard-working Black family gets poorer, that there is a God.

Try telling that Black mother who just lost her 3rd son to gang violence, and her only daughter to drugs and prostitution, that there is a God.

With all that pain, misery, and chaos going on, who can believe in God, let alone Honor Him?

I tell you truthfully:

There is a God, and all the death, disease, and destruction, and all the pain, misery, and chaos we see in the world, is the suffering that man, through his God-given power of choice and his self-centered arrogance, creates for himself.

We can't blame God for the suffering we see in the world.

God told man,

I will love you unconditionally, no matter what you do, but if you allow Me to, I will show you the way to peace, freedom, love, joy, and eternal life. All you have to do is follow My example. However, I will not make you choose My Way. But be forewarned, My Son, if you go your own way, and you choose your way of life over Mine, there will be dire conse-quences for your actions. Not of My making, but of yours, for I have given you the Power of Free Will. You can choose the Light of My uncon-ditional Love, or you can choose the darkness of your own selfish desires, but the choice is yours. Know this, My Son: whatever you decide to do, I will always Love you, and you can always come home to My Light, for the Light is in Me, and the Light is of Me, and the Light is by Me, and that Light is My Love which shines forever and ever, until the end of time.

Black men, I know how bad you are suffering out here in the streets and in the "hoods." I know from firsthand experience how painful it is to watch the people you love die from poverty, drug addiction, and black-on-black crime and violence.

BLACK SON RISING

I know how easy it is, and has been, to turn your back on God, because you think he has turned His back on you.

But have you stopped to consider that if every man, woman, and child on this planet were to follow the example God set for you, and live and walk in His Mercy, Kindness, Compassion, Truth, Peace, Justice, Wisdom, and Love, that world suffering would end in a day?

This is God's greatest hope and desire for mankind, that one day man will wake up to the truth of the darkness that *he* has created, and using his God-given Power of Choice, choose the Light of God's unconditional Love.

A minister in the Nation of Islam once said:

The mind of the Black man must look heavenward, not necessarily into the sky dreaming of some metaphysical land of milk and honey where angels with wings fly peacefully. Black men must elevate their thinking, as the Honorable Minister Louis Farrakhan has stressed, into the thinking of God, Himself.

God is a righteous God. The Black man must seek to become righteous. God is a producer. The Black man must become productive. God loves. The Black man must seek to demonstrate love, particularly for himself.

I believe this statement to be true for all men, but for Black men especially.

We can no longer afford to ignore God's example and continue perpetrating the evil that we see White men do. They will pay for their arrogance and their evil ways, I can assure you of that. And so will we, if we keep following in their selfish and arrogant footsteps. The law of reaping and sowing is unbreakable, and you cannot escape it. I don't care who you are, or what you own, or what you do, *you will pay for your actions*! One way or another.

I believe that God put the Black man, the "hue-man," the first man on this planet for a reason:

To be the shining, living example of how men should live and walk with God. I believe that in his natural state, prior to his fall into ignorance and arrogance, the Black man was the living example of God on earth, and that he honored his Father in the ways the Father desired to be honored.

I believe that God is calling us back to his example, and that the Black man is the only one who can restore the light of peace, love, and justice to this world of darkness.

I believe all of these things with my whole heart.

However, regardless of what I might believe about God, or what I might think about God's plan for man, I can't tell you what's right for your life. No man can or should.

But I am exercising my Power of Choice, and I'm choosing the Light, and I'm Honoring my Father, my God.

34

BREAKING THE CYCLE

Organizational Strategies for
Breaking the Cycle of Black-on-Black Crime and Violence

There is nothing more dangerous than to build a society with a large segment of people in that society who feel they have no stake in it, who feel that they have nothing to lose. People who have a stake in their society protect that society, but when they don't have it, they unconsciously want to destroy it.
- **Marcus Garvey, Nationalist Leader**

Black-on-black crime and violence has reached epidemic proportions in the Black community, and each of us as individuals has had our hand in perpetuating the cycle. Homicide is the number one killer of Black males between 15 and 24 years of age. There are more Black men in prison than there are in all of the colleges and universities combined.

This is a national crisis!

However, as we have learned throughout *Black Son Rising*, this cycle can be broken and this crisis can be averted!

In the last 15 chapter essays (*chapters 19 through 33*), I have described to you ways in which you as an individual can free yourself from the fear, false pride, social ignorance, mental laziness, self-hatred, and misplaced anger that keep you enslaved to your violent and criminal behavior. It is absolutely essential that you continue to do your part and do the difficult work to become a better man, a better father, a better son, a better mate, and a better human being overall, in order to help break the cycle of black-on-black crime and violence.

However, I never said that doing your part was going to be easy, and I never said you had to try to do this difficult work all by yourself.

Remember, there is strength in numbers, and a community of people working together for a common goal can be far more effective than one person acting alone. That's why it's vitally important that we not only work on ourselves by ourselves, but that we join forces with and seek out community support that can help us overcome many of the difficult challenges we face as Black men in America.

As Black males living in a racially hostile nation, we are constantly bombarded by socioeconomic conditions that place us at-risk for poverty, crime, violence, substance abuse, unemployment, and incarceration. We are going to need all the help we can get to assist us in overcoming these numerous overwhelming challenges. Therefore, we need to focus on developing a comprehensive array of social and community service programs that addresses our unique needs.

These service programs should be a combination of a faith-based, community-based, and correctional-based strategies and activities that focus on knowledge building skills, and social and moral development skills for Black males who are at-risk for crime, violence, and incarceration.

Reversing the Reactionary Masculinity Mindset in Black Males

According the late Professor Amos N. Wilson, to reduce black-on-black crime and violence, we have to first implement programs and strategies that can reverse the "reactionary masculinity" in Black males that gives rise to crime and violence. Professor Wilson theorized that,

If the characteristics of reactionary masculinity are to be reversed and prevented, then educational, communal, and manhood training programs should include as an important part of their programmatic mission the objectives listed below:

1. Identify the idea of masculinity with African-centeredness and consciousness, the idea of African communalism and a commitment to African collective goals; a sense of social responsibility and interest.

2. Associate masculinity with social service, community uplift and defense; with reason, sensitivity, tolerance, patience, flexibility, creativity, generosity; with productivity, economic self-sufficiency, teamwork, cooperation, reliability, trustworthiness, honor and courage; with the ability to attain and maintain feelings of love and intimacy for women, children, and males.

3. Encourage males to be motivated by positive drives and to strive for positive goals instead of by negative drives such as inordinate fear, anger, vanity, feelings of inadequacy and inferiority, and the need to "prove" masculinity.

4. Associate masculinity with self-control, the mastery of knowledge, technique, technology, craft and skills; with intellectual development, self-actualization, and positive interpersonal skills.

5. Encourage masculine self-definition in terms of productivity and nurturance instead of conspicuous consumption, parasitic exploitation, and faddish fashions.

6. Identify masculinity with self-determination, taking responsibility for personal failures as well as success.

7. Resist using avoidance, escape, withdrawal and retreat; evasion and denial, projection of false superiority complex, as methods of dealing with problems and painful, unpleasant, or unflattering situations.

8. Recognize that sexuality, sensuality and pleasurable excitements are important parts of life and among many of its important pursuits but not the whole life, not its only ends; that these passions can be the by-products of many other productive, positive personal and

social vocations and activities; that the mate is the person of equal value to oneself and is due all the deep respect and consideration, freedoms and privileges one demands for oneself; that children are to be nurtured and cared for and not merely utilized to demonstrate sexual prowess and sexual seductiveness.

Launching Minority Teacher Recruitment Campaigns

A number of studies, most notably those conducted by Dr. Jawanza Kunjufu in his world renowned publication, *Countering the Conspiracy to Destroy Black Boys*, have demonstrated that young Black boys are more positively responsive in educational environments where the teacher looks like them. Therefore, efforts to recruit, train, and employ Black male teachers could prove to be an effective deterrent to antisocial and criminal behavior in adolescent Black males.

Providing Transitional Services for Ex-Offenders

To reduce adult offender recidivism rates and assist them with their successful re-entry back into society, we need to provide them with the critical services that can make the difference between staying out of prison and being re-incarcerated, over and over again.

The transitional services needed by most ex-offenders include:

- Transitional Housing Placement
- Job Readiness Training
- Job Placement Assistance
- Drivers License Restoration Assistance
- GED Certification/College Preparation
- Life Skills Training
- Effective Parenting Workshops
- Vocational Training
- Computer Literacy Training
- Child Support Arrears Counseling
- Credit Repair Counseling
- Time and Money Management Training

Developing Micro-Enterprise Training Programs

The employment outlook for the country as a whole is uncertain, and job opportunities are scarce for adults without a felony record. How much more scarce are they for ex-offenders who have a felony conviction?

To address the issue of limited job opportunities for ex-offenders, we need to focus on developing micro-enterprise training programs and other entrepreneurial training programs that give adult ex-offenders the opportunity to start and manage their own small businesses. So that, instead of relying on and waiting for job prospects from employers who are reluctant to hire individuals with criminal records, the ex-offen- ders can become employers themselves and productive contributing members of society.

Providing Programs for Juvenile Offenders and At-Risk Youth

Juvenile offenders, and other at-risk youth, need a wide array of mentoring, counseling, and intervention programs to preclude them from becoming adult offenders and perpetuating the cycle. These programs need to address adolescent Black male behavior at all stages of their development, including:

- Long before they ever have negative contact with the criminal justice system
- After their initial contact with the criminal justice system
- Throughout their short-term and long-term detention
- Immediately upon their release from detention
- As part of an ongoing therapeutic remedy after their detention
- Throughout the remainder of their adolescent development

The mentoring, counseling, and intervention programs should include:

1. Character Education & Manhood Training Programs
2. Mentoring Programs
3. Life Skills and Social Skills Training
4. School-based Anger Management & Conflict Resolution Workshops
5. Intensive Case Management Programs
6. Early Detection & Intervention Programs
7. Violent Youth and Gang Outreach Programs

1.   Character Education & Manhood Training Programs

Many of our Black males, youth and adults alike, embrace a false, negative, destructive perception of what it means to be a "man." As we have learned from Professor Wilson's "reactionary masculinity" theory, this false perception of manhood often results in violent and criminal behavior. Males prone to reactionary masculinity often lack the moral and social character skills that allow them to have positive interactions with others, especially other Black males, outside their immediate peer group.

This type of program incorporates moral and social character education into a manhood (rites of passage) training program, by associating manhood with the tenets of moral and social character such as: discipline, respect, responsibility, courage, compassion, integrity, self-control, assertiveness, cultural pride, strong work ethics, and a sense of civic duty.

The curriculum activities can be designed to engage Black males around issues related to:

- Manhood & Masculinity
- Fatherhood & Absentee Fathers

- Conflict Resolution
- Anger & Rage
- Decision Making
- Loss and Grief
- Thug and Gangsta Mentality

2. Mentoring Programs

Mentors provide a positive, caring influence and standard of conduct for other youth. Mentors provide models for young people who have no models or they offer alternatives to negative role models. The attention and interest bestowed on the youngster by a peer who cares can enhance the youth's self-esteem, strengthening his ability to choose non-violent methods to resolve conflicts.

The mentoring programs should be designed to:

- Reduce juvenile delinquency and gang participation by at-risk youth.

- Improve academic performance of at-risk youth.

- Reduce the school dropout rate for at-risk youth.

- Provide general guidance and support to at-risk youth.

- Promote personal and social responsibility among at-risk youth.

- Discourage use of illegal drugs and firearms, involvement in violence, and other delinquent activity by at-risk youth.

- Discourage involvement of at-risk youth in gangs.

- Encourage participation in service and community activities by at-risk youth.

3. Life Skills and Skills Training

Teaching Black males social skills provides them with the ability to interact with others in positive and constructive ways. Aspects of social-skills training include self-control, communication skills, forming friendships, resisting peer pressure, being appropriately assertive, and forming honest and trusting relationships with adults.

4. School-based Anger Management & Conflict Resolution Workshops

School-based workshops are used as group intervention designed to reduce future conduct problems, delinquency, and substance abuse in adolescent Black males with a history of aggressive behavior. Classes in conflict resolution are designed to provide adolescent Black males with the opportunity to develop empathy with others, learn ways to control impulses, develop problem solving skills, and manage their anger. The methods used to teach conflict resolution usually include role-playing of conflict situations and analyzing the responses and consequences to violence.

Reinforcement and feedback are used to support skill acquisition. Groups are led by highly trained workshop facilitators. The program lessons are designed to improve perspective-taking skills, affect recognition, develop self-control, social problem solving, and social skills strategies for managing conflict situations.

5. Intensive Case Management Programs

Intensive Case Management (ICM) programs for high-risk adolescent males, are intensive, home-based, family-oriented programs that address the males behavioral problems in the context of their families and wider communities. Highly individualized treatment plans are developed.

ICM programs provide an intensive assessment period that enables caseworkers to more readily identify and coordinate the resources needed to deal with high-risk males. The caseworker meets regularly with family members and school personnel and may call on outside experts, including psychologists and substance-abuse counselors, when needed.

The close and intensive daily contact allows caseworkers to closely track the adolescent males progress and any obstacles that arise, and enables caseworkers to function as mentors and role models, offering consistent guidance and support.

6. Early Detection & Intervention Programs

Early intervention programs are an effective tool for identifying and precluding the potential for violence and/or delinquent behavior in adolescent Black males. The programs are designed to nip future behavioral problems in the bud by recognizing, acknowledging, and then treating those youth who exhibit the early warning signs of maladaptive and antisocial behavior.

The program is initiated at the time of their first criminal adjudication. It assigns one caseworker to each youth for an intensive and comprehensive programmatic agenda. Caseworkers intervene directly with parents in an attempt to model appropriate parenting techniques. They also develop individualized case plans using a team staff model with the goal of formulating strategies that are both creative and proactive to reduce problem behaviors.

Program participants may also undergo psychological assessments and be referred to individual, group, or family counseling services. Other activities include restitution and community services programs, academic exercises, and group events.

7. Violent Youth and Gang Outreach Programs

Youth and gang violence is particularly problematic in Black communities all across the country. To proactively address this problem, we have to develop outreach initiatives that draw upon extensive research regarding the best practices in youth and gang outreach.

The overall philosophy of the outreach program should be to provide at-risk adolescent Black males with what they seek through gang membership (supportive adults, challenging activities, and a place to belong) in an alternative, socially positive and constructive format.

There are 5 key components of the Violent Youth and Gang Outreach Programs:

1. Community mobilization of resources to combat the community gang problem.

2. Recruitment of youths that are at-risk of gang involvement (prevention) or youths already involved in gangs (intervention) through outreach and referrals.

3. Promoting positive developmental experiences for these youths by developing interest-based programs that also address the youth's specific needs through programming, and mainstreaming of youths into Clubs.

4. Providing individualized case management across four areas (law enforcement/justice, school, family, and activities) to target youths to decrease gang-related behaviors and contact with the juvenile justice system; and to increase the likelihood that they will attend school and improve academically.

5. Developing and promoting a public information and education campaign to draw greater attention, and resources, to the issue of youth and gang violence, utilizing gang workbooks, and a national youth and gang seminar that highlights the devastating effects of youth and gang violence.

Focusing Our Efforts

The programs and services outlined above are just the tip of the iceberg when it comes to implementing successful initiatives to break the cycle of black-on-black crime and violence.

We could literally implement another 1000 programs throughout the country, and it would still not be enough to address all of the issues of poverty, unemployment, illiteracy, child abuse and neglect, drug addiction, and the sense of hopelessness and despair that give rise to black-on-black crime and violence.

However, we have to recognize that to break this cycle of crime, violence, incarceration, and recidivism, we have to start somewhere. I believe that we need to focus our efforts on those areas, and on those populations, where we can have the greatest impact: *Black males at-risk for crime, violence, and incarceration.*

It's time to think and work outside the box!

That is the only way we are going to be able to break this cycle of black-on-black crime and violence, because simply locking people up and warehousing them in prison plantations does nothing to deter crime or criminals. It never has and it never will. At least not in Black communities, and not according to the black-on-black crime statistics.

Our ultimate goal should be to make all of our communities better and safer places to live for everyone in the Black community. If we focus our efforts and our resources, and start teaching these at-risk Black males the knowledge and skills they need to survive and succeed in this racially hostile nation, then we can get them off the streets, out of the drug game, out of their ignorance and slave mentality, and keep them from killing each other for nothing, and rotting their lives away in the modern day slavery called *prison.*

PART IV

THE THREE BLACK KINGS

We need leaders – neither saints nor sparkling television personalities – who can situate themselves within a larger historical narrative of this country and our world, who can grasp the complex dynamic of our peoplehood and imagine a future grounded in the best of our past, yet who are attuned to the frightening obstacles that now perplex us.
- **Cornel West, Philosopher and Activist**

35

TRIBUTE

Paying Respect to The Three Black Kings

*What we need are mental and spiritual giants who are aflame with a purpose....
We're a race ready for crusade, for we've recognized that we're a race on this
continent that can work out its own salvation.*
- **Nannie Burroughs, Civil Rights Pioneer**

There are Black men in our history who are so extraordinary that they defy all
standards of what we consider "Black manhood." These men uniquely exemplify
the true model of manhood to which all Black men should aspire. The moral
strength and courage they demonstrated despite the constant threat of physical
violence, and their willingness to assume leadership in the face of overwhelming
political and social adversity, forever defines them as Men of Honor and Respect.

On the following pages are the biographies of three such men. I call them
The Three Black Kings. They are:

Marcus Garvey, Malcolm X, and Dr. Martin Luther King, Jr.

Each of these men possessed all of the qualities and attributes that we as
Black men should strive to possess and demonstrate in our lives:

**Mental, physical, and spiritual strength; courage, intelligence, wisdom
compassion, dignity, honor, faith, truth, justice, and love.**

Brothers Marcus, Malcolm, and Martin each made monumental sacrifices
to light the way to our individual and collective freedom.

They used their moral strength and courage to overcome the challenges of
racism, discrimination, and racial oppression.

They used their extraordinary gifts and talents to touch the lives of millions
of people, Black and White.

They showed us by their living example what any Black man can
accomplish if he uses the strength, courage, and intelligence given to him by
God, toward a meaningful and worthwhile purpose.

They are truly "Kings" in every sense of the word.

BLACK SON RISING

Without their significant contributions to the struggle, I fear we would be much worse off than we are now. Thank God we never had to know what it would have been like if they had not taken the mantle of Black leadership in their hands.

It is for all of these reasons that I pay my respects to three of the greatest Black men throughout all history.

Please, study their biographies and their philosophies so that you can gain a better understanding of what it truly means to be a Man and a King.

36

MARCUS GARVEY
The Father of Contemporary Black Nationalism
(August 17, 1887 – June 10, 1940)

(source: The AfroCentric Experience at http://www.cbs.niu.edu)

Born in St. Ann's Bay, Jamaica, on August 17, 1887, Marcus Garvey was the youngest of 11 children. Garvey moved to Kingston at the age of 14, found work in a printshop, and became acquainted with the abysmal living conditions of the laboring class. He quickly involved himself in social reform, participating in the first Printers' Union strike in Jamaica in 1907 and in setting up the newspaper *The Watchman*. Leaving the island to earn money to finance his projects, he visited Central and South America, amassing evidence that black people everywhere were victims of discrimination. He visited the Panama Canal Zone and saw the conditions under which the West Indians lived and worked. He went to Ecuador, Nicaragua, Honduras, Colombia, and Venezuela. Everywhere, blacks were experiencing great hardships.

Garvey returned to Jamaica distressed at the situation in Central America, and appealed to Jamaica's colonial government to help improve the plight of West Indian workers in Central America. His appeal fell on deaf ears. Garvey also began to lay the groundwork of the Universal Negro Improvement Association, to which he was to devote his life. Undaunted by lack of enthusiasm for his plans, Garvey left for England in 1912 in search of additional financial backing. While there, he met a Sudanese-Egyptian journalist, Duse Mohammed Ali. While working for Ali's publication *African Times* and *Oriental Review,* Garvey began to study the history of Africa, particularly, the exploitation of black peoples by colonial powers. He read Booker T. Washington's *Up From Slavery,* which advocated black self-help.

In 1914 Garvey organized the Universal Negro Improvement Association and its coordinating body, the African Communities League. In 1920 the organization held its first convention in New York. The convention opened with a parade down Harlem's Lenox Avenue. That evening, before a crowd of 25,000, Garvey outlined his plan to build an African nation-state. In New York City his ideas attracted popular support, and thousands enrolled in the UNIA. He began publishing the newspaper *The Negro World* and toured the United States preaching black nationalism to popular audiences. His efforts were successful, and soon, the association boasted over 1100 branches in more than 40 countries. Most of these branches were located in the United States, which had become the UNIA's base of operations. There were, however, offices in several Caribbean countries, Cuba having the most. Branches also existed in places such as Panama, Costa Rica, Ecuador, Venezuela, Ghana, Sierra Leone, Liberia, Namibia, and South Africa. He also launched some ambitious business ventures, notably the Black Star Shipping Line.

BLACK SON RISING

In the years following the organization's first convention, the UNIA began to decline in popularity. With the Black Star Line in serious financial difficulties, Garvey promoted two new business organizations — the African Communities League and the Negro Factories Corporation. He also tried to salvage his colonization scheme by sending a delegation to appeal to the League of Nations for transfer to the UNIA of the African colonies taken from Germany during World War I.

Financial betrayal by trusted aides and a host of legal entanglements (based on charges that he had used the U.S. mail to defraud prospective investors) eventually led to Garvey's imprisonment in Atlanta Federal Penitentiary for a five-year term. In 1927 his half-served sentence was commuted, and he was deported to Jamaica by order of President Calvin Coolidge.

Garvey then turned his energies to Jamaican politics, campaigning on a platform of self-government, minimum wage laws, and land and judicial reform. He was soundly defeated at the polls, however, because most of his followers did not have the necessary voting qualifications.

In 1935, Garvey left for England where, in near obscurity, he died on June 10, 1940, in a cottage in West Kensington.

The following dialogue is an excerpt from Marcus Garvey's book entitled, *Marcus Garvey Life and Lessons*. The dialogue takes place between a Black father and his young inquisitive Black son who doesn't understand why the Black race is treated as an inferior race.

What this father tells his son is simple, yet powerful, and I wish to God that every Black man who has a son, or who is a role model to some young Black man, would sit down and read this passage with them, and then explain how important this message is to Black men and the Black race.

37

MALCOLM X

The Original "Street Soldier" of the Black Power Movement

(May 19, 1925 – February 21, 1965)

(source: The AfroCentric Experience at http://www.cbs.niu.eedu)

Malcolm X was born as Malcolm Little on May 19, 1925, in Omaha, Nebraska, the son of Louise and Earl Little. Louise Little was a mulatto born in Grenada in the British West Indies and Earl Little, a six-foot, very dark-skinned man from Reynolds, Georgia, was a Baptist minister and organizer for Marcus Garvey, who advocated that all Afro-Americans go back to the land of their ancestors, Africa.

Louise, his second wife, bore six children: Wilfred, Hilda, Philbert, Malcolm, Yvonne, and Reginald. Earl Little also had three children by a first wife: Ella, Earl, and Mary. Because of the father's advocacy for Garvey's movement, the whole family was terrorized by the Ku Klux Klan. To avoid any more harassment by these white racists, Little had to migrate with his family to Lansing, Michigan. It did not help. The white racists of Lansing killed Malcolm's father and laid him on a railway track, claiming he committed suicide. Alone and without money, Louise Little got more and more desperate, before the white authorities sent her to a mental hospital.

Malcolm attended school until eighth grade, living with different families. When his teacher stopped him from trying to become a lawyer, he dropped out of school and went to his older half sister, Ella, who lived in Boston. There, he took a job as a shoeshine boy at the Roseland Ballroom. A career as a hustler seemed a more tempting option, and he was soon peddling narcotics. He met a white girl called Laura who quickly became his girlfriend. Having a white girl and being a very good dancer, he soon was a notorious young man with crazy clothes and a haircut made to resemble the hair of white people, which he was very ashamed of later. But Roxbury proved to be too small for him, and in 1942 he took a job as a railroad dining-car porter, working out of Roxbury and New York. Settling in Harlem, New York, he became more and more involved in criminal activities. He robbed, worked as a pimp, and sold narcotics.

Malcolm soon learned to survive in the hustler society, which was constantly threatened by internal wars that could render every man your enemy. In Harlem he also got his nickname, "Detroit Red," because his home town Lansing was close to Detroit and his hair was red. After a year in Harlem, Malcolm was officially initiated into the hustler society. He returned to Boston in 1945 after falling out with another hustler, and continued a life of crime, forming his own house robbing gang. Arrested for robbery in February 1946, he was convicted and sentenced to prison for seven years.

While in prison, Malcolm became a follower of Elijah Muhammad, the leader of the "Nation of Islam," with branches in Detroit, Chicago, and New York. Malcolm and Elijah Muhammad corresponded by mail. Malcolm's brothers Philbert and Reginald, visiting him in prison, urged him to join Muhammad's "Nation of Islam" and while still in prison he did. He discarded his "slave name," Little, and took the new name "X." He improved his poor knowledge by reading encyclopedias and studying plenty of books as well as the Koran and followed strictly the Nation of Islam's dietary laws and moral codes.

After his parole in 1952, Malcolm X undertook organizational work for the "Nation of Islam" under the guidance of Elijah Muhammad. Minister Malcolm X founded mosques in Boston, Philadelphia, Harlem, and elsewhere and made the national expansion of the movement possible, so that the membership reached approximately 30,000 in 1963. Malcolm X's vision was expressed in speeches, a newspaper column, as well as radio and television interviews. In addition, he helped to found the Black Muslim newspaper "Muhammad Speaks." Minister Malcolm X was said to be the only Black person who "could stop a race riot-or start one." In January 1958 he married Betty X, who was also a member of the Nation of Islam.

Because of his success, other Ministers of the "Nation of Islam" grew jealous. Elijah Muhammad also began to be afraid of his best Minister who proved to be more famous than he himself. So, partly because of these tensions within the Black Muslim movement, Malcolm became critical of Elijah Muhammad. He was eventually "silenced" for 90 days after commenting on the assassination of President John F. Kennedy with the phrase "chickens come home to roost." But before his silence was lifted, Malcolm X left the Nation of Islam to form the Muslim Mosque, Inc. in March 1964. He began to advocate a more pragmatic black nationalism and said that blacks should control the politics within their own community and, through his speeches, encouraged his followers to make changes by voting.

At the height of his power Malcolm X was one of black America's most powerful voices. He had enormous influence among black youth and in progressive intellectual circles. He traveled widely in Europe and Africa and established his Organization of Afro-American Unity. He saw the black American struggle partly as a segment of the efforts of African, Caribbean, and other disadvantaged nations' struggles for human rights.

In 1964, Malcolm X went on his pilgrimage to Mecca, which is obligatory for orthodox Muslims, and there he began to consider changing his views toward integration. In Mecca, he saw that it was possible for black and white people to live in brotherhood, and he was deeply touched. After the pilgrimage, he adopted the name El-Hajj Malik El-Shabazz.

The angry members of the Nation of Islam began to threaten to kill him. His home in Queens, New York, which Malcolm X shared with his wife and his six children was firebombed in early February 1965. When Malcolm X was delivering a speech in the Audubon Ballroom in Harlem on February 21, 1965, he was shot down by Black Muslims; but it is widely suspected that there were higher powers behind his murder.

On the following pages is a portion of the speech Malcolm delivered on February 14, 1965, at the Ford Auditorium in Detroit, the very night that his home in New York was firebombed. Because of the length of the entire speech, I have only included his closing remarks, which are full of the fire and brilliance that Malcolm was known for.

38

DR. MARTIN LUTHER KING, JR.
The Leader of the Civil Rights Movement
(January 15, 1929 – April 4, 1968)

(source: The AfroCentric Experience at http://www.cbs.niu.eedu)

Martin Luther King, Jr., was born on Tuesday, January 15, 1929, at the family home, 501 Auburn Avenue, N.E., Atlanta, Georgia. Dr. Charles Johnson was the attending physician. Martin Luther King, Jr., was the first son and second child born to the Reverend Martin Luther King, Sr., and Alberta Williams King. Other children born to the Kings were Christine King Farris and the late Reverend Alfred Daniel Williams King. Martin Luther King's maternal grandparents were the Reverend Adam Daniel Williams, second pastor of Ebenezer Baptist, and Jenny Parks Williams. His paternal grandparents, James Albert and Delia King, were sharecroppers on a farm in Stockbridge, Georgia.

He married the former Coretta Scott, younger daughter of Obadiah and Bernice McMurray Scott of Marion, Alabama, on June 18, 1953. The marriage ceremony took place on the lawn of the Scott's home in Marion. The Reverend King, Sr., performed the service, with Mrs. Edythe Bagley, the sister of Mrs. King, maid of honor, and the Reverend A.D. King, the brother of Martin Luther King, Jr., best man.

Four children were born to Dr. and Mrs. King: Yolanda Denise (November 17, 1955, Montgomery, Alabama); Martin Luther III (October 23, 1957, Montgomery, Alabama); Dexter Scott (January 30, 1961, Atlanta, Georgia); Bernice Albertine (March 28, 1963, Atlanta, Georgia). He graduated from Booker T. Washington H.S. at 15 and Morehouse College at 19. He earned a Masters at 22 from Crozier and a Ph.D from Boston University at 26.

Martin Luther King entered the Christian ministry and was ordained in February 1948 at the age of nineteen at Ebenezer Baptist Church, Atlanta, Georgia. Following his ordination, he became Assistant Pastor of Ebenezer. Upon completion of his studies at Boston University, he accepted the call of Dexter Avenue Baptist Church, Montgomery, Alabama. He was the pastor of Dexter Avenue from September 1954 to November 1959, when he resigned to move to Atlanta to direct the activities of the Southern Christian Leadership Conference. From 1960 until his death in 1968, he was co-pastor with his father at Ebenezer Baptist Church and President of the Southern Christian Leadership Conference.

Dr. King was a pivotal figure in the Civil Rights Movement. He was elected president of the Montgomery Improvement Association, the organization which was responsible for the successful Montgomery Bus Boycott from 1955 to 1956 (381 days). He was arrested thirty times for his participation in civil rights activities. He was a founder and president of Southern Christian Leadership Conference from 1957 to 1968. He was also vice president of the national Sunday

BLACK SON RISING

School and Baptist Teaching Union Congress of the National Baptist Convention. He was a member of several national and local boards of directors and served on the boards of trustees of several institutions and agencies. Dr. King was elected to membership in several learned societies including the prestigious American Academy of Arts and Sciences.

Dr. King was shot while standing on the balcony of the Lorraine Motel in Memphis, Tennessee, on April 4, 1968, by James Earl Ray. James Earl Ray was arrested in London, England, on June 8, 1968, and returned to Memphis, Tennessee, to stand trial for the assassination of Dr. King. On March 9, 1969, before coming to trial, he entered a guilty plea and was sentenced to ninety-nine years in the Tennessee State Penitentiary. Dr. King had been in Memphis to help lead sanitation workers in a protest against low wages and intolerable conditions. His funeral services were held April 9, 1968, in Atlanta at Ebenezer Church and on the campus of Morehouse College, with the President of the United States proclaiming a day of mourning and flags being flown at half-staff. The area where Dr. King was entombed is located on Freedom Plaza and surrounded by the Freedom Hall Complex of the Martin Luther King, Jr., Center for Nonviolent Social Change, Inc. The Martin Luther King, Jr., Historic Site, a 23 acre area, was listed as a National Historic Landmark on May 5, 1977, and was made a National Historic Site on October 10, 1980, by the U.S. Department of the Interior.

PART V

THE FINAL CALL!

If there is no struggle, there is no progress. Those who profess to favor freedom, and yet depreciate agitation, are men who want crops without plowing up the ground. They want rain without thunder and lightning. They want the ocean without the awful roar of its many waters. This struggle may be a moral one, or it may be a physical one, or it may be both moral and physical, but it must be a struggle. Power concedes nothing without a demand. It never has and it never will.
- **Frederick Douglass, Abolitionist**

39

UNIFY OR DIE!

Black Power is a call for black people of this country to unite, to recognize their heritage, to build a sense of community.
- **Stokley Carmichael, Black Panther Party Leader**

Wake Up, Black Man! Prison is modern day slavery!

The laws and policies of this country - written by White men, for White men - were designed to rob Black men of their freedom, their respect, and their manhood.

We as Black men have to stop giving them that power!

That means as Black men, we have to stop giving the white law makers, and the white law enforcers, the excuse to put us where they want us anyway: *in graves or in prisons.*

That means as Black men, we have to put down the glocks and the gats, the AKs and the Mac10s, the "crunk" and the crack, the pills and smack, and the 40 ounces and the 5ths, that are killing our Black families and Black communities.

That means as Black men, we have to break free from our ignorance, and our slave mentality, and our false sense of manhood, to escape the traps and pitfalls that the *"whips"* have created for our demise.

That means as Black men, we have to stop making excuses for our negative, destructive, and irresponsible behavior, and start finding positive, constructive, and responsible solutions to the drugs, the crime, and the violence that are plaguing the Black race.

That means as Black men, we have to start becoming strong, courageous, intelligent, and responsible protectors of the Black race, instead of drug-dealing, gun-toting, gang-banging, back-stabbing murderers of our own people.

That means we have to Unify or Die!

Wake Up, Black Man!

You are being *used* as a pawn of the white racist power structure to commit Black racial genocide!

Every time a Black man goes to prison, that's one less Black man to raise and support his Black children.

Every time you abandon your child, and your child's mother, you are reinforcing negative stereotypes of Black men as immature, irresponsible, trifling, and disloyal fathers and mates.

Every time you commit a crime of violence, you are reinforcing negative stereotypes of Black men as ruthless, dangerous, and out-of-control hoodlums.

Every time you sell crack, cocaine, heroin, or some other dangerous drug to another Black man or women, you are helping to destroy at least two generations of Black families.

Every time you put a liquor bottle to your lips, or a crack pipe in your mouth, or a heroin needle in your veins, you weaken your mind, body, and spirit, and destroy any chance of uplifting yourself, your children, the Black family, or the Black community.

Every time you kill another Black man, you are killing another potential Black father, and making it more difficult for the Black race to reproduce itself.

Every time you kill another Black man, you are killing the next Malcolm X, Marcus Garvey, Dr. Martin Luther King, Jr., or some other potential great Black leader.

Every time you kill another Black man, you are helping the white racist power structure is this country, and hate groups like the KKK become more powerful.

Black men, we have two extremely powerful enemies in this country that are hell bent on our destruction. I call them the *Evil Twin Sisters*. They are:

The criminal (in)justice system and the prison industrial complex, both of which are owned, operated, and funded by the white racist power structure.

The Evil Twin Sisters and everybody who works for them are making money hand over fist off of your misery and continued slavery. That includes the cops, the lawyers, the judges, the parole/probation agents, the correctional officers, and the privatized prison corporations.

We as Black men have the power to break the back of The Evil Twin Sisters, and put all of these modern day slave plantation owners and overseers out of business, permanently.

How do we do that? Simple:

STOP GIVING THEM THE POWER AND THE EXCUSE AND THE REASON TO TAKE AWAY YOUR FREEDOM, YOUR RESPECT, AND YOUR MANHOOD!

In other words:

STOP BREAKING THE LAW!
STOP COMMITTING CRIMES!
STOP PUTTING YOURSELF IN HARM'S WAY!
STOP MAKING YOURSELF AN EASY TARGET!

Think about it:

If we make up the majority of the people getting arrested, prosecuted, sentenced, convicted, and incarcerated, doesn't it stand to reason that if we stop giving the system the excuse to arrest us and put us in prison that the system would eventually break down and fall apart?

Don't forget that Black men make up 60% of the entire prison population.

Hell, we are the criminal justice system and the prison industrial complex! That means they need police to arrest us, prosecutors to prosecute us, defense attorneys to defend us, judges to hear our cases, prisons to house us, correctional officers to oversee us, and parole/probation officers to keep us in line after we are released.

If they are not locking up Brothers, who are they gonna lock up, White folks?

Yeah, right!

If we stop killing each other and selling drugs, who will the FBI, DEA, ATF, and the local and state law enforcement agencies investigate and arrest?

If there are no more Black men to arrest, they don't need police officers!

If there are no more Black men to charge with crimes, they don't need prosecuting attorneys!

If there are no more Black men to defend in court, they don't need public defenders!

If there are no more Black men to bring to court, they don't need judges!

If there are no more Black men to convict for crimes, they don't need prisons!

If there are no more Black men to send to prison, they don't need correctional officers or parole/probation officers!

We can break the back of The Evil Twin Sisters without raising a finger!

All we have to do is stop doing what gives them the power and excuse to rob us of our freedom, our respect, and our manhood!

I'm challenging all you Brothers, right here and right now, to protest against The Evil Twin Sisters.

Here's my challenge:

STOP ASSAULTING EACH OTHER, STOP STEALING FROM EACH OTHER, STOP ROBBING EACH OTHER, STOP KILLING EACH OTHER, AND STOP SELLING THE WHITE MAN'S POISON, FOR JUST 1 YEAR!

If we stop all of these criminal and violent activities for just 1 year, I guarantee you that the criminal (in)justice system and the prison industrial complex will slowly begin to crumble and break down!

The Evil Twin Sisters are like two big grizzly bears living in the same woods. If the bears run out of food long enough and get hungry enough, they will eventually turn on each other, start fighting each other, and start eating their own cubs.

Similarly, if there are no more Black men to investigate, arrest, prosecute, and incarcerate, The Evil Twin Sisters will eventually start turning on themselves and start eating their own children.

That means in order for them to survive without us as a food source, they will have to turn their attention to their own kind (i.e., young White men and boys).

Wouldn't you like to see for yourself what would happen to the criminal justice system and the prison industrial complex if we stop feeding it with our Black fathers, sons, and brothers?

But what do you do in the meantime, while we are actively engaged in this protest?

What do you do to feed your families without jobs and other legitimate sources of income?

How are you supposed to survive without the underground economy that puts money in your pocket and food on your table?

Simple:

You come together and unite for the purpose of supporting each other through this difficult period of protest and resistance!

That means we make this protest a national movement and let everybody in the world know that for 1 whole year no Black man will commit a crime or an act of violence against another Black man, woman, or child.

If we proceed as a united national protest, you will be amazed at how many people and organizations will come to your aid, including churches, community organizations, and private citizens.

Remember Rosa Parks and the bus boycott she helped launch in Montgomery, Alabama, when she refused to give her seat to a White man? That bus boycott lasted for more than 365 days. Most of those people never met Rosa Parks or knew anything about her before that fateful day, but not one Black person in that city rode the public bus system, to show their support for her courage and strength.

After more than 365 days of Black protest, they had to change the laws about Black people riding the bus. Before the boycott was over, they cost the city and the bus company several million dollars in lost revenue.

That's the power of protest!

There's strength in numbers!

We are going to have to take a united stand against these two Evil Twin Sisters, if we hope to put them out of business and keep them from profiting from the misery of Blacks!

This is the final call to all Black men in America!

Unify or Die!

I'm calling on all of you Brothers, right here and right now, to join me and join forces to protest against the criminal justice system and the prison industrial complex, the Evil Twin Sisters, by not giving them the power and the excuse to take away our freedom, our respect, and our manhood!

40

RISING UP, FIGHTING BACK, AND BREAKING FREE!

Reflections of a Rising Son

Salvation for a race, nation, or class must come from within. Freedom is never granted; it is won. Justice is never given; it is exacted, Freedom and justice must be struggled for by the oppressed of all lands and races, and the struggle must be continuous.
- **A. Phillip Randolph, Labor Leader**

My name is Michael Samir Mohamed, and I am a Black Son Rising!
I am rising up, fighting back, and breaking free!
I am rising up as a man, and taking responsibility for educating, uplifting, and empowering Black men.
I am fighting back against the systems of oppression that perpetuate the cycle of black-on-black crime and violence.
I am breaking free from the chains of mental, physical, and emotional bondage that were placed on my people through the institution of American slavery.
I am a Black Son Rising!

Together, we can become Black Men Rising!

Together, we can Rise Up, Fight Back, and Break Free!

Freedom is the Goal. Knowledge is the Key. Faith is the Way.

As I end this book, I want to leave you with a few last thoughts to put into perspective everything you just read and learned.

For the record, you have every right to be angry and hostile and aggressive. After all that has been done to Black men and Black people by white racists, who could blame you?

But you have absolutely no right whatsoever to direct your anger, hostility, and aggression toward your own people.

They are not the ones who infected you with the disease of mental slavery; the European and American racists did that.

Therefore, from here on, I want all you Brothers to take your foot off your own people's neck, take your hands out of their pockets, remove your knives from their backs, get your coke out of their noses and your needles out of their veins.

I'm not judging you for your behavior, Black man, for I understand its roots.

It's not my place to judge you, I'm not God. But like a good father or uncle, I have to call you on your behavior, because I love you enough to tell you the truth, and I hate to see you being manipulated and tricked into destroying your own people.

Why do I love you so much?

BLACK SON RISING

I love you because I can see you in a way that no other man can, or will see you.

As a Black man myself, I see your strengths and weaknesses without looking at them through the muddy lenses of white racism.

I see your strengths and weaknesses in the way a father sees his own son's strengths and weaknesses, with the desire to help his son grow stronger and overcome his weaknesses, rather than exploiting those weaknesses for selfish ends.

I see you in a way that no other man is able to see you, because I can see you without the stereotypes, positive and negative, that are all too commonly associated with Black men.

I see you as more than just outstanding athletes.

I see you as more than just violent thugs, hoodlums, and criminals.

I see you in all your glory and all your shame.

I see your highs and your lows, and your valleys and mountains, because I eat with you, live among you, hang out with you, talk with you, listen to you, think like you, and in most cases, act like you and do what you do – including all the good and the bad.

I see you when you are at your best as fathers, husbands, and friends, but I also see you at your worst as murderers, drug dealers, thieves, dead-beat fathers, alcoholics, and drug abusers.

I see, and have seen every aspect of your life, and every dimension of your being, and every scope of your character.

Who but another Black man can say that?

I understand better than any White man ever could, what motivates, inspires, strengthens, angers, frustrates, and weakens you, Black man, because I have had to experience all of these emotions myself, not just as a man, but as a Black man.

Therefore, I have earned the right to tell you what I think and what I know, because I love you unconditionally, and I don't have a hidden agenda.

I'm not trying to hurt you, I'm only trying to help you save your own life, because no one can save it but you.

I can only show you the door, but you're the one who has to walk through it.

Black-on-black crime and violence is a "Black problem," requiring a "Black solution."

That means we have to stop looking to White people for the solutions to the problems that they created in the first place.

We want them to *give us* more rights.

We want them to *give us* more opportunities.

We want them to *give us* more jobs.

Instead of us *asking* them to give us this and give us that, we need to be focusing on developing our individual and collective strength, wealth, and power, and start demanding our rights and opportunities, instead of begging for them like some pathetic charity cases.

Power perceived is power achieved.

And power, or the perception of it, is the only thing that white racists respect.

White people are not going to spend any time and energy trying to resolve this issue of black-on-black crime and violence. Nor should they. It doesn't affect them directly.

Their kids are not the ones going to prisons.

Their kids are not the ones dying in the streets like dogs.

Their kids are not the ones murdering each other by the thousands.
Their kids are not the ones standing in the unemployment lines.
Their kids are not the ones dropping out of school like flies.
Their kids are not the ones dropping babies like rabbits.

You know what though? White people are funny. They are quick to point out how other people need to accept responsibility for their actions. But White people have yet to admit responsibility for creating the horrible conditions in which Black people live.

They have yet to even apologize for dragging us in chains, kicking and screaming, from our motherland, raping our women and children, lynching and castrating our men, and scattering our families and loved ones to the four corners of the globe.

Yet they apologized to the Japanese for bombing Hiroshima and Nagasaki, and built a beautiful multi-million dollar monument in their honor.

Where is the apology to the Black race?

Where is the Slave Holocaust museum or monument?

White people don't give a damn about the plight of the Black race. Half the time they are so-called "helping us" it's out of guilt for being part of a race that has subjugated another race by using lies and deceit and violence to achieve those ends.

Therefore, no White man, even the few who do sincerely care, can ever solve the problems of the Black race. He doesn't even think we have any real problems, other than laziness and lack of ambition.

That means that the Black race has to stop looking to the White race as the *cause* of our problems, and the *solutions* to them. They can't be both.

This is our problem, not theirs. And we can't continue to let racism, or any other *ism*, keep us from taking full advantage of our rights as human beings, and full advantage of the opportunities that were bought and paid for in this country – with the blood, sweat, and tears of our forefathers.

But what about racism and discrimination? How do we get around that? They aren't just going away.

You and I both know that racism is forever, and that discrimination is here to stay, but if we let any man tell us what we can and can't have because of the color of our skin, that's our fault, not theirs.

Personally, I'm not going to let any man tell me what I can and can't do. I may have to work five times harder than the White man to get what I want, but that's not going to stop me from trying to get it, and I'm not going to blame racism for my failure to try.

Therein lies the problem. Too many of you Brothers are using racism and discrimination as an excuse to fail, or to quit even before you try. That's a self-defeatist attitude, and that's exactly what they are hoping for: that you will quit in the face of adversity instead of fighting their racist and oppression tooth and nail.

Look, I know it ain't easy out here, and I know how bad you're suffering, Black man. I'm right there with you, but you and I both know that Black men have opportunities today that their fathers, just 50 years ago, didn't have.

Yet, we have lost more Black men to drugs (that we sell and use) and violence (that we commit) in the past 20 years, than we have lost at the hands of White men in the past 100 years, and we are doing this to ourselves.

Today, there are more Black men in prison (1.5 million) than there are in all of the colleges in this country combined (650,000). That's a tragic waste of humanity. And all of the current criminal and social statistics indicate that the problem is getting worse for Black men, not better.

BLACK SON RISING

What does this mean for us Black men in America?

This means, Black man, that *we* are doing something wrong, not the White man, because *we* are responsible for our individual and collective destinies.

The White man "ain't going" to do no more for us than we are prepared to do for ourselves.

And regardless of what happened to us in the past, no one can keep us in mental or physical slavery without our consent.

The bottom line is this: Despite racism, discrimination, and racial oppression, we have come a long way in this country, but we still have so much more to accomplish.

However, we can't accomplish the things we need to accomplish, like protecting our families, or raising our children, or building our own homes and businesses, if we are locked-down in prison, strung out on drugs, or wasting our lives as drug-dealing, gun-toting, gang-banging, back-stabbing murderers of our own people.

I have spent the last 39 chapters of this book telling you how and why the Black race was deceived, manipulated, and mis-educated into its mental, physical, and emotional bondage.

I told you about the disease of mental slavery and its symptoms of fear, false pride, material greed, mental laziness, social ignorance, self-hatred, and misplaced anger.

I told you that this disease is the true cause of black-on-black crime and violence, and how to rid yourself of this disease in order to break the cycle.

And now that you know all of these things, it is now your responsibility, from this point forward, to rise up, fight back, and break free from your disease, and to help others do the same.

Once you know the truth, you can no longer claim ignorance as an excuse.

Once you know better, you must do better.

I know that *Black Son Rising* may have seemed offensive to some, but "right-on-point" to others. My intention was not necessarily to offend *anyone*, but to awaken *everyone* to the truth about the causes and effects of black-on-black crime and violence, and the role we each play in perpetuating the cycle.

And sometimes the truth hurts!

I wrote this book primarily as an educational tool for my Brothers, to help them break the chains of mental, physical, and emotional bondage that give rise to black-on-black crime and violence.

I wrote this book to provide my Brothers with a powerful new definition of African American "manhood" that allows them to live and survive in this racially hostile nation with their pride and dignity intact.

I wrote this book because I love Black people, and I hate to see them suffer. It is my greatest desire to see them succeed and prosper in all aspects of their lives. I especially love Black men, because of the struggles we constantly endure, and the incredible degree of strength and courage it requires to endure them.

We are the original "Survivors"!

Why did I bother writing a book like this? Because despite all the negativity you hear about Black men, and no matter how many people might turn their backs on us, the truth is:

Rising Up, Fighting Back, and Breaking Free!

Black men are worth saving!

Why? Because without Black men, there is no Black family, and without the Black family, there is no Black race! That means *"they"* win.

Is there anyone among you who doesn't know by now who *"they"* are?

If we don't do something right now to liberate Black men from their slave mentality, and show them how to rid themselves of their fear, false pride, material greed, social ignorance, self-hatred, and misplaced anger, we are going to lose thousands, if not millions, more of our Black men, women, and children to the streets, the prisons, and the graveyards of this racially hostile nation we call "America."

This is *our* problem. This is *our* responsibility. And as Black men, we are the potential solution. However, if you are not going to be part of the solution, then you *are* automatically part of the problem.

I'm urging each of you to join me and become part of the solution, by Rising Up, Fighting Back, and Breaking Free!

I truly believe there is a *Black Son Rising* in our midst. The time is ripe. The moment is at hand. . .

Let the revolution begin!

Peace & Blessings,

Michael Samir Mohamed
(fna Michael Curtis Jones)
The Rising Son

BLACK SON RISING

A PRAYER FOR SUCCESS

The LORD shall open unto thee His good treasure, the heaven to give the rain unto thy land in His season, and to bless all the work of thine hand.
-   **DEUTERONOMY 28:12**

Father, my life abounds with Your blessings: a strong mind, a healthy body, and a good heart. Everything I need is given to me as a gift, and I am free (or will soon be free) to use it all.

You have given me stewardship of this world, but I have often failed in my responsibilities to You, myself, my family, and my community.

Father, I have lied, stolen, cheated, exploited charitable acts, and worst of all, I have harmed Your children in my selfish and greedy pursuit of pride, pleasure, and possessions.

Father, please forgive me for my trespasses against You and all of Your creations. Show me where I have done wrong. Teach me how to correct my selfish acts and childish ways. Teach me how to live in peace, respect, and harmony with my family, my community, and my fellow man.

When I do, that will be the true measure of my success.

Not what I own, or how much money I have, or what kind of cars I drive, or how many children I sire, or how many women I can exploit;

But when I'm drug-free, crime-free, and mentally liberated; when I'm raising and supporting my children, and protecting my Black Queen; when I'm doing everything in my power to live as a man of honor; when I'm wholly responsible for my actions and no longer making excuses for my failures and weaknesses; when I'm no longer full of false pride and arrogance; when I'm living and walking in Your example of Mercy, Compassion, Truth, Justice, Peace, Wisdom, and Love;

That's when I will know that I have truly succeeded!

I pray these things in the name of the Almighty, the Most-High, the Supreme Creator of all that exists.

Amen

APPENDIX

The slave master will not teach you the knowledge of self, as there would not be a master-slave relationship any longer.
- **Elijah Muhammad, Nation of Islam Leader**

APPENDIX A

AFRICAN AMERICAN QUOTATIONS

Since the time of their enslavement, African Americans have relied on oral tradition for sustenance and inspiration, often using words in a simple yet profound way to convey ordinary and exceptional sentiments.
-   **Richard Newman, Editor**

Black people have always demonstrated a unique and colorful way of expressing common sense wisdom and philosophy in life. We have a way of saying things that we can relate to and that hit close to home, and give us pause for deep, personal reflection. I have read many of the so-called European philosophers and have found no more wisdom or knowledge in their works than what can be found within our own Black community.

I never doubted my ability, but when you hear all your life you're inferior, it makes you wonder if the other guys have something you've never seen before. If they do, I'm still looking for it.
–   **Hank Aaron (Henry Louis Aaron)**

I'm not comfortable being preachy, but more people need to start spending as much time in the library as they do on the basketball court. If they took the idea that they could escape poverty through education, I think it would make a more basic and long-lasting change in the way things happen. What we need are positive, realistic goals and the willingness to work. Hard work and practical goals.
–   **Kareem Abdul-Jabbar (Ferdinand Lewis Alcindor, Jr.)**

Champions aren't made in gyms. Champions are made from something they have deep inside them- a desire, a dream, a vision. They have to have last-minute stamina, they have to be a little faster, they have to have the skill and the will. But the will must be stronger than the skill.
–   **Muhammed Ali, World Championship Boxer**

None of us is responsible for the complexion of his skin. This fact of nature offers no clue to the character or quality of the person underneath.
–   **Marian Anderson**

Africa is herself a mother. The mother of mankind.
–   **Maya Angelou (Marguerite Johnson), Poet**

If we lose love and self-respect for each other, this is how we finally die.
–   **Maya Angelou**

Your ancestors took the lash, the branding iron, humiliations, and oppression because one day they believed you would come along to flesh out the dream.
–   **Maya Angelou**

BLACK SON RISING

Egypt is to African American culture as Greece to white culture.
- **Molefi Kete Asante**

Ignorance is the root of all evil, pain, and suffering; therefore, the end of ignorance is the main goal of the teachings [Egyptian Yoga].
- **Dr. Muata Ashby, Author and Philosopher**

Hatred, which could destroy so much, never failed to destroy the man who hated, and this was an immutable law.
- **James Baldwin, Author**

I imagine that one of the reasons that people cling to their hates so stubbornly is because they sense, once hate is gone, that they will be forced to deal with the pain.
- **James Baldwin**

The most dangerous creation of any society is the man who has nothing to lose.
- **James Baldwin**

The only thing that white people have that black people need, or should want, is power – and no one holds power forever.
- **James Baldwin**

To act is to be committed, and to be committed is to be in danger.
- **James Baldwin**

Whatever the white man has done, we have done, and done better.
- **Mary Macleod Bethune, Social Activist**

The most potent weapon in the hands of the oppressor, is the mind of the oppressed.
- **Steven Biko, South African Revolutionary**

Blackness has been a stigma, a curse with which we were born. Black power means that henceforth this curse will be a badge of pride rather than of scorn.
- **Robert S. Browne**

To struggle and battle and overcome and absolutely defeat every force designed against us is the only way to achieve.
- **Nannie Burroughs**

Fear of something is at the root of hate for others, and hate within will eventually destroy the hater.
- **George Washington Carver**

Sins, like chickens, come home to roost.
- **Charles W. Chesnut**

Brothers, we have striven to regain the precious heritage we received from our fathers...I am resolved that it is better to die than to be a white man's slave, and I will not complain if by dying I save you.
- **Joseph Cinque, Leader of the Amistad Revolt**

Appendix A: African American Quotations

Pride, like humility, is destroyed by one's insistence that he possesses it.
- **Kenneth B. Clarke**

You're either part of the solution or part of the problem.
- **Eldridge Cleaver**

Respect commands itself and can neither be given nor withheld when it is due.
- **Eldridge Cleaver**

You don't have to teach people how to be human. You have to teach them how to stop being inhuman.
- **Eldridge Cleaver**

When you educate a man you educate an individual, but when you educate a woman, you educate a nation.
- **Johnetta B. Cole**

Truth knows no color; it appeals to intelligence.
- **James Cone**

The past is a ghost, the future a dream, and all we ever have is now.
- **Bill Cosby**

Train your head and hands to do, your head and heart to dare.
- **Joseph Seamon Cotter**

Revolution is a serious thing, the most serious thing about a revolutionary's life. When one commits oneself to the struggle, it must be for a lifetime.
- **Angela Davis, Revolutionary**

Jails and prisons are designed to break human beings, to convert the population into specimens in a zoo- obedient to our keepers, but dangerous to each other.
- **Angela Davis**

When you get real old, honey, you realize there are certain things that just don't matter anymore. You lay it all on the table. There's a saying: Only little children and old folks tell the truth.
- **Sarah Louise Delany**

It has been the fashion of American writers to deny that the Egyptians were Negroes and claim that they are of the same race as themselves. This has, I have no doubt, been largely due to a wish to deprive the Negro of the moral support of ancient greatness and to appropriate the same to the white race.
- **Frederick Douglass**

You are not judged by the height you have risen, but from the depths you have climbed.
- **Frederick Douglass**

Men must not only know, they must act.
- **W.E.B. Dubois**

BLACK SON RISING

Men talk of the Negro problem; there is no Negro problem. The problem is whether American people have the loyalty enough, honor enough, patriotism enough, to live up to their own Constitution.
- **Paul Laurence Dunbar**

Don't feel entitled to anything you didn't sweat and struggle for.
- **Marian Wright Edelman**

Speak truth to power.
- **Marian Wright Edelman**

I am not ashamed of my grandparents for having been slaves. I am only ashamed of myself for having at one time being ashamed.
- **Ralph Ellison, Author of *Invisible Man***

When I discover who I am, I'll be free.
- **Ralph Ellison**

I am invisible, understand, simply because people refuse to see me.
- **Ralph Ellison**

To identify the enemy is to free the mind.
- **Mari Evans**

The black man must first find himself as a black man before he can find himself as an American.
- **James Farmer**

You are the ancient builders of civilization. Before there was civilization you were there, and when civilization was built, your fathers built it.
- **Louis Farrakhan (Louis Eugene Walcott)**

Never exalt people because they're in your family; never exalt people because they're your color. Never exalt people because they're your kinfolk. Exalt them because they're worthy.
- **Louis Farrakhan**

Just don't give up trying to do what you really want to do. Where there's love and inspiration, I don't think you can go wrong.
- **Ella Fitzgerald**

Trying to grow up is hurting, you know. You make mistakes. You try to learn from them, and when you don't, it hurts even more.
- **Aretha Franklin**

Question everything. Every stripe, every star, every word spoken. Everything.
- **Ernest J. Gaines**

Words mean nothing. Action is the only thing. Doing. That's the only thing.
- **Ernest J. Gaines**

Appendix A: African American Quotations

Sometimes you got to hurt something to help something. Sometimes you have to plow under one thing in order for something else to grow.
- **Ernest J. Gaines**

The moment the slave resolves that he will no longer be a slave, his fetters fall. He frees himself and shows the way to others. Freedom and slavery are mental states.
- **Mohandas K. Gandhi**

Black men and Black men alone hold the key to the gateway leading to their freedom.
- **Marcus Garvey**

All of us may not live to see the higher accomplishments of an African empire, so strong and powerful as to compel the respect of mankind, but we in our lifetime can so work and act as to make the dream a possibility within another generation.
- **Marcus Garvey**

When Europe was inhabited by a race of cannibals, a race of savage men, heathens and pagans, Africa was peopled with a race of cultured Black men who were masters in art, science, and literature.
- **Marcus Garvey**

Teach your children they are the direct descendants of the greatest and proudest race who ever peopled the earth.
- **Marcus Garvey**

I really don't think life is about the I-could-have-beens. Life is only about the I-tried-to-do. I don't mind the failure but I can't imagine that I'd forgive myself if I didn't try.
- **Nikki Giovanni**

I like to tell the truth as I see it. That's why literature is so important. We cannot possibly leave it to history as a discipline nor to sociology nor science nor economics to tell the story of our people. It's not a ladder we are climbing, it's literature we're producing, and there will always be someone to read it.
- **Nikki Giovanni**

I never learned hate at home, or shame. I had to go to school for that.
- **Dick Gregory**

They have forgotten the struggle....and they have forgotten the road over which we have come, and they are not teaching it to their children.
- **Alex Haley, Writer**

You can jail a revolutionary, but you can't jail the revolution.
- **Fred Hampton, Black Panther Party Leader**

Dope never helped anybody sing better or play music better or do anything better. All dope can do for you is kill you- and kill you the long, slow, hard way.
- **Billie Holiday**

BLACK SON RISING

Many of our institutions apparently are not trying to make men and women of their students at all. They are doing their best to produce spineless Uncle Toms, uninformed, and full of mental and moral evasions.
- **Langston Hughes, Poet and Writer**

The Burden of being black is that you have to be superior just to be equal. But the glory of that is that, once you achieve, you have achieved indeed.
- **Jesse Jackson Sr.**

A man must be willing to die for justice. Death is an inescapable reality and men die daily, but good deeds live forever.
- **Jesse Jackson Sr.**

As a people, we must remember that we are not as weak as we have allowed ourselves to be painted, and we are not as strong as we can be.
- **John E. Jacobs**

We can go on talking about racism and who treated whom badly, but what are you going to do about it? Are you going to wallow in that or are you going to create your own agenda?
- **Judith Jamison**

The civil rights discourse was a moral discourse based on an appeal to whites to recognize their own humanity and act accordingly. The presumption that the people who hold power are moral rather than amoral is the fatal flaw of the movement; it depends so much on the good will of the oppressor....
- **Maulana Karenga, Educator**

We are not fighting for the right to be like you. We respect ourselves too much for that.
- **John O. Killens**

A man who won't die for something is not fit to live.
- **Martin Luther King, Jr.**

It may get me crucified. I may even die. But I want it said even if I die in the struggle that "He died to make men free."
- **Martin Luther King, Jr.**

An individual who breaks a law that conscience tells him is unjust, and who willingly accepts the penalty of imprisonment in order to arouse the conscience of the community over its injustice, is in reality expressing the highest respect for the law.
- **Martin Luther King, Jr.**

Schooling is what happens inside the wall of the school, some of which is educational. Education happens everywhere, and it happens from the moment a child is born – some say before – until it dies.
- **Sara Lawrence Lightfoot, Educator**

Appendix A: African American Quotations

From 1863, when slavery was abolished in this country, down to the present time history reveals to us the fact that the Negro race, though spurned at every hand, has made the most rapid progress, under the most trying circumstances, of any race on the globe.
- **W.A. Luis, Educator**

There is no easy walk to freedom anywhere, and many of us will have to pass through the valley of the shadow of death again and again before we reach the mountaintop of our desires.
- **Nelson Mandela**

The mind is like the body. If you don't work actively to protect its health, you can lose it, especially if you're a black man, 19 years, old and wondering, as I was, if you were born into the wrong world.
- **Nathan McCall, Journalist and Author of *Makes Me Wanna Holler!***

I learned very quickly that education was the best vehicle to begin overturning a status quo that historically repressed and marginalized our race.
- **Kweisi Mfume, NAACP Official**

If you can't count, they can cheat you. If you can't read, they can beat you.
- **Toni Morrison, Novelist and Nobel Laureate**

The education and training of our children must not be limited to the "Three Rs" only. It should instead include the history of the black nation, the knowledge of civilizations of man and the universe, and all sciences.
- **Elijah Muhammad, Nation of Islam Leader**

America is the world's greatest jailer, and we are all in jails. Black spirits contained like magnificent birds of wonder.
- **Larry Neal, Writer**

I suggested [in 1966] that we use the panther as our symbol and call our political vehicle the Black Panther Party. The panther is a fierce animal, but he will not attack until he is backed into a corner; then he strikes out.
- **Huewy Newton**

Stand up for your rights, even if it kills you. That's all that life consists of.
- **Clarence Norris, Scottsboro Victim**

One ought to struggle for its own sake. One ought to be against racism and sexism because they are wrong, not because one is black or female.
- **Eleanor Holmes Norton, Lawyer and Activist**

In theory, the Emancipation Proclamation had been a wonderful thing. But in 1915 in Alabama, it was only a theory. The Negro had been set free to work 18 hours a day, free to see all his labor add up to a debt at the year's end, free to be chained to the land he tilled but could never own any more than if he were still a slave.
- **Jesse Owens, Olympic Track Star**

BLACK SON RISING

The battles that count aren't the ones for gold medals. The struggle within yourself – the invisible, inevitable battles inside all of us – that's where it's at.
- **Jesse Owens**

Until my mid-teens I lived in fear; fear of being shot, lynched, or beaten to death – not for any wrong doing of my own.... I could have easily been the victim of mistaken identity or an act of terror by hate-filled white men.
- **Gordon Parks, World Famous Photographer**

I had felt for a long time, that if I was ever told to get up so a white person could sit, that I would refuse to do it."
- **Rosa Parks, Civil Rights Activist**

Black men must make a special effort to become spiritual and psychological fathers to needy black children within their extended families and community.
- **Alvin Poussaint, Psychiatrist**

Many interviewers when they come to talk to me, think they're being progressive by not mentioning in their stories any longer that I'm black. I tell them, "Don't stop now. If I shot somebody you'd mention it.'
- **Colin Powell**

I have nothing more to offer than what General Washington would have to offer had he been taken by the British and put to trial by them. I have adventured my life in endeavoring to obtain the liberty of my countrymen, and am a willing sacrifice to their cause; and I beg, as a favor, that I may be immediately led to execution. I know that you have predetermined to shed my blood; why then all this mockery of a trial?
- **Gabriel Prosser, Insurrectionist**

This is the red man's country by natural right, and the black man's by virtue of his suffering and toil.
- **Robert Purvis, Abolitionist**

Freedom is never given; it is won.
- **A. Philip Randolph, Labor Leader**

My father was a slave and my people died to build this country, and I am going to stay and have a piece of it just like you.
- **Paul Robeson, Singer and Activist**

I learned that along with the towering achievements of the cultures of ancient Greece and China there stood the culture of Africa, unseen and denied by the looters of Africa's material wealth.
- **Paul Robeson**

African Americans ought to care about Africa and the Caribbean because we are much stronger together than separate. Our potential as black people is to harness our power globally.
- **Randall Robinson**

Appendix A: African American Quotations

Love yourself, appreciate yourself, see the good in you, see the God in you, and respect yourself.
 - **Betty Shabazz, Educator and Malcolm X's Wife**

Before you can understand what I mean, you have to know how I lived or how the people I'm talking to lived.
 - **Tupac Shakur, Rap Artist**

Great careers don't come without sacrifice. Something in your life will probably have to go. Decide, now, what you're willing to forfeit to get what you want.
 - **Cydney and Leslie Shields, Entertainers**

It is of no use for us to sit with our hands folded, hanging our heads like bulrushes, lamenting our wretched condition; but let us make a mighty effort and arise; and if no one will promote or respect us, let us promote and respect ourselves.
 - **Maria Stewart, Lecturer**

If women want any rights more than they's got, why don't they just take them, and not be talking about it.
 - **Sojourner Truth, Revolutionary**

I believe that the two or three million of us should return to the land of our ancestors, and establish our own civilization, laws, customs.... What the black man needs is a country.
 - **Henry McNeal Turner, Minister and Militant Activist**

I heard a loud noise in the heavens, and the Spirit instantly appeared to me and said the Serpent was loosed, and Christ had laid down the yoke he had borne for the sins of men and that I should take it on and fight against the Serpent, for the time was fast approaching when the first should be the last and the last first.
 - **Nat Turner, Prophet and Insurrectionist**

Remember that ours is not a war for robbery, or to satisfy our passions; it is a struggle for freedom.
 - **Nat Turner**

Nothing ever comes to one, that is worth having, except as a result of hard work.
 - **Booker T. Washington, Inventor**

White supremacists' ideology is based first and foremost on the degradation of black bodies in order to control them...by convincing them that their bodies are ugly, their intellect is inherently underdeveloped, their culture is less civilized, and their future warrants less concern than that of other peoples.
 - **Cornel West, Philosopher**

I was raised to believe that excellence is the best deterrent to racism or sexism. And that's how I operate my life.
 - **Oprah Winfrey, Actress and Entertainer**

Black people have been mis-educated into confusing their interests with those of the dominant society.
 - **Carter G. Woodson, Historian**

BLACK SON RISING

We must recapture our heritage and our ideals if we are to liberate ourselves from the bonds of white supremacy. We must launch a cultural revolution to unbrainwash an entire people.
– **Malcolm X, Nationalist Leader**

You don't have a peaceful revolution. You don't have a turn-the-other-cheek revolution. There's no such thing as a nonviolent revolution. Revolution is bloody. Revolution is hostile. Revolution knows no compromise. Revolution overturns and destroys everything that gets in its way.
– **Malcolm X**

History is a people's memory, and without a memory, man is demoted to the lower animals.
– **Malcolm X**

I believe in the brotherhood of all men, but I don't believe in wasting brotherhood on anyone who doesn't want to practice it with me. Brotherhood is a two-way street.
– **Malcolm X**

It is a blessing to die for a cause, because you can so easily die for nothing.
– **Andrew Young, Politician**

Every black person who rises is subject to a greater degree of criticism and more than any other segment of the population.
– **Coleman Young, Former Mayor of Detroit**

APPENDIX B

SUGGESTED READING LIST

One of the joys of reading is the ability to plug into the shared wisdom of mankind.
– **Ishmael Reed, Dramatist**

Black people have a long proud tradition of literary and scholarly excellence. We have hundreds of African and African American scholar warriors who have vigorously searched for, recorded, and published the anthropology, sociology, and psychology of Black and White people, in order to arrive at an objective, color-blind truth about the human condition throughout history. I am grateful for their valiant efforts, and pay homage to them and their significant contributions. Below are just a few of the literary and scholarly works that were produced by some of our best and brightest minds, and that I used as the basis of my research for *Black Son Rising*.

I highly recommend that at your earliest convenience, each of you buy, borrow, or "steal" a copy of these great works and read them as often as possible so that you can discover for yourself the depth and breadth of knowledge that our people possess. I think you will be as surprised and amazed as I with the sheer volume of information found in these texts.

This list is just the scratch of the surface. There are literally thousands of such books in publication, if you bother to go looking for them.

Remember: To be free, you must think free. To think free, you must educate yourself. To educate yourself, you must read!

The Top 100 Must Read Books for All African Americans

1. THE AUTOBIOGRAPHY OF MALCOLM X, ALEX HALEY
2. AFRICA, DR. YOSEF BEN-JOCHANNAN
3. A CHRONOLOGY OF THE BIBLE, DR. YOSEF BEN-JOCHANNAN
4. HOW EUROPE UNDERDEVELOPED AFRICA, WALTER RODNEY
5. THE AUTOBIOGRAPHY OF MARTIN LUTHER KING, JR., CLAYBORNE CARSON
6. I HAVE A DREAM, MARTIN LUTHER KING, JR.
7. MARCUS GARVEY: LIFE & LESSONS, ROBERT HILL
8. THE SOULS OF BLACK FOLK, W.E.B. DU BOIS
9. UP FROM SLAVERY, BOOKER T. WASHINGTON
10. FREDERICK DOUGLASS: AUTOBIOGRAPHIES, FREDERICK DOUGLASS
11. THE MIS-EDUCATION OF THE NEGRO, CARTER G. WOODSON
12. MESSAGE TO THE BLACKMAN, ELIJAH MUHAMMAD
13. THE FALL OF AMERICA, HONORABLE ELIJAH MUHAMMAD
14. BEFORE THE MAYFLOWER, LERONE BENNETT
15. NELSON MANDELA: THE STRUGGLE IS MY LIFE, NELSON MANDELA

16. BROTHERMAN: THE ODYSSEY OF BLACK MEN IN AMERICA, HERB BOYD
17. RACE MATTERS, DR. CORNEL WEST
18. THE COLUMBUS CONSPIRACY, MICHAEL BRADLEY
19. NEO-COLONIALISM, KWAME NKRUMAH
20. COINTELPRO, CATHY PERKUS
21. BLACK POWER, STOKELY CARMICHAEL (KWAME TOURE)
22. AFRICAN WORLD REVOLUTION, JOHN HENDRIK CLARKE
23. OPPRESSION: A SOCIO-HISTORY OF BACK-WHITE RELATIONS IN AMERICA, JONATHAN H. TURNER
24. COUNTERING THE CONSPIRACY TO DESTROY BLACK BOYS, VOLUMES I THROUGH IV, DR. JAWANZA KUNJUFU
25. STATE OF EMERGENCY: WE MUST SAVE AFRICAN AMERICAN MALES, DR. JAWANZA KUNJUFU
26. CIVILIZATION OR BARBARISM, CHEIKH ANTA DIOP
27. THE DESTRUCTION OF BLACK CIVILIZATION, CHANCELLOR WILLIAMS
28. FIGHT THE POWER, CHUCK D
29. THE SPOOK WHO SAT BY THE DOOR, SAM GREENLEE
30. BLACK FACE, NELSON GEORGE
31. THE BLACK PANTHER SPEAKS, PHILIP S. FONER
32. THE GENIUS OF HUEY P. NEWTON, ELDRIDGE CLEAVER
33. FROM SUPERMAN TO MAN, J.A. ROGERS
34. 100 AMAZING FACTS ABOUT THE NEGRO, J.A. ROGERS
35. BREAKING THE CHAINS OF PSYCHOLOGICAL SLAVERY, DR. NAIM AKBAR
36. VISIONS FOR BLACK MEN, DR. NAIM AKBAR
37. CHAINS AND IMAGES OF PSYCHOLOGICAL SLAVERY, DR. NAIM AKBAR
38. THE WRETCHED OF THE EARTH, FRANTZ FANON
39. THE PSYCHOLOGY OF OPPRESSION, FRANTZ FANON
40. SOCIAL DOMINANCE, JIM SIDANIUS
41. WHAT THEY NEVER TOLD YOU IN HISTORY CLASS, INDUS KUSH
42. MUHAMMAD ALI, THOMAS HOUSER
43. THE SCIENCE OF RAP, KRS-ONE
44. THE PECULIAR INSTITUTION, KENNETH M. STAMPP
45. THE TURNER DIARIES, ANDREW MACDONALD
46. DARK ALLIANCE, GARY WEBB
47. BLACK LIKE ME, JOHN HOWARD GRIFFIN
48. NIGGER, DICK GREGORY
49. WHY BLACK PEOPLE TEND TO SHOUT, RALPH WILEY
50. MANCHILD IN THE PROMISED LAND, CLAUDE BROWN
51. AFRICANS IN AMERICA, CHARLES JOHNSON & PATRICIA SMITH
52. THE BLACK 100, COLUMBUS SALLEY
53. THE DEBT & THE RECKONING, RANDALL ROBINSON
54. CAPITALIST NIGGER, CHIKA ONYEANS
55. MODERN BLACK NATIONALISM, WILLIAM L. VAN DEBURG
56. IT'S ABOUT THE MONEY, JESSE JACKSON
57. WOMEN, RACE & CLASS, ANGELA Y. DAVIS
58. FROM BABYLON TO TIMBUKTU, RUDOLPH R. WINDSOR
59. AFRICAN AMERICAN VOICES OF TRIUMPH: PERSEVERANCE, TIME-LIFE BOOKS
60. ONE MILLION STRONG, RODERICK TERRY

61. NATION CONSCIOUS RAP, JAMES SPADY
62. MILLION MAN MARCH, MICHAEL COTTMAN
63. STOKELY CARMICHAEL: THE STORY OF BLACK POWER, JACQUELINE JOHNSON
64. WHAT BLACK MEN SHOULD DO NOW, K. THOMAS OGLESBY
65. SOUL ON ICE, ELDRIDGE CLEAVER
66. THE HEAD NEGRO IN CHARGE SYNDROME, NORMAN KELLEY
67. FROM NIGGAS TO GODS, VOLUMES I & II, AKIL
68. THE ASSASSINATION OF THE BLACK MALE IMAGE, EARL HUTCHINSON
69. THROUGH THE EYES OF A CONVICT, BLAKE HOLMES
70. POST TRAUMATIC SLAVERY DISORDER, DR. OMAR REID
71. FROM THE BROWDER FILE, ANTHONY BROWDER
72. STOLEN LEGACY, GEORGE G. M. JAMES
73. INTRODUCTION TO BLACK STUDIES, MAULANA KARENGA
74. A TORCHLIGHT FOR AMERICA, MINISTER LOUIS FARRAKHAN
75. BLACK ROBES/WHITE JUSTICE, BRUCE WRIGHT
76. CAN BLACK MOTHERS RAISE OUR SONS, LAWSON BUSH V
77. TWO NATIONS: BLACK & WHITE, SEPARATE, HOSTILE, UNEQUAL, ANDREW HACKER
78. THE ISIS PAPERS, DR. FRANCES CRESS WELSING
79. UNDERSTANDING BLACK MALE ADOLESCENT VIOLENCE, AMOS N. WILSON
80. THE DEVELOPMENTAL PSYCHOLOGY OF THE BLACK CHILD, AMOS N. WILSON
81. BLUEPRINT FOR BLACK POWER, AMOS N. WILSON
82. SEIZE THE TIME, BOBBY SEALE
83. STREET SOLDIER, DR. JOSEPH MARSHALL, JR.
84. MAKES ME WANNA HOLLER, NATHAN MCCALL
85. EMPOWERING AFRICAN AMERICAN MALES TO SUCCEED, MYCHAL WYNN
86. AS A MAN THINKETH, JAMES ALLEN
87. THINK & GROW RICH: A BLACK CHOICE, DENNIS KIMBRO
88. HOW TO SUCCEED IN BUSINESS WITHOUT BEING WHITE, EARL GRAVES
89. THE LAWS OF SUCCESS, NAPOLEAN HILL
90. THE TWELVE UNIVERSAL LAWS OF SUCCESS, HERBERT HARRIS
91. THE POWER OF WILL, FRANK HADDOCK
92. THE POWER MIND SYSTEM, MICHAEL KIEFER
93. THE POWER OF YOUR SUBCONSCIOUS MIND, DR. JOSEPH MURPHY
94. AFRICAN HOLISTIC HEALTH, LAILA AFRICA
95. THE HOLY BIBLE
96. THE HOLY QURAN
97. SON OF MAN: THE MYSTICAL PATH TO CHRIST, ANDREW HARVEY
98. THE HISTORY OF THE NATION OF ISLAM, AKBAR MUHAMMAD
99. EGYPTIAN YOGA, VOLUMES I & II, DR. MUATA ASHBY
100. THE EGYPTIAN BOOK OF THE DEAD: THE BOOK OF COMING FORTH BY DAY, DR. MUATA ASHBY

NOTES